PAGAN
REGENERATION

PAGAN REGENERATION

A Study of Mystery Initiations in the
Graeco-Roman World

By

HAROLD R. WILLOUGHBY

THE UNIVERSITY OF CHICAGO PRESS

The University of Chicago Press, Chicago 37
The University of Toronto Press, Toronto 5, Canada

MMC   FRW
EBW   EES
————

AMABILES ET DECORI
IN VITA SUA
IN MORTE QUOQUE
NON SUNT DIVISI

PREFACE

IT MUST frankly be confessed that this study of mystery initiations in the Graeco-Roman world is but a prolegomenon to further research in early Christian origins. For some years the author has been fascinated by the problem of the genesis of Pauline mysticism. How did it come about that, with Judaism and primitive Christianity essentially unmystical in character, Pauline Christianity developed in a way to accentuate the mystical phases of religious experience? The writer hopes that some day circumstances will permit him to make a contribution toward the solution of this problem. In order to answer this question it is patently necessary to investigate the gentile religious milieu in which Pauline Christianity had its development.

Researches in the field of Graeco-Roman religions prove conclusively that apologists for early Christianity and even eminent classicists have been inclined to underestimate the genuineness of gentile religious interests and the extent to which religion dominated life in pagan lands when Christianity was emerging. Of the gentile cults probably the most popular in the first century, and certainly the least known and understood in the twentieth, were the so-called mystery religions. Notwithstanding the protestations of apologists there is ample evidence that in both the west and the east the mystery cults were widely disseminated and very influential before Christianity appeared on the scene. In the following pages care is taken to exhibit this evidence in relation to each of the mystery systems.

A detailed investigation of typical cult experiences

further convinced the author that the central meaning of mystery initiation—the regeneration, both essential and ethical, of the individual devotee—has largely escaped the notice of even sympathetic researchers. To bring out this meaning in the terminology and thought-forms of the initiates themselves, as recorded in scattered and fragmentary remains both monumental and literary, is one of the major purposes for which these studies are published.

Additional researches in Hermetic and Philonian literature demonstrated how important this mystical type of religious experience was considered to be, not only by religio-philosophical groups but also by individual thinkers quite outside the circle of gentile cult brotherhoods. To the writer Philo's case was particularly interesting, because it illustrated the extent to which the thought and experiences of a diaspora Jew might be influenced by gentile religious practices.

An analytical investigation of the social milieu in which the mystery cults operated brought to light the fundamental character of the interests and needs met by mystery initiation. On the one hand this made intelligible the undoubted popularity of the mystery cults themselves; on the other hand it served to suggest why it was that early Christian propagandists, in order to win gentile adherents to their cult, came to place such insistent emphasis on the experience of individual regeneration.

By means of the dedicatory page the author has tried to express a gratitude and appreciation that lie too deep for words. He would also make grateful acknowledgment to Professor Shirley Jackson Case, who guided his early studies in the mystery religions, and to Professor Edgar J. Goodspeed, who gave helpful advice and encouragement. The reading of proof, the verification of references, and the preparation of the Index have been largely the work of

Dr. A. D. Beittel and Mr. R. B. Brewer. Their painstaking exactness is deserving of commendation. Above all the writer would express his appreciation to a number of his own students who with patience more than Christian have endured tedious lectures about pagan mysteries.

H. R. W.

GOODSPEED HALL
THE UNIVERSITY OF CHICAGO
July 4, 1929

CONTENTS

xi

CHAPTER I

PAGAN PIETY IN THE GRAECO-ROMAN WORLD

THERE is a vague but widespread impression that the age that saw the emergence of Christianity was religiously destitute and morally decadent. The general and orthodox conviction of today is that all pagan religions current in the first century A.D. were in a bad state of degeneration. Originally they may have started with a modicum of light and revelation from above, but that original good had been corrupted by false beliefs and evil practices to such an extent that in the first century the gentile world was in a worse state than it had ever been before. People of all classes, wearied of the apparent futility of contemporary cults, were quitting them wholesale, or were giving them a merely formal adherence. In an abandon of atheism they were surrending themselves to unrestrained indulgence in immoral practices. Approximately this is still the popular impression of religious conditions in the Graeco-Roman world.

This misconception, so far as it has any basis at all in ancient sources of information, results from a piecing together of notions derived from certain readily accessible writings, pagan and Christian. On the one hand, philosophical writings in Greek and Latin record the rationalist criticism to which the polytheistic systems of the Gentiles were subjected. Furthermore, the Roman satirists of the early imperial period, superlatively skilful in the practice of their art, painted the immoralities of the upper classes in Roman society in colors that could not be forgotten. On the other hand, the later Christian apologists delighted to represent their pagan competitors in as unfavorable a light as possible. They pilloried the faults and failures of gentile religions and sought to establish the point that the inadequacies of paganism were a part of the providential preparation of the world for the outburst of true revelation in Christianity itself. This admittedly apologetic position, familiar alike in ancient and modern times, was given its classic statement in the *Praeparatio Evangelica* composed early in the fourth century A.D. by Eusebius of Caesarea.

Concerning the literary sources involved it is sufficient to observe, first of all, that the Greek and Roman authors cited represent the attitudes and customs of limited classes in contemporary society: the skepticism of the intellectuals and the excesses of the *nouveaux riches*. As to the Christian sources, they betray a frank bias both in the selection of discreditable data and in the utilization of that data to serve a polemic purpose. Because of this misuse of inadequate materials the point of view which posits a dearth of real religion in the Graeco-Roman world is itself clearly discredited.

Completely contradictory to such an estimate was the judgment of the earliest Christians concerning rival religious movements. They, who knew competition with gentile cults as a matter of vivid present experience, did not question the strength or reality of gentile loyalties to heathen systems. Not because Gentiles were irreligious but because they were so incurably and tenaciously religious, Christian propagandists actually made little headway with them at first. In face of this discouraging situation the missionaries explained their early failures as due to the infatuated devotion of Gentiles to gods who were really demons. The earliest historian of Christianity, writing at the end of the first century, represented Paul, the outstanding missionary to the Gentiles, as saying to a typical pagan audience, "Men of Athens, from every point of view I see that you are extremely religious."

During the last quarter-century the detailed researches of specialists in the field of Graeco-Roman religions have fully confirmed this ancient appreciation of pagan piety.[1] The propagandist vigor of diaspora Judaism in seeking for proselytes from among the heathen was fully understood before the beginning of our century; but recently discovered non-literary papyri and similar unpretentious remains have revealed a not less vigorous gentile propaganda carried on by members of voluntary religious associations. That the *princeps* of the Roman Empire was responsible for an official revival of antique Roman religion was well known to earlier generations than our own; but only recently have students been aroused to a realization that the developing imperial cult, focused on the person of the *princeps*, was an expression of genuinely religious hopes and appreciations and interests on the part of the people of the empire. That Graeco-Roman philosophy came to a religious climax in Neo-Platonism has long been a matter of common knowledge; but only in our generation have serious scholars given sympathetic attention to the mystical literatures of similar systems previous to Plotinus. The net result of all this fresh investigation in new fields has been to prove that the Mediterranean world in which early Christianity emerged was indeed "extremely religious." It is perhaps not exaggeration to affirm of the first century A.D., as Francis Legge does of the six centuries from Alexander to Constantine, "there has probably been no time in the history of mankind when all classes were more given up to thoughts of religion, or when they strained more

[1] The main results of these investigations are reviewed by the author in summary fashion in *Religious Thought in the Last Quarter-Century*, edited by G. B. Smith (Chicago, 1927), pp. 51 ff.

fervently after high ethical ideals"[1] than at just this period. To this extent do the actual records of gentile religious experience in the first century belie the traditional estimate of the age.

I

Fundamentally the *weltanschauung* generally prevalent during the early imperial period was emphatically a religious view of the universe and of life. By far the majority of people in all strata of society held a supernaturalistic conception of the universe that presupposed the existence of a spirit world above and beyond the world known to ordinary sense perception. In the presence of the mystery which lies back of all human experience, even the most ordinary, there were few in the Julian or Flavian periods who were content to maintain a position of agnosticism and say, "The mystery cannot be understood: therefore it may be ignored." The more curious majority sought in one way or another to penetrate the mystery and were satisfied that it held the key to an understanding of the meaning of existence. Furthermore, so far as the ordering of the universe was concerned, the supernatural realm was conceived to be far more important than the natural world; for the ultimate forces which controlled all things were believed to be the occult spiritual powers above and not the forces of nature operative in the world below. Only a very few strenuous thinkers had attained to anything approximating the modern scientific conception of natural law, i.e., the uniform sequence of natural events apart from the ordering of a will or mind responsible for the succession. Most men in the first century tended rather to think

[1] *Forerunners and Rivals of Christianity*, I, xlix. Similar views are recorded by Angus, *The Mystery Religions and Christianity*, pp. 4 ff.; Case, *The Evolution of Early Christianity*, pp. 31 ff.; and *The Social Origins of Christianity*, pp. 79 ff.; and Deissmann, *Light from the Ancient East*, pp. 284 ff.

of events as the result of the more or less capricious activities of spirits or demons who peopled the supernatural area. Some, to be sure, personalized these spiritual powers but ostracized them completely from effective human relationships. This was the Epicurean way. Others depersonalized and rationalized all supernatural power, connected it most intimately with the world of experience, and made it the very essence of things, the ordering mind of the universe itself. This was the Stoic way. Between these rival camps the masses of men continued to think of the supernatural powers as personal beings who governed the affairs of men in ways that were whimsical and freakish.

A person's attitude toward the supernatural powers and his conception of them varied considerably according to his particular circumstances in life. To many minds it seemed that experience was chiefly characterized by the element of uncertainty. Nature was sometimes hostile and sometimes kind. Business was now a success and now a failure, with no fully apparent reason for either result. A man who had such experiences, if he were skeptical of the traditional gods of paganism, was likely to hold chance responsible for the inexplicable permutations of fortune. Still others were more impressed by the orderliness of the universe. The fortunes of men might vary, but the processes of nature continued in a more or less invariable sequence over long periods of time. To them the universe seemed not conspicuously friendly, perhaps, but at least it could be depended on. Under such circumstances it was reasonable to attribute the ordering of events to a stern and inflexible Necessity, and the corresponding religious attitude was to be submissive to the rulings of Fate. In general, when one's lot in life was notably favorable and success crowned one's efforts, one could easily maintain an optimistic attitude toward the universe and regard the supernatural with equanimity. Providence was obviously kind to the prosperous man and it was his religious duty to be correspondingly grateful.

The masses of humanity in the Graeco-Roman world were not so well situated as this, and consequently they found it difficult to maintain an attitude of grateful appreciation toward the powers controlling the universe. To be sure society was more stable in the first century of the empire than in the last century of the republic; but the injustices of that social order were flagrant, the mood of the *princeps* was changeable, and the uncertainties of life were great. Experience seemed to indicate that on the whole the supernatural powers were more likely to be unfriendly than favorable. Accordingly, the ordinary man of that time was inclined to regard the spirits and demons of his universe with fear and blank terror even. Out of this unfortunate attitude there developed irrational beliefs and absurd practices, difficult to understand at this distance in time, but broadly intended to establish and maintain safe relationships with man's spiritual environment.

The growth of superstition in the Roman Empire during the first century A.D. was immense.[1] All classes in society from the *princeps* down were infected by it to a greater or less degree. Augustus, when a thunderstorm arose, used to retire to the cellar, and Caligula by preference crawled under the bed. Nero, like Orestes, only more deservedly, was haunted by the furies of his murdered mother just as Otho, later, was tortured by the unquiet spirit of his predecessor Galba. The Flavian emperors were not less addicted to superstition. Domitian, the last of the line, had the worst experiences of them all. During the last months of his life he was in constant terror while the lightning struck,

---

[1] Dill, *Roman Society from Nero to Marcus Aurelius*, pp. 443–83. See also Cumont, *Astrology and Religion among Greeks and Romans* (New York, 1912).

one after the other, the Roman Capitol, the Flavian temple, and the imperial palace. The very men of letters, Suetonius and Dio Cassius, who regale us *ad nauseam* with these and similar tales, confess their own credulity by the way in which they handle their narratives. Petronius and Apuleius introduce us to more superstitions of the same sort in their romances of society life in Cumae and village life in Thessaly. Almost anywhere that a test is made in contemporary Mediterranean life, the result is to disclose a fantastic assortment of grotesque superstitions.

The prevalence of superstition in the Roman world together with concomitant evils caused real concern on the part of intelligent and conscientious religionists. In the last century B.C. the enthusiastic Epicurean, Lucretius, faced the problem squarely and proposed a rigorous remedy. He identified superstition and religion, and emphasizing the disquieting character of fears inspired by supernaturalism, he unhesitatingly pronounced religion a curse on the human race. In his account of religious origins in relation to the development of human society he burst out in passionate invective:

O unhappy race of mankind, to ascribe such doings to the gods and to add thereto bitter wrath! What groans did they then create for themselves, what wounds for us, what tears for generations to come! It is no piety to show oneself often with covered head, turning towards a stone and approaching every altar, none to fall prostrate upon the ground and to spread open the palms before shrines of the gods, none to sprinkle altars with the blood of beasts in showers and to link vow to vow; but rather to be able to survey all things with mind at peace.[1]

To Lucretius the remedy seemed obvious: to do away altogether with contemporary supernaturalism and to substitute instead rational views of nature. Because Epicurus in his philosophy had accomplished this very thing and so

[1] Lucretius *De Rerum Natura* v. 1194 ff.

freed mankind from unnecessary fears, Lucretius expressed his unbounded admiration for the achievement.[1]

Plutarch, of Chaeronea, facing essentially the same problem in the first century A.D., took a more moderate position.[2] He contrasted religion with superstition on the one hand and with atheism on the other. The latter he defined as insensibility to the gods, and the former he characterized as the excessive and irrational fear of the gods. In origin the two were closely related. A fundamental misconception of the gods as malignant beings gave rise to the fears of superstition, and these in turn caused the extreme reaction of atheism. Of the two the latter was certainly preferable. But for himself Plutarch preferred to choose neither. The remedy, as he saw it, was at just a happy medium between the two; and this was the position of true religion. The gods, in Plutarch's judgment, were the friends of mankind and chiefly concerned with their welfare. Hence they should be approached without dread, but with gratitude and confidence. Plutarch's own testimony was: "What we esteem the most agreeable things in human life are our holidays, temple-feasts, initiations, processions, with our public prayers and solemn devotions."[3] In the "golden mean of true piety" Plutarch found the antidote for both the practical atheism of the Epicurean and the terrors of the superstitious. The miscellanarian of Chaeronea did not stand alone in this position, but was typical of a large number of sane, thoughtful, conservative Gentiles who were his contemporaries.

II

Broadly speaking, the religious situation in the Graeco-Roman world was as varied and complex and syncretistic

---

[1] *Op. cit.* i. 62 ff.

[2] Plutarch *De Superstitione.*   [3] *Op. cit.* 9.

as Mediterranean society itself was at this period. All peoples included as citizens or provincials within the limits of the empire and all previous ages of religious experience in the Mediterranean area made some characteristic contribution to the religious life of Roman times. Prominent in the complex, and thoroughly typical of the particular races and geographical areas involved, were the survivals of the nationalistic type of religion in vogue before the Roman and Macedonian conquests. The Jahvism of the Jews is the best known of this group, and the propagandist vigor of Judaism in the early Roman Empire is unquestioned. All the world was missionary territory for the Jews. In their zeal for proselytes they "scoured land and sea to make one convert." But equally the Roman world was missionary territory to the devotees of Syrian Baals, to the priests of Egyptian gods, and to the Magi of Ahura Mazda. If the missionaries of polytheistic systems were less exclusive than the rabbis in their demands for religious loyalty, at least they were not less sincere in their devotion to their own particular cults. Outstanding among the traditional survivals and providing the standard paganism of the day was the merged Olympian-Capitoline system, the joint contribution of Greece and Rome. It has become a habit to think and speak of these cults as practically dead when Christianity came to birth. A close study of the archaeological and literary remains of first-century life, however, shows that not only were the traditional religions of Greece and Rome surviving, but they were also actually functioning with considerable vigor; perhaps not as robustly as at an earlier period, but still vitally enough to make them a noteworthy element in the Graeco-Roman situation as a whole.

A peculiarly Roman current in contemporary life was the religion of the home magnified in adaptation to the needs of the state.[1] In its primitive development Roman piety was the cult of a household living in a rural environment and engaged in ritual practices intended to placate the powers on which the welfare of the family was chiefly dependent. The *paterfamilias* of the household was the high priest of the family cult, the *mater* was the priestess of the Penates, and the daughters who tended the hearth fire, were the ministrants of Vesta. So Rome, grown to a city-state, then to a republic, and finally to an empire, continued to maintain both the organization and the practices of the domestic religion. The *pontifex maximus*, the official head of the state religion, was the "father of his people," and the vestal virgins, the daughters of the state, kept the fire burning on the public hearth in the Forum. But the antique Latin religion, developed in a rural setting and essentially conservative in character, could not possibly be enlarged to meet the needs of the expanding Roman state. So the attempt was made to supplement Latin religion from the outside. The *numina* of primitive thought were personalized and individualized; *di novensiles* were imported from south Italy and Greece and the Orient, and they almost crowded out the *di indigetes;* Greek rites were introduced to supplement the native Roman rites, and, finally, the Olympian and Capitoline pantheons were merged, with the Hellenic elements distinctly dominant in the combination.

It is true that there was a pitiful decline of Latin religion during the last century of the republic. But that is

[1] The following titles selected from an extensive list of standard works on Roman religion are recommended: G. Boissier, *La religion Romaine d'Auguste aux Antonins* (Paris, 1909[7]); J. B. Carter, *The Religious Life of Ancient Rome* (London, 1912); W. W. Fowler, *The Religious Experience of the Roman People* (London, 1911); W. R. Halliday, *Lectures on the History of Roman Religion from Numa to Augustus* (Boston, 1923); Kurt Latte, *Die Religion der Römer und der Synkretismus der Kaiserzeit* (Tübingen, 1927); G. Wissowa, *Religion und Kultus der Römer* (Munich, 1912[2]).

not the end of the story. Simultaneous with the establishment of the principate by Augustus there was an official
revival of state religion under his immediate direction.[1]
Just why Augustus, who was both cynical and superstitious, should be interested in doing this is still a matter for
debate. The probability is that his motives were mingled.
In part to cloak his actual autocracy and make the principate a safe and secure office; in part to further the fortunes
of himself and his family, and to stimulate patriotism at
the same time; and in part, surely, to reinculcate the old
Roman type of virtue, he sought the renaissance of the
primitive Latin religion. He restored decayed sanctuaries
and built new temples. He revived priesthoods that had
lapsed and filled colleges with men of distinction. He himself carefully observed all the required forms of religion
and gave special prominence to cults associated with his
own career or his family. In 17 B.C. he had the "secular
games" celebrated in honor of the new order of things and
appointed Horace to write the *Carmen Saeculare* for the
occasion. This and other literature of the Augustan age,
particularly the poems of Vergil, give the impression of a
religious revival actually in progress. Following the chaos
and excesses of the last century of the republic, the old
Roman character asserted itself once more and reverted
anew to the familiar *religio*.

It is quite probable that in all this Augustus was less
a leader and more a follower of public opinion than he is
usually supposed to have been. Notwithstanding the scan-
tiness of literary records there are yet data enough to prove

---

[1] Important chapters on the Augustan revival are to be found in the follow-
ing works: A. W. Benn, *The Greek Philosophers* (1914²); pp. 474–522; Samuel
Dill, *Roman Society from Nero to Marcus Aurelius*, pp. 529–46; L. Friedlander,
Roman Life and Manners under the Early Empire, III, 84–170; W. W. Fowler,
The Religious Experience of the Roman People, pp. 403–51; W. R. Halliday,
Lectures on the History of Roman Religion, pp. 160 ff.

that the ancient Latin religion was still a considerable factor in Italian life. Originally developed to meet family needs in a rural type of society, it continued to function in country districts and in cities, even, where family life survived. The charming pictures of the actual operations of the religion of Numa in *Marius the Epicurean* are just as true of first-century Italy as of the age of the Antonines.[1] They can be matched by a dozen delightful sketches in the minor poets of the Augustan age and by more serious representations in Cato's treatise on agriculture. Also in the city milieu the religious routine of family life, the offerings to Vesta and the Penates at mealtime, and the celebrations at birth, marriage, or death, continued to be observed to the very end of paganism. In the Theodosian code of the late fourth century are the following prohibitions: "Let no man in any place in any city make sacrifice or worship the Lar with burnt offering, or the genius with wine, or the Penates with perfumes—let them light no lamp, burn no incense, hang no garlands." Conscientious Romans habituated to the religious customs of family life were ready to give support to such a revival as history associates with the name of Augustus.

The cults devoted to the Olympian gods of Greece were far more widely influential over the Mediterranean area than Roman religion ever was.[2] Originally the various Olympians had been local divinities merely, charged with

[1] Walter Pater, *Marius the Epicurean*, chap. i.

[2] Olympian religion is given due prominence in the following manuals which are standard for Greek cults generally: A. Fairbanks, *A Handbook of Greek Religion* (New York, 1910); L. R. Farnell, *Cults of the Greek States*, 5 vols. (Oxford, 1896–1909); L. R. Farnell, *The Higher Aspects of Greek Religion* (London, 1912); O. Gruppe, *Griechische Mythologie und Religionsgeschichte* (München, 1906); Jane Harrison, *Prolegomena to the Study of Greek Religion* (Cambridge, 1922[3]); Jane Harrison, *Themis* (Cambridge, 1927[2]); M. P. Nilsson, *A History of Greek Religion* (Oxford, 1925); C. H. Moore, *The Religious Thought of the Greeks* (Cambridge, 1916); Gilbert Murray, *Five Stages of Greek Religion* (New York, 1925); T. Zielinski, *The Religion of Ancient Greece* (Oxford, 1926).

the protection of people living in a given territory. Gradually, as the Hellenes came to associate together in larger political and social units, certain of the local cults acquired significance for the Greeks generally and then a society of Olympian gods was organized paralleling in its main features the social organization of the Greeks themselves. By the conquest of Alexander the Olympian cults were disseminated throughout the east and by a process of peaceful penetration they came to dominate the Capitoline pantheon in the West. The very conquests which brought disaster to other national and racial systems brought a new accession of influence to the calm Olympians. During the Hellenistic and Roman periods the gods of Greece stood out before the world as the personifications of Hellenic ideals and as departmental deities representing important interests in life.

It is only fair to recognize that among the traditional religions of the day the Olympian cults possessed certain distinct advantages not enjoyed by other systems. There was, first of all, the aesthetic monopoly they held. The most impressive public buildings in the Graeco-Roman world were consecrated as temples to them and the most beautiful statues wrought by Greek artists were their cult images. They were the inspiration of the best literature as of the finest art: the epics of Homer and Vergil, the tragedies of Aeschylus and Euripides, the Homeric Hymns and the odes of Pindar, the lyrics of Sappho, and the poems of Horace. The greatest public festivals of the time were celebrated in their honor—witness the Olympian games. Their temples were banks as well as sanctuaries, and the records of dedications and mortgages and sacred manumissions suggest the influence they had in the control of economic processes. In a variety of ways the Olympian cults dominated important phases of contemporary life.

Concerning the traditional religions generally, it may be said that the extent of their popularity and influence in the first century was dependent on their capacity to meet real social needs. There was still a demand for cults to take care of the larger group and community interests of Mediterranean peoples. This condition obtained even after the Greek city-states had lost their political identity and the native kingdoms of Anatolia had given way to Roman provincial units. The economic prosperity of cities as well as of individuals must be assured. The health of large aggregations of humanity living in restricted areas was an ever serious problem. Homes and the food supply must be protected against destruction by fire and flood and earthquake. In all such instances religion seemed to furnish the best guaranties of security. By the very circumstance of their local genesis the traditional survivals were well equipped to meet this range of community needs; and the civic pride manifested in the first century in the maintenance of particular cults attests the fact that they had functional value. The author of Acts, in a vivid scene, reflected the pride of Ephesus to be the "temple-keeper" for Artemis,[1] and the Christian prophet of the Apocalypse, in his bitter words about "Satan's throne," rebuked the satisfaction that the Pergamenes took in the great altar of Zeus.[2] Typically the gods of Greece continued to function as municipal saviors for cities widely scattered over the eastern half of the Mediterranean world, older local divinities frequently adopting the names and symbols of the Olympians. Altogether a greater vitality must be granted to established cults in their communal functioning than is usually allowed.

[1] Acts 19:23 ff.

[2] Rev. 2:12 ff.

III

It was a characteristic Roman conviction that the primary function of religion was to serve the interests of the
state and that as a guaranty of political prosperity the
rites of religion were potent in the extreme. There was
nothing individualistic about Roman *religio*. The individual had significance only as a member of a household and
the household had significance only as a unit in the state.
Just as the welfare of the family group was considered to
be mainly conditioned by the preservation of *pax* with the
numina, so the prosperity of the state was conceived to
depend mainly on the maintenance of right relations with
spiritual powers. Accordingly the Romans made their *ius
divinum* as much a part of their civil law as the Jews did.
Again and again during the centuries that saw Rome's
rise to greatness and empire, the idea was emphatically
expressed that her success was due to the scrupulous way
in which the Romans observed their religious obligations.
" 'Tis by holding yourself the servant of the gods that you
rule," said Horace, addressing the typical Roman of his
day.[1] Livy composed his history and Vergil his epic to enforce the point. Equally when disaster befell the Roman
state, the tragedy was attributed to the neglect of religious
rites. According to the best Roman traditions political developments were, in the last analysis, determined by religious observances.

Because the Romans believed so strongly in the political efficacy of religion they made the extended effort, covering long centuries of their history, to adapt the religion of
the home to the uses of the state. In this they signally
failed. But in the first century A.D. the Romans were responsible for a unique religious development that temporarily seemed to meet their political needs with marked

[1] Horace *Odes* iii. 6.

success. This was the Roman development of the oriental
cult of the monarch, focused in imperial times on the person of the deified *princeps*.[1]

During the century which began with Augustus and
ended with Domitian, the cult of the ruler had its greatest
growth and became an effective force throughout the
Mediterranean world. Through the first half of the century
the personal policy of the *princeps* himself in regard to
apotheosis was marked by strange retroversions, each emperor almost invariably reversing the policy of his predecessor. With Augustus the divinization of the ruler became an established fact in the popular mind, even though
it was not officially authorized in Rome and Italy. Tiberius
encouraged the deification of Augustus, but was modest
about claiming like honors for himself.[2] Then Caligula became so insane in his demand for apotheosis that he incited
serious race riots in the Semitic portions of his empire.
Claudius, by contrast, practiced the reserve of Tiberius in
the matter. By the beginning of the second century, however, the worship of the ruler was such a well-established
and generally accepted phase of imperial policy that the
growing Christian movement found itself seriously involved and its loyalty to the state definitely challenged

[1] In addition to the general manuals on Roman religion the following works
which deal specifically with the imperial cult should be consulted: E. Beurlier,
Le culte impérial, son histoire et son organization (Paris, 1891); E. Lohmeyer,
Christuskult und Kaiserkult (Tübingen, 1919); L. M. Sweet, *Roman Emperor
Worship* (Boston, 1919).

The following sections are also indicated to emphasize important phases and
relationships of the Roman cult of the ruler: S. J. Case, *The Evolution of Early
Christianity* (Chicago, 1914), pp. 195–238; A. Deissmann, *Light from the Ancient
East* (New York, 1927[4]), pp. 338–78; Foakes-Jackson and Lake, *The Beginnings
of Christianity* (London, 1920), I, 199–217; J. Toutain, *Les cultes païens dans
l'empire romain* (Paris, 1911), I, 19–179.

[2] Note particularly the admirable statement of Tiberius regarding himself
recorded by Tacitus in *Annals* iv. 38.

because of non-participation in the cult.[1] So important had ruler worship become in the minds of patriotic Roman citizens.

The political usefulness of the imperial cult in providing a religious sanction for the unification of the various races living within the Roman empire has not been seriously questioned either in the early Christian centuries or in our own. An exaggerated importance, however, has been assigned to this function, and the religious significance of the cult has been largely ignored. Nevertheless in the first century the primary meaning of the imperial cult was religious and only incidentally did it serve the practical purpose of a political expedient. When the student of history views the imperial cult in relation to the contemporary desire of Mediterranean peoples for peace and security and also in relation to similar quests conspicuous in the Orient from the very beginning of the historical period, he comes to a realization of what concrete and widespread cravings were met and answered by imperial religion.

The current belief in the ancient world was that the evils of present experience were too stupendous for human management. If they were to be cured, the remedy must come from beneficent spiritual powers above. Out of this fundamental conviction grew a great yearning for a heaven-sent, divinely equipped savior who could deliver men from their wretchedness. From early times this desire for a savior was associated with and found appropriate expression in the cult of the ruler. The Babylonian legend of the divine king Marduk who vanquished the monster Tiamat was a mythological reflection of this association. In the Jewish anticipation of a Messianic deliverer the idea was projected into the future. Egyptian and Assyrian and Hebrew prophets who contrasted the distressful conditions of the

[1] Pliny *Epistolae* x. 96.

immediate present with the blessings certain to be realized under an ideal ruler gave iteration to the same yearning for a kingdom of God here on earth.

At the beginning of the Christian era these ancient hopes came to an impressive culmination with the reorganization of the Roman empire by Augustus. Wearied beyond expression by the continuous wars of the last hundred years and more, large numbers of people actually hoped and believed that Augustus himself would bring the iron age of strife to an end and usher in the new golden age of Saturn. In the well-known *Fourth Eclogue* of Vergil, in the sixth book of the *Aeneid*, and over and over again in the *Odes* of Horace, this confidence was repeated.[1] Provincial inscriptions in honor of Augustus were keyed even higher in their expressions of appreciation and expectation.[2] This mass of literary and epigraphic evidence cannot fairly be treated as fulsome compliment intended to flatter an egotistical prince. It is nearer the truth to regard it as a sincere expression of gratitude for real benefits. Augustus gave the world what it most needed at the time: peace and stable government. The people and especially the provincials responded by according him divine honors. So with the successors of Augustus, when the ruler was an able prince and the benefits realized were substantial, the apotheosis of the ruler was a popular expression of gratitude in religious terminology. The deified *princeps* was, to the Roman people, a symbol of social safety guaranteed by supernatural power.

[1] See particularly Horace *Odes* i. 2. 41 ff.; iii. 5. 1 ff.; iv. 2. 37 ff.; iv. 5. 25 ff.

[2] Especially interesting in its terminology is a calendar inscription from the market in Priene, dated *ca.* 9 B.C., which refers to the birthday of Augustus as a veritable evangel: "The birthday of the god was for the world the beginning of good tidings because of him" (Dittenberger, *Orientis Graeci Inscriptiones Selectae*, No. 458).

IV

Genetically related to the Roman imperial cult, yet persisting in an independent line of development and meeting a distinctive range of religious needs, were the various hero cults of the Greeks.[1] It was a typical Hellenic point of view of great social and ethical significance that humanitarian activity was one of the surest ways of attaining divinity. *Deus est mortali iuvare mortalem et haec ad aeternam gloriam via*, wrote the elder Pliny, probably translating Posidonius.[2] The hero-gods of the Greeks were the personifications of this great idea. They were divine beings of the second order, less than the gods yet more than men. Usually they were thought of as descended from at least one divine parent, as having lived on earth and performed some signal service for mankind, in consequence of which they had risen to rank as demigods after death. Heracles was one of the best loved of these Greek heroes. By his twelve labors he had proved himself the friend of humanity and in the end had been welcomed to Olympus. "Heracles has passed into the number of the gods," wrote Cicero. "He would never have so passed if he had not built up that road for himself while he was among mankind."[3] In this laborious way the mortal son of Zeus and Alcmene became the immortal husband of the Olympian Hebe. The number of similar demigods thus revered by the Greeks was legion. This is not the place to debate the question as to which

[1] Hero worship in Greek and Roman times may conveniently be studied in the following works: Jean Bayet, *Herculé*, 276 pp. (Paris, 1926); Jean Bayet, *Les Origines de l'Herculé Romain*, 502 pp. (Paris, 1926); L. R. Farnell, *Greek Hero Cults and Ideas of Immortality*, 434 pp. (Oxford, 1921); J. R. Harris, *The Cult of the Heavenly Twins*, 160 pp. (Cambridge, 1906); Jane Harrison, *Prolegomena to the Study of Greek Religion*, pp. 322–62 (Cambridge, 1922³); Jane Harrison, *Themis*, pp. 260–444 (Cambridge, 1927²); B. Schweitzer, *Herakles, Aufsätze zur griechische Religionsgeschichte und Sagengeschichte*, 247 pp. (Tübingen, 1922).

[2] Pliny *Historia Naturalis* ii. 7. 18.   [3] Cicero *Tusculan Disputations* i. 32.

element was primary in this combination, the divinity of the god or the humanity of the hero. Were these demigods originally gods who had degenerated to the level of glorious mortals, or were they able men and women who became minor gods? Suffice it to observe that in the development of these cults believers found in divine parentage a reasonable explanation for exceptional ability and in the beneficient activity of heroes an ethical justification for their apotheosis.

It is more important to note the distinctive functioning of these demigods in comparison with other divinities during the Alexandrian and imperial eras. The great gods of Olympus and the Capitol looked out for the protection of cities and states. But even in Periclean Athens the individual was not completely submerged by the *polis*. As an individual he was conscious of personal needs and interests that were outside the scope of his responsibility as a citizen. He was naturally ambitious to succeed in his vocation. There were times in life when he felt acutely the need for personal guidance or for recompense from disaster. Health must be conserved. He felt that he had a right to a full share in the good things of life, and he was not adverse to having special privileges, even, not shared with his fellowmen. In the cosmopolitan environment of Hellenistic and Roman times, such personal demands became more emphatic than ever before and religion was expected to serve these special purposes. It was here that the hero cults came in to take care of the more minute personal concerns of everyday life. Because the hero-gods had been human themselves they were very sympathetic with human needs and were experienced in meeting them. In their intimate, personal functioning the demigods of antiquity resembled the Roman Catholic saints of today.

This group of religions came to prominence in the Hel-

lenic world about the fifth century B.C. During the Hellenistic age the cult nexus had an amazing growth, and again
in the early imperial period there was a pronounced revival
of hero worship. Hence it is possible by studying the cults
of real persons in the historic period to form a vivid impression of the actual operations of this type of religion and
of the kind of interests represented by it.

In classical times when civic interests were predominant
in Greek states the founders of cities and colonies, and men
otherwise pre-eminent in public service, were honored by
divinization. Plutarch told of an annual commemorative
service for the Greeks who fell at Plataea, which was celebrated down to his own day,[1] and Pausanias noted that the
heroes of Thermopylae and Marathon were accorded a like
religious reverence.[2] Later, as political interests tended to
recede somewhat, more refined, cultural interests became
prominent in connection with hero worship. Literary skill
and intellectual acumen were given their meed of recognition by apotheosis. By command of the Pythoness herself
Pindar was awarded equal first fruits with Apollo at
Delphi.[3] Homeric cults were practiced by the litterati at
Smyrna and Alexandria.[4] Schools of philosophy adopted
the custom. So scientific a thinker as Aristotle consecrated
at Stagira an altar in honor of Plato. Even Epicurus made
provision in his will for regular memorial services of a
religious character.[5] While the imperial cult was at its
height in Roman times there was a persistence of hero cults
in private practice as well. No one was more extravagant
in observances of this sort during the early second century
than was the Emperor Hadrian in ordering the worship of
his dead favorite Antinous. Strangely, this exotic cult con-

[1] Plutarch *Aristides* 21.

[2] Pausanias i. 32. 4; iii. 12. 9.   [4] Strabo 646.

[3] *Op. cit.* ix. 23. 3.   [5] Diogenes Laertius x. 18.

tinued for more than a hundred years after the emperor's death.[1] The saintly Marcus Aurelius was not only the object of the usual official apotheosis, but his own statues were given a place among the household penates in many a pious Roman home. That the ambition for apotheosis might amount to a suicidal mania in a given instance was shown by the self-immolation of Perigrinus at Olympia.[2] There is no doubt that he was quite as eager to become an immortal as were his Cynic brothers to hail the event. Famous instances indicate that hero cults in great variety were widely popular in imperial times.

By far the most popular of the hero-gods of Greece was Asclepius, the divine patron of the healing art.[3] His cult was concerned with such fundamental and practical matters that it could not be otherwise than of general interest. Problems of sickness and health are universal, vital, precarious. Ancient theories usually attributed disease to the wrath of a justly angry god or to infection by a malignant demon. On either theory, the cure of disease was a concern of religion and the remedy must be supplied by beneficent spiritual power. Asclepius was the hero-god who specialized in operations of this kind and his sanctuaries were the sanitoria of the Graeco-Roman world. The most famous of them was at Epidaurus on the east coast of Greece, but there were others of great repute: at Athens close under the Acropolis, at Pergamum and Smyrna in Asia Minor,

---

[1] Dio Cassius lxix. 11.   [2] Lucian *De Morte Perigrini.*

[3] The following works deal significantly with the Asclepius cult: R. Caton, *The Temples and Ritual of Asklepios*, 49 pp. (London, 1900[2]); L. Deubner, *De Incubatione*, 48 pp. (Leipzig, 1900); L. Dyer, *The Gods in Greece* (New York, 1894), pp. 219–69; L. R. Farnell, *Greek Hero Cults and Ideas of Immortality* (Oxford, 1921), pp. 234–79; Mary Hamilton, *Incubation, or Cure of Disease in Pagan Temples and Christian Churches*, 223 pp. (London, 1906); Alice Walton, *The Cult of Asklepios*, 136 pp. (Boston, 1894); O. Weinrich, *Antike Heilungswunder*, 212 pp. (Giessen, 1909).

on Cos and other islands of the Aegean, and at the imperial
capitol on the Tiber island. Indeed the Asclepius cult was
ubiquitous in the Roman world.

At the various *Asclepeia* healings were accomplished in
different ways. There was a good deal of thaumaturgy involved, doubtless, but there was also much sound and
scientific medical practice as well. Archaeological remains
make it plain that a healthful location, a pleasing environment, a sane regimen, a variety of recreational activity,
and a great confidence in the power and benevolence of
the god, all contributed to the results obtained at the
Asclepius sanctuaries.[1]

So great was the gratitude of the Graeco-Roman world
to this hero-god for his beneficence that there was a spontaneous movement to make him a god of the first rank and
to identify him with the supreme god, Olympian Zeus himself. To quote the words of one of his enthusiastic devotees, Asclepius was "the one who leads and controls all
things, the savior of the whole world, and the guardian of
mortals."[2] In art the bearded Asclepius type became ca-
nonical and there are cases in which it is difficult to determine whether the god represented was Zeus or the human
son of Apollo. Thus by his healing activity the man-god
won a place for himself at the very head of the Olympian
pantheon. Because the benefits guaranteed by the hero-
gods were concrete and generally desired, hero worship was
a popular religious usage among Gentiles.

V

It is a curious circumstance that the very cults which
were most widely and genuinely popular in the Graeco-

---

[1] Walter Pater in chapter iii of *Marius the Epicurean* gives the reader a lively
and true impression of experiences at a healing shrine.

[2] Aelius Aristides *Oratio* 6.

Roman world are the least known in detail to religio-historical students today. The mystery religions of Greece and the Orient which came the nearest to satisfying the religious needs of the average man in the early imperial era are today still much of a mystery, and it is altogether likely that they will remain so. Under the circumstances it could not be otherwise; for the only people in a position to give dependable information concerning these cults were the initiates themselves, and they were pledged to absolute secrecy concerning the essential features of the mystery system. Almost without exception the vow was conscientiously observed, being enforced both within the brotherhood and from the outside with a rigor that amazes the inquisitive modern mind. The uninitiated, even, resented the illegitimate disclosure of matters supposed to be kept secret and united with the initiated to prevent such a violation of sacred things.

There are historical incidents that illustrate the reverential attitude of the ancients toward the secrets of the mysteries. Andocides, the Attic orator, and Alcibiades, the spoiled favorite of the Athenians, were both implicated in the serious charge of profaning the mysteries.[1] The former was condemned to forfeit certain civil rights and went into exile, while the latter was recalled from the ill-fated Sicilian expedition to stand trial for his impiety. Widely traveled and well-informed Greeks like Herodotus and Pausanias might have written much about the mysteries—and in fact they did tell something. But invariably, when they were on the verge of some significant disclosure, they would stop short and follow the traditional custom of maintaining a propitious silence. "I could speak more exactly of these matters," Herodotus acknowledged regarding the Egyptian mysteries, "for I know the truth." Then he quickly added,

[1] Plutarch *Alcibiades* 19.

"But I will hold my peace."[1] In like manner, Pausanias, after conducting his reader to the very portal of the Eleusinian precinct, there left him disappointed with the unsatisfying explanation: "My dream forbade the description of the things within the wall of the sanctuary, and the uninitiated are of course not permitted to learn that which they are prevented from seeing."[2] Lucius Apuleius, of Madaura, who detailed an extensive account of his own initiation without telling precisely what was said or done, could affirm of his narrative: "I have told you things which, although you have heard them, you cannot know the meaning."[3] When he himself was on trial for magical practices he stoutly declared that he could not be compelled to disclose to the uninitiated what he had received under vow of secrecy.[4] This in its bare simplicity was the typical pagan attitude toward the privacy of the mysteries. To the modern scholar it is inconvenient and annoying. At the same time it is worthy of admiration.

As a result of this ancient conspiracy of silence, the actual literary remains of the mystery cults are scanty and fragmentary in the extreme. Here and there obscure formulas are quoted; a few hymns and prayers have been preserved in part; a comic poet parodies an initiation and a devotee describes the process in figurative language; finally, Christian propagandists denounce the mysteries wholesale as a part of the Satanic system of paganism. The other literary remains of these cults are but chance references and vague allusions from which little can be learned. When all these literary data are assembled and

---

[1] Herodotus ii. 171. Cf. ii. 61.

[2] Pausanias i. 38. 7. Cf. i. 37. 4.   [3] Apuleius *Metamorphoses* xi. 23.

[4] Apuleius *Apologia* 56. In maintaining this position Lucius had Roman legal practice on his side. It was accepted Roman procedure to prosecute anyone guilty of profaning the mysteries.

combined with the equally slight amount of archaeological material extant, the sum total of it all seems meager and unimpressive, particularly when compared with the great monuments of traditional paganism, literary, epigraphic, and artistic.

Although sources of information concerning the mystery cults are notably defective in quantity, yet the popularity of these religions and their widespread influence in the Roman world cannot be doubted. Indirectly this is proved by the blistering vigor of Christian denunciations leveled against the gentile religions of redemption. From Paul to Augustine the mysteries bore the brunt of the Christian polemic against paganism. The fathers of the early church knew these cults as the strongest rivals that Christianity had, and with sour eloquence they testified to the popularity of the mysteries among gentile religionists.

Very directly the scattered fragments of mystery literature—the testimony of initiates and eyewitnesses—attest the strength and quality of mystery influence. One cannot read the *Odes* of Pindar, devout Orphic that he was, or the prayers of a fervent Isiacist like Lucius, or the *Consolatio* of a serious-minded Plutarch, or the *encomia* of Aristides and Julian, without realizing that the mysteries were real means of grace to many a convinced and sincere pagan. These cults had their apologists; Iamblicus, for example, and Porphyry, and Proclus. If their testimony has to be reduced somewhat in evaluation because of its apologetic character, full value must be allowed to the objective statements of disinterested witnesses like Cicero and Epictetus.[1] Mystery literature may be defective in quantity, but it is truly impressive for its fervor and the undoubted tone of sincerity that pervades it.

[1] Cicero *In Verrem* v. 72. 187; *De Deorum Natura* i. 42. 119; *De Legibus* ii. 14. 36. Epictetus *Dissertationes* iii. 21.

A realistic impression of the extent of mystery influence in the ancient world may be secured by observing the distribution of mystery chapels and other archaeological remains. For the most part the tangible monuments of the mysteries were very unpretentious in character, and were concentrated at the centers of population. The inscriptions which glimpse the group life within gentile religious brotherhoods have been found in a majority of cases in the great seaports. Mystery chapels have been unearthed in cities all over the Roman empire. They vary all the way from great and world-famous shrines, like the Eleusinian, to small chapels in private houses. In Rome a subterranean pagan basilica was recently discovered near the Porta Maggiore;[1] and Rome had also her temple to the Phrygian Mother crowning the Palatine itself. It is a familiar fact that the *limes* of the Roman Empire can be roughly sketched simply by marking the *mithraea* located in the frontier camps of the Roman army. And it is also a matter of common knowledge that Rome's nearest seaport, Ostia, was thickly dotted with mithraic chapels.[2] In view of the distribution of mystery monuments and the character of mystery sources generally, we may conclude, in the words of a well-known historian, "It would not be a mere rhetorical figure if one were to designate the religious history of the Mediterranean world in the early imperial period as the age of the mysteries."[3]

When the reason for the immense popularity of this group of religions is sought, it is found in their capacity to

[1] Cumont, "La Basilique souterraine de la Porta Maggiore," *Revue archéologique* (1918), pp. 52–77. See also Strong and Joliffe, "The Underground Basilica near the Porta Maggiore," *Journal of Hellenic Studies*, XLIV (1924), 65–111. Also Rostovtzeff, *Mystic Italy* (New York, 1928), pp. 130 ff.

[2] See Taylor, *The Cults of Ostia* (Bryn Mawr, 1912).

[3] Case, *The Social Origins of Christianity*, p. 113.

meet the most insistent religious demands of the age. They gave assurances to the restless, questing masses of people in the Roman empire such as neither philosophy nor ethics nor traditional religion could give. More particularly they answered to the demand of the individual man for special and unusual privileges in his religious relationships. The public performances of traditional religion, the healings accomplished by Asclepius and the oracles vouchsafed by Apollo, the omens interpreted by the augur and the charms formulated by the magician—these were more or less common property shared by all who could pay the price. But the average individual in the Roman Empire was not satisfied with these common goods. He desired unique religious privileges, made certain through personal attachment to a particular god who was especially interested in him. Dulled by the monotony and discouragements of everyday experience, he felt the need for emotional stimulation and uplift. Depressed by the injustices and defeats of life, he craved the assurance of recompense in the future. The demand for emotional stimulation and for the assurance of a happy immortality were among the most important religious needs that the mysteries aimed to satisfy.

There were other less important and more superficial reasons for the success of these cults. Their rites were exceedingly attractive. The pageantry and processionals of the public celebrations appealed to Mediterranean tastes and had no little propaganda value, while the intimate rites of the esoteric services were designed to stimulate a varied and richly emotional type of religious experience. The doctrines of the mysteries, cast in mythological forms, were to a degree satisfying to the intellect. They gave a comprehensive and intelligible explanation of the universe, and provided pictorial answers to inevitable questionings as to the how and why of things. The very antiquity of the mysteries was in their favor and there was a tendency for each cult to claim precedence on the basis of greater age. Also the secrecy and esoteric character of the gentile religions further enhanced their reputation. Finally, it should be asserted that the mystery religions, particularly in their Roman development, were readily responsive to the ethical demands of the age.[1] In summarizing the reasons that account for the remarkable diffusion of mystery cults throughout the Roman world, M. Cumont concludes:

> These religions gave greater satisfaction first of all to the senses and emotions, in the second place to the intelligence, and finally and chiefly to the conscience. . . . . They offered, in comparison with previous religions, more beauty in their ritual, more truth in their doctrines, and a superior good in their morality.[2]

A great variety of mystery religions flourished in the Roman empire. Almost every separate geographical area east of the Adriatic developed and contributed to the mystery group a typical cult of its own. The Phrygian plateau and the plains of Thrace, where emotionalism ran high, seem to have been the great primitive centers for this type of religion. Thrace was the homeland of the Dionysian and Orphic movements, which spread broadly over Hellas and Magna Graecia in recurrent tides of religious revival. To Eleusis in Attica the world was indebted for the evolution of the Eleusinian mysteries, the very finest product of the religious genius of the Greeks. Nor should the Samothracian or Andanian mysteries be forgotten, for they were well known both to Greeks and to Romans. Anatolia gave to

---

[1] Recent and well-informed discussions of the moot question of mystery morality may be found in Angus, *The Mystery Religions and Christianity* (London, 1925), pp. 235–46, and Halliday, *The Pagan Background of Early Christianity* (London, 1925), pp. 265–80.

[2] Cumont, *Religions orientales dans le paganisme romain*, pp. 43–68; English translation, pp. 28–44.

Rome the cult of the Great Mother of the Gods and Syria shared with the empire in devotion to a goddess who was known simply as *Iasura*, i.e., the Syrian goddess. Also there flourished in the east Mediterranean territory the cult of Aphrodite and Adonis, a divine pair known to Phoenicia as Ashtart and Eshmun and to Mesopotamia as Ishtar and Tammuz. On the Iranian plateau the mysteries of Mithra had their initial growth and in the Nile valley the cult of Isis and Osiris originated, each embodying characteristic phases of Persian and Egyptian culture. These were only the most famous of the Graeco-Oriental mysteries. Apart from them many an ignored local cult functioned significantly in its own day and place.

As a result of their diversity of origin, the Graeco-Oriental mysteries exhibited many differences in detail. In fundamental character, however, they were alike, and so markedly differentiated from contemporary systems as to warrant grouping them together under the common classification of mystery religions. By contrast with the established gentile cults they were purely individualistic in character, concerned not with the material welfare of a particular race or nation or city, but with the salvation of the individual soul instead. It is but a complementary statement to add that because of this individualistic emphasis the mysteries came to assume the character of cosmic religions to a degree that was impossible for other gentile systems. Furthermore, the mystery cults were outstanding as religions of redemption par excellence. The salvation they had to offer was spiritual and other-worldly. The individual could not hope to attain it as a result of his own unaided efforts. What the mysteries guaranteed was that on account of the devotee's attachment to the lord of the cult his salvation could and would be fully accomplished for him. Uniformly, the mystery deities were conceived as

hero-gods of the dying and rising type, who had suffered
to an exaggerated degree the ills to which flesh is heir; but
in the end they had gloriously triumphed. Because of this
archetypal experience of the god, the initiates might feel
sure of a similar victory over the evils of human experience.
"Be of good cheer, you of the mystery. Your god is saved.
For us also there shall be salvation from ills." This in exact
mystery terminology was the guaranty of each cult. The
mysteries were also distinguished as sacramental religions wherein salvation was conditioned upon participation in a prescribed ritual. By means of initiatory rites
which included ablutions and purifications the candidate
was made a fit person to approach deity. Finally, in culminating rites of communion and revelation and deification,
the union of divinity and humanity was experientially accomplished. But the chief distinction of the mysteries in
comparison with other gentile cults was the fact that they
were eschatological religions which had to do with the ultimate issue of death itself. When the imperial cult promised
a kingdom of God on earth and the state religions granted
an Elysian land to the favored few, the mysteries gave to
the ordinary man the prized assurance of immortality of
soul in a happy hereafter.

Because of these common characteristics and the non-
exclusive religious habits of the Gentiles and the eclectic
tendencies of the age, it was inevitable that the mysteries
should undergo a considerable degree of fusion during the
Graeco-Roman period. None of the mysteries demanded
an exclusive religious loyalty on the part of its adherents.
Hence it was a common custom for initiates to belong to
more than one religious brotherhood at the same time.
Lucius Apuleius actually bankrupted himself in order to
secure initiation into various secret cults,[1] and Tatian, in

[1] Apuleius *Metamorphoses* xi. 26 ff.

his quest for truth, joined one mystery after another.[1] Plutarch's friend Clea, to whom the treatise on *Isis and Osiris* was inscribed, was equally a devotee of the Delphic Dionysus and the Egyptian Isis.[2] Among the clergy as well as the laity non-exclusive religious practices were in vogue. An Attis of the Phrygian Mother might at the same time be a Father in the Mithraic mysteries. Lucius, before his Isiac initiation, was assigned to the tutelage of a mystagogue who bore the significant name "Mithra."[3] A more striking case of varied clerical functioning was recorded in a Latin inscription which designated one and the same man as *Pater Patrum Dei Solis invicti Mithrae, Hierofanta Hecates, Dei Liberi Archiboculus, taurobolio criobolioque in aeternum renatus.*[4]

Under conditions such as these an interchange of formulas and symbols and beliefs and practices was the natural consequence. There was a *theocrasia* in the mystery group of religions corresponding to that accomplished between the Capitoline and Olympian systems. The likenesses of the various pairs of mystery divinities were unmistakable, the mother goddess embodying all the powers of nature and the suffering son or lover exhibiting life in action. So the Phrygians recognized their *Magna Mater* in the Syrian goddess and the Greeks saw Dionysus in the person of Osiris. This tendency to identify deities with one another culminated in the assertion, not infrequent in mystery documents, that a given god or goddess represented the totality of the divine nature.[5] Picturesque rites, even, passed from one cult to another. The *taurobolium*, histori-

---

[1] Tatian *Ad Graecos* 29.

[2] Plutarch *De Iside et Osiride* 35.   [3] Apuleius *Metamorphoses* xi. 22.

[4] *Corpus Inscriptionum Latinarum*, Vol. VI, No. 510.

[5] For this affirmation regarding Isis see Apuleius *Metamorphoses* xi. 5 and the "Invocation of Isis" in *Oxyrhynchus Papyri*, Vol. XI, No. 1380.

cally the great sacrament of the *Magna Mater*, was so conspicuously appropriated by the Mithraists that it is popularly associated with the Persian rather than with the Phrygian cult.

To a greater or less degree all the mystery religions were subject to the process of fusion, but none to a greater extent than the Orphic movement, which in Roman times largely lost its identity. In fact the process of syncretism, which was characteristic of almost every phase of Graeco-Roman thinking, cannot be studied more effectively than by investigating the development of the mysteries in Hellenistic and Roman times.

The fact of fusion among the mysteries causes peculiar problems to the modern student. This is the dilemma: either to study the various cults separately, as Loisy does, for example,[1] or to view them *en masse* as a single great religious system. The latter is the method of Reitzenstein, in whose latest volume the "mystery religions" become "the Hellenistic mystery religion."[2] The former method is apt to give a false impression of the whole religious situation in the Graeco-Roman world and to picture it as more chaotic than it actually was. On the other hand, the synthetic study of the mysteries is apt to neglect the distinctive contribution of each to the religious life of the age and, at the same time, to attribute to a given cult phases of some other system. Under the circumstances, the most nearly exact procedure would seem to be to emphasize those fundamental aspects of the mystery type of religion which were characteristic of all the cults in common and to balance this with a detailed investigation of the idiosyncrasies of each particular cult.

For membership in each and all of the mysteries there

[1] Loisy, *Les Mystères païens* (Paris, 1921²), pp. 1–203.

[2] Reitzenstein, *Die Hellenistischen Mysterienreligionen* (Leipzig, 1927³).

was one absolute *sine qua non*—participation in special rites of initiation. Membership in national religions was an involuntary matter. The accident of birth into a given race or nation made one automatically a member of the state church. In the case of the mysteries, however, membership was a volitional matter. It was contingent, first of all, upon the individual's own personal choice and his further willingness to submit to the prescribed rites. Thus it was that mystery initiation came to be considered a matter of very great importance by many gentile religionists. Without this single prerequisite there could be no share in the religious privileges that the mysteries and the mysteries alone could guarantee.

What, more precisely, was the central meaning of mystery initiation for the individual neophyte? What difference did it make for the person who shared in the rite? What, if anything, was actually accomplished by the antique liturgy? In view of the general social situation in the Graeco-Roman world, what was the functional significance of mystery initiation in relation to contemporary social processes generally? These are fundamental questions that can be answered, if at all, only after a detailed study of actual initiation experiences in the various cults, together with an equally analytical investigation of the social milieu in which the mysteries operated.

BIBLIOGRAPHY

ANGUS, SAMUEL, *The Mystery Religions and Christianity*. New York, 1925.

CASE, S. J., *The Evolution of Early Christianity* (Chicago, 1914), pp. 195–330.

CUMONT, F., *Religions orientales dans le paganisme romain*, Paris, 1909². English translation by Grant Showerman, *Oriental Religions in Roman Paganism*. Chicago, 1911.

CUMONT, F., *Astrology and Religion among Greeks and Romans*. New York, 1912.

DILL, SAMUEL, *Roman Society from Nero to Marcus Aurelius* (London, 1920²), pp. 443–626.

GLASSÉ, JOHN, *The Mysteries and Christianity*. Edinburgh, 1921.

GLOVER, T. R., *The Conflict of Religions in the Early Roman Empire*, London, 1920⁹.

GLOVER, T. R., *Progress in Religion to the Christian Era*. London, 1922.

HALLIDAY, W. R., *The Pagan Background of Early Christianity* (London, 1925), pp. 168 ff.

DE JONG, K. H. E., *Das antike Mysterienwesen*. Leiden, 1919².

LEGGE, F., *Forerunners and Rivals of Christianity*, 2 vols. Cambridge, 1915.

LOISY, A. F., *Les Mystères païens et le Mystère chrétien* (Paris, 1921²), pp. 1–203.

OTTO, WALTER, *Priester und Tempel im hellenistischen Ägypten*, 2 vols. Leipzig, 1905–8.

REITZENSTEIN, R., *Die hellenistischen Mysterien-religionen*. Leipzig, 1927³.

ROSTOVTZEFF, M. I., *Mystic Italy*. New York, 1928.

SCHMIDT, E., *Kultübertragungen*. Giessen, 1910.

TOUSSAINT, C., *L'Hellénisme et l'Apôtre Paul* (Paris, 1921).

TOUTAIN, J., *Les Cultes païens dans l'empire romain*, 3 vols. Paris, 1911–20.

WISSOWA, G., *Religion und Kultus der Romer*. Munich, 1912².

CHAPTER II

THE GREATER MYSTERIES AT ELEUSIS

A MONG the cults of Greece none was more favorably known in the first century of the Christian era than the Eleusinian mysteries. Although it was more definitely localized and centralized than were the other Greek mysteries, this circumstance did not detract from either its reputation or its influence. Locally it was associated with an antique tradition that ran back to prehistoric times, and such antiquity was a valued credential for any first-century religion. The home of this cult was the town of Eleusis on the fertile Rharian plain a few miles from Athens, where in prehistoric times the cereal goddess Demeter was revered by an agricultural community. Legends of the special initiation of foreigners like Heracles and the Dioscuri recall the primitive time when membership in the cult was open to citizens of Eleusis only. With the political fusion of Eleusis and Athens, however, the local barriers were broken down and rebuilt along much extended lines. The dominant city-state of Athens adopted the cult as her own, brought it under state supervision, and entrusted the general management of the mysteries to the *Archon Basileus*. Inscriptions of the Periclean period attest the well-considered plan of Athens to use the mysteries as a religious support for her political hegemony.[1] This combination of ancient Eleusinian tradition and the official patronage of the Athenian state gave dignity and prestige to the mysteries of Demeter even in the first century.

But this cult was more than merely a state religion of

[1] *Corpus Inscriptionum Atticarum*, Vol. I, 1.

the usual Greek model. In the first century its appeal and its guaranties were for the individual rather than for the citizen. On the one hand not all Athenians, by any means, were members of the cult. The citizen of Athens did not automatically come under the protection of Demeter by natural birth as he found himself under the aegis of Athena. It was by special initiation alone, conceived and represented as a process of rebirth, that he could avail himself of the cult privileges. No less an Athenian than Socrates was reproached for not seeking initiation into these mysteries. The state cult of Demeter operated as a voluntary religious association in which Athenian citizens were eligible for membership; but their adherence was a matter of their own volition.

Conversely, eligibility for admission was not limited to Athenians only. When, as a result of the absorption of Eleusis by Athens, the mysteries lost their local exclusiveness, they further took on a pan-Hellenic character. The so-called Homeric Hymn to Demeter,[1] one of the earliest and most valuable of Eleusinian documents, invites the whole Greek world to come and participate in the mysteries. Herodotus states that in his day whoever wished to do so, whether they were Athenians or other Greeks, might come to be initiated.[2] Later, even the Hellenic limitation was removed and persons of any nationality were received, providing they understood the Greek language in which the ritual was conducted. In the time of Cicero, just before the beginning of our era, "the most distant nations were initiated into the sacred and august Eleusinia."[3]

[1] For a critical edition see Sikes and Allen, *Homeric Hymns* (London, 1904). Lang, *Homeric Hymns* (New York, 1899) contains a good English translation. See also the critical text and translation by H. G. Evelyn-White in the "Loeb Classical Library" (London, 1920).

[2] Herodotus viii. 65.   [3] Cicero *De Deorum Natura* i. 42.

It is interesting to note further that women and slaves, even, were admitted to this cult. The author of the oration *In Neaeram*, which was once attributed to Demosthenes, states that Lysias, without any difficulty, was able to arrange for the initiation of his mistress Metanira.[1] That slaves were admitted is suggested by a fragment from the comic poet Theophilus in which a slave speaks with gratitude of his beloved master who taught him his letters and got him initiated into the sacred mysteries.[2] An inscription dated in the administration of Lycurgus (329–328 B.C.) further puts the question of the admission of slaves beyond doubt. It is an expense account of an Eleusinian official, and among the items included is the following: "For the initiation of two public slaves; thirty drachmae."[3] The mysteries of Demeter, therefore, once a local cult and later a state religion, came in the end to assume an international character and to make an individualistic appeal. In its developed form, the cult received into membership not only Greeks but also "barbarians," and women and slaves as well as free men.

I

It is indubitable that the influence of the Eleusinian mysteries was widespread in the Graeco-Roman world. Though localized at Eleusis this cult influenced rites that were celebrated elsewhere in widely scattered centers. In Ionia, at Ephesus[4] and Mycale,[5] and again in the Arcadian city of Pheneus,[6] Demeter Eleusinia was worshiped and her cult was related in local legend to the Attic foundation. Pausanias vouches for the statement that Celeae near

---

[1] (Demosthenes) *In Neaeram* 21–23.

[2] *Fragmenta Comicorum Graecorum*, III (Meineke), 626.

[3] *Ephemeris Archaiologike* (1883), pl. 10, l. 71.

[4] Strabo 633.

[5] Herodotus ix. 97.   [6] Pausanias viii. 15. 1.

Phlius, and Megalopolis in Arcadia each had an "initiation mystery of Demeter" in which the proceedings were conducted "in imitation of those at Eleusis."[1] According to a late inscription (third century A.D.), a mystery of Demeter flourished at Lerna in Argolis, and the hierophant in charge was the son of an Athenian priest.[2] There are further records that Demeter Eleusinia was worshiped in Boeotia and Laconia on the Greek mainland, and in Crete and Thera among the Greek islands. At Naples, in Italy, mysteries in honor of Demeter were celebrated after the Attic manner.[3] It is even possible that the Andanian mysteries in Messenia, which Pausanias regarded as second in dignity and prestige to the Eleusinian alone,[4] were also related to the Attic cult. In each of these instances two possibilities are to be considered. Either the similar rites had their origin in the Eleusinian ceremonies or else both came from a common parentage.[5] In either case it is patent that there was widespread interest in Demeter cults in the Graeco-Roman world.

Quite apart from the question of related Demeter cults, however, there is an abundance of *testimonia* to prove the world-wide reputation of the Eleusinian rites themselves at the beginning of the common era. Crinagoras, the Greek epigrammatist of Mytilene, writing in the time of Augustus, advised his friend by all means to go to Athens and see the mysteries, even though he traveled nowhere else.[6] If we may credit Philostratus, his hero Apollonius of Tyana,

[1] Pausanias ii. 14. 1; also viii. 31. 7.

[2] *Corpus Inscriptionum Atticarum*, Vol. III, No. 718.

[3] Statius *Silvae* iv. 8. 50.

[4] Pausanias iv. 33. 4 *et passim*.

[5] For further and detailed discussion of this moot question see Farnell, *Cults of the Greek States*, III, 198 ff.

[6] *Anthologia Palatina* xi. 42.

certainly one of the most famous and respected religionists of his day, applied in person for admission to the Eleusinian mysteries. "But the hierophant was not disposed to admit him to the rites, for he said he would never initiate a wizard and charlatan, nor open the Eleusinian Mysteries to a man who dabbled in impure rites."[1]

During the early imperial period some very famous non-Greeks showed their deep interest in the mysteries at Eleusis, among them the Emperor Augustus himself. Though normally not attracted by foreign religions, he was initiated at Eleusis in 21 B.C. Later, according to Suetonius, he gave signal proof of his reverence for the mysteries.

He was hearing a case at Rome which involved the privileges of the priests of the Attic Ceres. When some of the mysteries of their sacred rites were to be introduced into the pleadings, he dismissed those who sat upon the bench with him as judges, as well as the bystanders, and heard the arguments upon these points himself.

Seutonius also tells us that when Nero was in Greece, "he dared not attend the Eleusinian Mysteries at the initiation of which impious and wicked persons are warned by the voice of the herald from approaching the rites."[2] However, there were other emperors who like Augustus attained the goal which Nero failed to gain. Marcus Aurelius and Commodus were two of these illustrious *mystae*. The epitaph of an Eleusinian priestess mentions it as a matter of special pride that she set the crown upon their heads as they participated in the solemn rites.[3] The fact that the first citizens of the Roman Empire sought membership in the Eleusinian cult is striking proof of its great influence.

Other significant testimony is given by the philosophers and moralists of this period. At the close of the pre-Chris-

---

[1] *Philostratus* iv. 18.

[2] Suetonius *Augustus* 93; also *Nero* 34.

[3] *Ephemeris Archaiologike* (1885), p. 150.

tian era, Cicero declared it was his personal opinion that Athens had given nothing to the world more excellent or divine than the Eleusinian mysteries.[1] At the beginning of the Christian centuries, the Stoic Epictetus spoke of the impressiveness of these mysteries in terms of genuine appreciation.[2] Thus, at the beginning of our era, when Olympian Zeus had lost his ancient supremacy and Delphian Apollo, though reviving, was yet reduced in influence, Demeter of Eleusis still enjoyed a high reputation. The influence of her mysteries was literally world-wide during the early imperial period.

II

In order to understand the type of religious experience represented by this important cult, it is necessary clearly to keep in mind the main points of the Eleusinian myth which was developed to explain and justify the cult rites. These are stated with sufficient elaboration in the Homeric Hymn to Demeter, although this document does not give the myth in its fully developed form. According to the story, Persephone, daughter of Demeter, "giver of goodly crops," was stolen by Pluto and carried off to the underworld to be his bride. This was done with the knowledge and tacit approval of Zeus himself. The mother, frenzied with grief, rushed about the earth for nine days, torch in hand, abstaining from eating and drinking, and searching wildly for her lost daughter. As she rested at the "maiden well of fragrant Eleusis" she was welcomed by the daughters of Celeus, who took her to their father's house for refreshment. Here she finally broke her fast and dwelt for a time. In her resentment against Zeus, she brought famine upon the fruitful earth so that no crops grew for men and no offerings were made to the gods. Finally, an arrangement was made with Pluto whereby Persephone was

[1] *De Legibus* ii. 14.   [2] *Discourses* iii. 21.

restored to her sorrowing mother. Since, however, the daughter had eaten a sweet pomegranate seed in the underworld she was forced to return there regularly for a portion of each year. Demeter, in her joy at the restoration of her lost daughter, allowed the crops to grow once more and instituted in honor of the event the Eleusinian mysteries which gave to mortals the assurance of a happy future life. Such was the myth which stood in the background of thought for one who participated in the Eleusinian rites.

The experiential basis for this story is quite clear. It was a nature myth, a vivid depiction of the action of life in the vegetable world with the changing of the seasons. Each year nature passed through the cycle of apparent death and resurrection. In winter vegetable life was dead while Demeter, the giver of life, grieved for the loss of her daughter. But with the coming of spring the life of nature revived again, for the sorrowing mother had received her daughter back with rejoicing. Through the summer the mother abundantly maintained the life of nature until autumn, when again her daughter returned to the underworld and earth became desolate once more. Thus year after year nature re-enacted the myth of Eleusis.

It was also a reflection of poignant human experiences, mirroring the joys, sorrows, and hopes of mankind in face of inevitable death. The three actors of the Eleusinian tragedy, the *mater dolorosa* as the protagonist, the maiden daughter as the deuteragonist, and the sinister figure of the ravisher as the mysterious third actor, these three enacted the mystery of human life and death. The god of death himself stole the beloved daughter away from the life-giver; but the divine mother would not give up her loved one, and in the end she accomplished her daughter's resurrection. Here was human experience made heroic and divine; for man has ever loved and lost, but rarely has he ceased to hope for reunion with the loved one. The Eleusinian myth told of these fundamental human experiences as well as of the life of nature.

III

With this mythological background in mind the Eleusinian ritual should be examined, at least in its more important features, in order to define the variety of religious experience fostered by this cult. It was an elaborate ceremonial, extending over a long period of time. The classical analysis of the Eleusinian rite divided it into four distinct stages: the *katharsis*, or preliminary purification, the *sustasis*, or preparatory rites and sacrifices, the *teletē*, i.e., the initiation proper, and the *epopteia*, or highest grade of initiation.[1] Of these various stages the first two were public, and concerning them there is a large amount of information. But the last two were very strictly private and therefore they remain for us shrouded in mystery. Unfortunately, it is these very private ceremonials that are most important for the student who is interested in the personal religious experiences of paganism. The elaborate preliminary ceremonies do not concern us in detail except as a preparation for the all-important rites which followed.

More than six months before the "great mysteries" in September the "lesser mysteries" were celebrated at Agrae, a suburb of Athens, on the banks of the Illisus. Clement of Alexandria spoke of "the minor mysteries which have some foundation of instruction and of preliminary preparation for what is to come after."[2] This statement emphasizes what for our purpose was the most significant feature of the mysteries at Agrae—they were important as a prerequisite for the "great mysteries."

[1] Cf. Lobeck, *Aglaophamus* I, 39 ff.

[2] Clement *Stromateis* v. 11.

On the thirteenth of September the "great mysteries" began and they lasted over a full week. Early in the festival there was a solemn assembly in the *Stoa Poicilē*, the main item of which was a proclamation by the hierophant. This was not a sermon but rather a warning to depart, addressed to those who for one reason or another were disqualified or unworthy of initiation. As to the content of the formal warning, Libanius states that the "leaders of the *mystae*" proclaimed to those seeking initiation that they must be "pure in hand and soul and of Hellenic speech." These terms are confirmed in part by a mathematician of the imperial period who compared his studies to the mysteries. "Not all who wish," he said, "have a share in the Mysteries. But there are some who are forewarned to abstain; such as those whose hands are not clean and whose speech is unintelligible." Celsus, as reported by Origen, gives two formulas of invitation, one altogether similar to those already cited and the other of a somewhat different character. He is quoted as follows:

Those who invite people to other mysteries make proclamation thus: "Everyone who has clean hands and intelligible speech," others again thus: "He who is pure from all pollution, and whose soul is conscious of no evil and who has lived well and justly." Such is the proclamation made by those who promise purification from sins.[1]

These quotations from late pagan writers indicate that the Athenian proclamation included not only ritualistic requirements but elements of moral scrutiny as well. One may say that over the Eleusinian shrine as over the doorway of the Rhodian temple were inscribed the words "[Those can rightfully enter] who are pure and healthy in hand and heart and who have no evil conscience in themselves."[2]

[1] Origen *Contra Celsum* iii. 59.

[2] *Inscriptiones Graecae Insularum Maris Aegaei* Vol. I, No. 789.

On the day following the assembly came the cry, "To the sea, O *Mystae!*" and the candidates for initiation ran down to the sea, there to purify themselves in its salt waves—a lustration believed to be of greater virtue than that of fresh water. "Sea waves wash away all sin," said Euripides. The potent effect of the cleansing by salt water was further enhanced by sprinkling with pig's blood. Each of the *mystae* carried with him a sucking pig which he purified by immersion in the waters of the sea. Later the pig was sacrificed and its blood sprinkled on the candidate. Tertullian, in speaking of this rite, declared, "At the Eleusinian mysteries men are baptized and they assume that the effect of this is their regeneration and the remission of the penalties due to their perjuries."[1] This striking affirmation by a Christian writer shows that the initiates themselves applied the new birth comparison to their own experiences in Eleusinian baptism. The rite was believed to be more than cathartic, merely. Regenerative powers were credited to it which operated to make the initiate in some sense a new being. It was with this rite particularly that the Eleusinian devotees associated the idea of personal transformation.[2]

After the preliminary rites at Athens, the purified candidates formed in solemn procession on the nineteenth of September and marched to Eleusis, there to complete the celebration of the festival. Along the Sacred Way leading from Athens there were many holy places, and since the *mystae* performed ritualistic observances en route the company arrived at Eleusis by torchlight late in the evening. The long march was followed by a midnight revel under the stars, a ceremony that Aristophanes described in glowing terms.[3] This was held on the Rharian plain,

[1] Tertullian *De Baptismo* 5.

[2] Aristophanes *Acharnians* 747; *Pax* 374; *Ranae* 337.

[3] Aristophanes *Ranae* 324 ff.

and it is not improbable that it partook of the nature of a mimetic ritual. Near the great propylaea of the sacred precinct was the Well of Callichoros, where the first choral dances were organized by the women of Eleusis in honor of Demeter. Close at hand was the Unsmiling Rock, where the desolate mother sat when she first came to Eleusis. Not far away were the meadows which had seen her torchlit wanderings. It would not be strange if the *mystae* beginning their choral dances at the Well of Callichorus, continuing their revel by torchlight in the meadows, or resting at the Unsmiling Rock—it would not be strange if they felt that they were really sharing in the antique experiences of their goddess. Certainly in their wearied state, weakened by fasting, they would be peculiarly susceptible to such mystical emotions.

Thus the *mystae* were prepared for the climactic feature of the celebration which took place in the *telestērion*, or Hall of Initiation. This sacred place was closed to all save the initiated, and the events which occurred there were strictly private and shrouded in the densest mystery. The initiates were under pledge of secrecy not to divulge the revelation there given. Apparently public opinion enforced this pledge in a very remarkable manner. Once when Aeschylus was acting in one of his own tragedies the audience became suspicious that he was betraying certain secrets of the Eleusinian mysteries. They arose in real fury and attacked the author-actor, who saved his life only by fleeing to the altar of Dionysus, a refuge that the Athenian mob respected. Later, however, Aeschylus was brought to trial before the Areopagus for revealing forbidden secrets and was acquitted quite as much because of his bravery at Marathon as because of his plea of ignorance. Alcibiades, on the eve of his departure for the Sicilian expedition, was charged with "impious mockery of the goddesses Demeter and Persephone" because he had "profanely acted the sacred mysteries at a drunken meeting."[1] Even such a garrulous historian as Herodotus, though he was "accurately acquainted with the sacred rites of Demeter" yet felt that he "must observe a discreet silence" concerning them.[2] The secret of Eleusis was guarded all too well and as a result we know almost nil concerning the central rites of the mysteries of Demeter.

One of the incidents just mentioned, however, makes it clear that the heart of the Eleusinian ritual was in the nature of a religious drama. The accusation against Alcibiades very definitely specified actors in a mock pageant which he staged at his drunken revel. "Theodorus represented the herald, Polytion the torch-bearer, and Alcibiades the chief priest, while the rest of the party appeared as candidates for initiation and received the title of initiates."[3] This describes the situation in the *telestērion* at Eleusis on the night of initiation; the priests took the part of actors in a religious drama or pageant of which the initiates were the spectators. The archaeological remains of the Hall of Initiation at Eleusis bear out this theory. It was a great square hall around the four sides of which ran stone seats eight steps high, one above the other. Here the initiates sat and watched the spectacle staged in their midst.

Of what did the dramatic action in the *telestērion* consist? Only hints are given; yet these are sufficient to suggest what was probably the subject matter of the mystery play. Clement of Alexandria tells us that "Deo [Demeter] and Kore became [the personages of] a mystic drama, and Eleusis with its *dadouchos* celebrates the wandering, the

[1] Plutarch *Alcibiades* xix. 1.

[2] Herodotus ii. 171.

[3] Plutarch *Alcibiades* xxii. 3.

abduction, and the sorrow."[1] Apparently the drama of the *telestērion* was a sort of passion play, the subject matter of which was essentially the same as that of the Homeric Hymn. It concerned the loss of the daughter, the sorrow of the mother, and the final return of the loved one from Hades. This view is further confirmed by the words which Apuleius puts into the mouth of Psyche when she appeals to Demeter "by the unspoken secrets of the mystic chests, the winged chariots of thy dragon ministers, the bridal descent of Proserpine, the torchlit wanderings to find thy daughter, and all the other mysteries which Attic Eleusis shrouds in secret."[2] From these two references it is evident that the important parts of the great myth of Demeter were enacted as a drama before the eyes of the *mystae* gathered in the *telestērion*.

Various writers, pagan as well as Christian, furnish additional evidence on this point and emphasize certain crises in the unfolding plot of the passion drama. Apollodorus, an Athenian historian and mythographer of the second century B.C., is quoted as saying, "The hierophant is in the habit of sounding the so-called gong when Kore calls for aid." Undoubtedly this statement has reference to the Eleusinian ritual, as the mention of the hierophant proves. One can easily understand that the cry of Persephone marked a high point of interest in the course of the Eleusinian drama, and that it was accentuated by the sounding of a gong. The effect of this on the devotees can easily be imagined. It was an unexpected sound coming suddenly in the midst of a solemn ceremonial. It focused attention entirely and sharply on the immediate action. In emotional effect, it was probably not unlike the sounding of the gong during the celebration of mass. By this simple ex-

---

[1] Clement of Alexandria *Protrepticus* iv. 27.

[2] Apuleius *Metamorphoses* vi. 2.

pedient, the abduction of Persephone was made a memorable part of the passion play of Eleusis.

The statement already quoted from the Alexandrian Clement concerning the actors in the Eleusinian drama makes specific reference to the grief of Demeter as constituting a part of the action. This reference is further confirmed by a quotation from a late pagan author, Proclus, who asserts, "The ceremonies of the Mysteries in their secret part, transmit certain sacred lamentations of Kore, of Demeter, of the Great Goddess herself." Thus again it becomes clear that the Eleusinian passion play was not merely a pantomine, reproducing the actions and gestures of the divine personages, but that it included vocal expression as well. By recitative or chant the actors who impersonated the goddesses gave expression to the emotions of the moment. The text suggests that these chants were traditional and were characterized by the fixity of form usual in ritual. Such being the case, the sorrow of Demeter which formed a distinct episode in the Eleusinian drama was further made impressive by traditional liturgical expression.

An important but very vague reference to the secret part of the Eleusinian mysteries is found in the Panegyric oration of Isocrates. "In her wanderings after the abduction of Persephone, Demeter came into our land. She wished to give testimony of her benevolence to our ancestors in recompense for the good offices of which initiates alone are permitted to hear."[1] What were these services with which only initiates into the Eleusinian mysteries were familiar and of which they could speak only among themselves? Obviously it could not be the welcome given to Demeter by the household of Celeus. That was known to the wide world through the Homeric Hymn. A Latin

[1] Isocrates *Panegyricus* 28.

poet of the first century furnishes a possible explanation of this veiled reference in Isocrates. Addressing the goddess herself, Statius says:

> Tuque, Actaea Ceres, cursu cui semper anelo
> Votivam taciti quassamus lampada mystae.[1]

Here the Latin poet speaks as an initiate himself. He is contemplating a ceremony which is not a mere spectacle but a religious rite, shared in by the devotees. In solemn silence, torch in hand, they accompanied Demeter in her breathless wanderings. Just as the priestess personified the goddess, they temporarily represented the legendary inhabitants of Eleusis who not only welcomed the goddess but also assisted her in her search. These were probably the services of which Isocrates hinted with such reserve. In the wanderings of Demeter, then, the initiates actually participated by mimetic action. They did the very things which would enable them best to share emotionally in the profound experiences of their goddess.

A quotation from a fourth-century Christian writer, Lactantius, adds confirmatory evidence here and further suggests what was probably the closing scene of the Eleusinian drama. Referring specifically to the mysteries of Demeter, Lactantius says, "With burning torches Proserpina is sought, and when she is found, the rite is closed with general thanksgiving and a waving of torches."[2] The search was not in vain. The lost daughter was found and restored; and the initiates who had shared in the anxious wanderings of the mother now shared in her happiness at the recovery of her daughter. With joyous acclamation and the waving of torches the return of the lost daughter was hailed by the initiates. This scene of happiness, according to Lactantius, closed the drama of Eleusis.

[1] Statius *Silvae* iv. 8. 51.

[2] Lactantius *Institutiones Divinae* (*Epitome*) 23.

Thus, notwithstanding the meagerness of information concerning the Eleusinian passion play, we can yet distinguish the main episodes of its action. The abduction of Persephone, the grief of her mother, the search for the lost daughter, and the reunion of the two goddesses—these were the principle scenes. The indecent actions suggested by a few Christian writers must be ruled out as vouched for only on the testimony of prejudiced and highly interested witnesses.[1] On the other hand, the well-certified scenes, though so few in number, constitute the basis for a religious rite of impressive possibilities.

True, the actors in this passion play were few. But classical Greek tragedy at its best boasted of but three actors. And in the *telestērion* the protagonist was Demeter, the goddess of grain, and the deuteragonist was Persephone, the goddess of the underworld. Clad in gorgeous and traditional costumes the personages of the Eleusinian passion play must have been very impressive figures. Of scenic effect there was little or nothing. The architectural remains of the *telestērion* show no provision for anything like stage settings or machinery. There was not even a stage, and the properties were probably the simplest possible—torchlight and rich robes. Again the familiar effects of Greek drama may serve to account for this absence of properties. On the Greek stage all was simplicity and convention. Greek audiences, like the spectators of the Elizabethan drama, were trained to depend upon their imaginations to supply what was lacking in stage settings. So at Eleusis, the effectiveness of the passion play depended much upon the cultivated imaginations of the *mystae*. Moreover, by simple expedients the participation of the initiates in the action of the drama was brought about.

---

[1] Clement of Alexandria *Protrepticus* ii *passim*; Arnobius *Adversus Gentes* v. 25; Gregory of Nazianzen *Orations* xxxix. 4.

They were not merely spectators of a pageant; they were participants in a ritual. The gong focused their attention upon the first great crisis of the drama, the abduction of the daughter. With torches they followed the mother in her frantic search and again with the waving of torches they expressed their joy at the return of her daughter. Thus, by participation in the dramatic action, as well as by active imagination, the *mystae* were enabled to share emotionally in the experiences of the great goddesses.

Does the plot centering around the abduction of Persephone and her restoration to her sorrowing mother mark the limits of the dramatic representation in the *telestērion?* Many students believe it does not. M. Foucart, for example, goes so far as to distinguish a second drama, enacted at Eleusis on the evening following the passion play just outlined.[1] According to M. Foucart, the main features of this second mystery drama were a sacred marriage and the birth of a holy child.

The citations supporting this view are not numerous. A commentator on a passage in Plato's *Gorgias* says, "The Mysteries are celebrated in honor of Demeter and Kore, because the latter was abducted by Pluto and because Zeus was united with Demeter."[2] This reference does suggest the possibility of two different Eleusinian dramas along the lines indicated. From the context, however, it is evident that the scholiast is drawing uncritically from Christian sources; hence the value of his testimony is not certain. Tertullian's question, "Why is the priestess of Ceres ravished, unless Ceres herself suffered the same sort of thing?"[3] is a passage of doubtful reference and interpretation that can scarcely be cited in proof of a sacred

---

[1] Foucart, *Les Mystères d' Éleusis*, pp. 475 ff. Farnell's position on this point, however, is reserved.

[2] Scholion on *Gorgias* 497C.   [3] Tertullian *Ad Nationes* ii. 7.

marriage at Eleusis. It is most reasonable to think that Tertullian in speaking thus merely confused Demeter and Persephone. As a subsidiary bit of evidence from a pagan source, it should be noted that Lucian had his false-prophet Alexander introduce a sacred marriage into his mysteries, which were modeled in part after the Eleusinian rites.[1] However, the clearest passage in support of the sacred marriage idea is found in the writings of Asterius, a fourth-century Christian bishop. With unpleasant insinuation, he speaks of "the underground chamber and the solemn meeting of the hierophant and the priestess, each with the other alone, when the torches are extinguished, and the vast crowd believes that its salvation depends on what goes on there."[2]

If this passage may be taken as conclusive evidence of a sacred marriage in the Eleusinian *telestērion,* then it has a further significance that is noteworthy. It shows that the marriage was a representative act whereby the initiates entered into mystical communion with their deity. As such it would be a more or less realistic rite after the order of the marriage of the *Basilinna* at Athens with the god Dionysus, in which the city was united by proxy to the god. The point has this importance: if a sacred marriage was part of the Eleusinian ritual, then this rite assured the initiates of a more direct and immediate communion with the goddess than would otherwise be possible. Whether or not the testimony of Asterius is accepted, his insinuations deserve to be repudiated. There is no reason to assume that any part of the rites were indelicate or were regarded otherwise than with reverence by the initiates. We may be sure of this, that if there was a sacred marriage at Eleusis it was a solemn ceremonial, probably a liturgical

[1] Lucian *Alexander* 38, 39.

[2] *Encomium in sanctos martures* 113B.

fiction, and not an exhibition of licentiousness. Indeed, we have the positive statement of Hippolytus as to the scrupulous purity of the hierophant.[1]

Closely connected with the question of a sacred marriage is that relative to a holy birth at Eleusis. Hippolytus, in the Naassenic sermon just cited, is almost the only authority for this episode. He says:

> The hierophant himself . . . . celebrating at Eleusis the great and ineffable mysteries beside a huge fire cries aloud and makes proclamation, saying: "August Brimo has brought forth a holy son, Brimos," that is, the strong has given birth to the strong. For august, he says, is the generation which is spiritual, or heavenly, or from above, and strong is that which is thus generated.

Such a holy birth as this would normally follow the marriage rite just discussed. What lends exceptional interest to the rite is the idea suggested unclearly in a brief word study that follows. Quoting from "those initiated into the mysteries," the name Eleusis is derived from *eleusesthai* (to come) "because we spiritual ones came on high." This suggests that the holy birth of the Eleusinian drama, a birth "spiritual, heavenly, and from above" was viewed as typifying the new birth of the initiate which translated him from the earthly, human sphere to the heavenly, spiritual realm. On this interpretation the rite came to be viewed as a dramatic enactment of a spiritual rebirth experienced individually by the initiates themselves.

The possibility of such a two-act drama as this at Eleusis must certainly be allowed. With lights extinguished, the initiates may have waited in breathless silence for the consummation of a sacred marriage, believing that it involved their own direct communion with the goddess. Again in a blaze of light they may have welcomed the announcement of a holy birth, believing that their own

[1] Hippolytus *Philosophoumena* v. 1. 8.

rebirth as spiritual beings was involved in the process. If so, the rites of Eleusis held out to the whole body of initiates the possibility of immediate communion with deity and complete personal transformation guaranteed by appropriate rites. The mystical communion fostered by the problematic second drama at Eleusis was even more intimate and realistic than that cultivated by the passion play.

Distinct from the dramatic part of the initiation ceremony at Eleusis was the exhibition of sacred objects. This part of the service was at least of equal importance with the passion play. The title of the hierophant was "he who displays the sacred things," and his exhibition of these objects was an act of the utmost solemnity. Only a part of them were shown during the celebration at which the neophytes witnessed the mystic drama and attained the grade of *mystae*. Others were reserved for exhibition a year later at the *epopteia*, or final grade of initiation, when the *mystae* became *epoptae*. Thus the display of venerable objects marked the culmination of the "great mysteries" and, so far as we know, was the all-important feature of the final grade of initiation.

Just what the "sacred things" were is a question not clearly answered. It is but reasonable to suppose that they were the very objects which were solemnly escorted to Athens at the beginning of the festival and were later returned to Eleusis in the procession of the candidates on the nineteenth of September. In these processions they were treated with the highest honors and were carefully guarded from public view. Probably they included statues of the goddesses, images of great antiquity and sanctity. We know how the crude old wooden statues of the gods were venerated in other cults. Ordinarily their origin was a matter of marvel. At Athens, for example, the wooden image

of Athena Polias, which was believed to have fallen from
heaven during the reign of Cecrops, was inextricably bound
up with the fortunes of the city. Tertullian speaks not only
of a wooden statute of Athena but also of a like image of
Demeter as well.[1] Accordingly, we may infer that Eleusis
had its wooden image of Demeter even as Athens had its
xoanon of Athena Polias, and in all probability this was
the most sacred of all the sacred objects at Eleusis. Quite
certainly it was accompanied also by an image of Persephone. Within the sacred area at Eleusis, these statues
were housed in the *anactoron*, or chapel, of Demeter which
crowned the citadel. This was the holy of holies in the
Eleusinian precinct and none but the hierophant might
enter here. An Epicurean who had the hardihood to violate
the shrine perished miserably as a result of his impiety.[2]
In this *anactoron* the sacred objects were carefully guarded
from profanation until the time came for their exhibition.

The display of the *hiera* was contrived in a most impressive manner. When the door of the shrine was opened
the hierophant, clad in his festival robes, came out into
the full blaze of a bright light and revealed the sacred
objects to the gaze of the initiates. It was an awesome
spectacle. The hierophant in his priestly vestments was
himself an impressive figure. Eleusinian inscriptions also
suggest how effective was the lighting of this scene. One
of them speaks of the "holy night, clearer than the light
of the sun." Another one, a metrical inscription engraved
on the base of the statue of a hierophant, exclaims: "O
mystae, formerly you saw me coming from the shrine and
appearing in the luminous nights."[3] Being in an impressionable state of mind, the *mystae* must have felt themselves very near to divinity when objects so jealously

---

[1] Tertullian *Apologeticus* 16; *Ad nationes* i. 12.

[2] Aelian *Fragmenta* 12.   [3] *Ephemeris archaiologike* (1883), p. 79.

guarded and of such sanctity were finally exposed to view. The emotional effect of the exhibition is well suggested by a passage from Plutarch. In discussing "Progress in Virtue," he used a figure of speech derived from the initiation ceremony of these mysteries. According to Plutarch, "He who once enters into philosophy and sees the great light, as when shrines are open to view, is silent and awestruck."[1] This passage probably well describes the impression made by the spectacle at Eleusis on a company of initiates.

Of the *epopteia* attained a year after the *teletē*, our knowledge is most scanty. Apparently it was in the nature of a further revelation of sacred tokens. But a single rite is known to us and this only on the authority of Hippolytus. With a fine show of sarcasm he speaks of "the Athenians initiating people at Eleusis and showing to the *epoptae* that great and marvellous mystery of perfect revelation, in solemn silence, a cut cornstock!"[2] There are two points of emphasis in this passage: first, that the exhibition of a corn token formed a part of the Eleusinian mystery, and, second, that this exhibition was reserved for the *epoptae*. On these two points there can be little doubt. Indeed, considering the agricultural background of the Eleusinian festival, it is not only credible, but even probable that a corn token should be among the most sacred things of the Eleusinia. The solemnity of this final exhibition is emphasized by the phrase "in silence." In this case the display took place without a word of elucidation from the hierophant, whereas the year before the spectacle had been accompanied with an explanatory discourse throughout. As to the meaning of this silent exhibition, we are left entirely to conjecture. It is not unreasonable to suppose that the corn was regarded as the symbol of

[1] Plutarch *De profectus in virtute* 10.

[2] Hippolytus *Philosophoumena* v. 1. 8.

a birth and rebirth in man paralleling the vernal rebirth of nature. This, at least, is the explanation suggested by Farnell.[1] To the gentile mind of the first century, however, it was not merely a matter of symbolism, but rather a conviction arising "in accordance with the naïve and primitive belief in the unity of man's life with the vegetative world." In this final exhibition, therefore, the initiate would find a proof as well as an illustration of a personal rebirth like that of the grain in springtime. The emotional effect of this rite was probably not unlike that of the hieratic spectacle a year previous. But the conviction arising from it would be rather the assurance of individual rebirth to new life, instead of communion with deity.

The revelation in silence at the *epopteia* serves to throw into relief a third distinctive element of the Eleusinian mysteries, the discourse or verbal explanation which accompanied the ceremonial. A quaint rhetorical fragment preserved under the name of Sopatros suggests the importance of this discourse. It recounts the dream of a young man who saw the spectacle of the mysteries. Because he did not hear the words of the hierophant, however, he could not consider himself initiated.[2] Without the priestly discourse, then, the initiation was incomplete.

It is difficult to determine precisely what the content of the discourse was. The references at hand concerning these utterances, however, make it clear that it was not an isolated speech but rather a running commentary which served to explain to the *mystae* the meaning of the tableaux and the significance of the sacred objects. In all probability the formulas used were liturgical in character, though some freedom of utterance may have been allowed the hierophant. In the course of the explanation,

---

[1] *Cults of the Greek States*, III, 184.

[2] *Rhetores graeci* viii. 110 (ed. Walz).

he probably descanted on the blessings assured by the initiation ceremonies, and he may have included moral exhortation as well. About all that can be said, therefore, concerning the sacred discourse is that it was an oral interpretation of the Eleusinian ceremonial intended to give to tableau and drama and exhibition their full meaning.

Having canvassed the drama, the spectacle, and the discourse, have we exhausted the significant elements in the Eleusinian ceremonial? Clement of Alexandria has preserved a formula that suggests the possibility of a different type of ritualistic observance. His statement is, "The password of the Eleusinian Mysteries is as follows: 'I have fasted, I have drunk the barley drink, I have taken things from the sacred chest, having tasted thereof I have placed them into the basket and again from the basket into the chest.' "[1] There is no reason for doubting the genuineness of this password. The meaning of the first two elements in the process is fairly clear. The fasting of the *mystae* corresponded to that of the sorrowing goddess Demeter who "sat smileless, nor tasted meat nor drink, wasting with long desire for her deep-bosomed daughter." Likewise the drinking of the barley drink corresponded to the breaking of her fast; for the goddess had refused a cup of sweet wine, "but she had them mix meal and water with the tender herb of mint, and give it to her to drink." This mixed potion the goddess accepted. Accordingly, in drinking a similar potation the *mystae* shared the cup from which the great goddess drank in her sorrow. It was a direct and sympathetic participation in the experiences of the goddess, an action expressive of attained fellowship with the deity.

Just what the eating of food from the chest meant to

[1] Clement of Alexandria *Protrepticus* ii. 21. The translation follows Lobeck's emendation (*Aglaophamus*, p. 25) which is commonly accepted.

the participant is less obvious. Like the drinking of the barley drink, it was probably a sacrament of communion, and it may have implied an even more realistic communion than was involved in the act of drinking. If, as is most likely, the sacred food consisted of cereals, then the assimilation of this food meant a direct and realistic union with Demeter, the goddess of grain. It meant an incorporation of divine substance into the human body. However the idea was arrived at, this rite clearly involved a mystical communion by the act of eating, even as the barley drink stood for mystical fellowship through the act of drinking.[1] Already emotionally united with Demeter through participation in her passion, the initiates now became realistically one with her by the assimilation of food and drink.

IV

It is further important to note the effects, both immediate and ultimate, of this elaborate ceremonial upon the lives of the devotees. According to Aristotle, the mysteries did not teach rules of conduct but rather stimulated the emotions. "Aristotle is of the opinion," Synesius affirms, "that the initiated learned nothing precisely, but that they received impressions and were put into a certain frame of mind."[2] To use the Aristotelian formula, not *mathein* (to learn) but *pathein* (to suffer) was the reason for participation in the Eleusinian ritual; and in its immediate aspect this was exactly the effect of the celebration.

This stimulation of emotion is so frequently mentioned in Eleusinian sources that there is little danger of exaggeration at this point. Plutarch drew several striking comparisons illustrating the emotional effect of the rites of Eleusis.

[1] See Jevons, *Introduction to the History of Religion*, pp. 363 ff.; also Dieterich, *Eine Mithrasliturgie*, p. 164.

[2] Synesius *De Dione* 10.

In his treatise on "Progress in Virtue" he compared the effect of initiation on a confused and jostling crowd of candidates to the influence of philosophy on a noisy and talkative group of students.

Those who are initiated, come together at first with confusion and noise, and jostle one another, but when the mysteries are being performed and exhibited, they give their attention with awe and silence. . . . . So also at the commencement of philosophy, ... you will see round its doors such confusion and assurance and prating, some rudely and violently jostling their way to reputation; but he who once enters in assumes another air and is silent and awestruck, and in humility and decorum follows reason as if she were a god.[1]

Plutarch used yet other striking similes to illustrate more specifically the emotional effect of participation in the mysteries. The joy of the initiated, he affirmed, was like that of the ostracized returning to their native land after banishment.[2] Again he took advantage of the mingled trouble and apprehension, the peculiar hope and final joy of the initiated to describe the feelings of the soul at death. According to Plutarch:

When a man dies, he is like those who are being initiated into the mysteries. The one expression *teleutan* the other *teleisthai* correspond. . . . . Our whole life is but a succession of wanderings, of painful courses, of long journeys by tortuous ways without outlet. At the moment of quitting it, fears, terrors, quiverings, mortal sweats, and a lethargic stupor, come over us and overwhelm us; but as soon as we are out of it pure spots and meadows receive us, with voices and dances and the solemnities of sacred words and holy sights. It is there that man, having become perfect and initiated—restored to liberty, really master of himself —celebrates crowned with myrtle the most august mysteries, and holds converse with just and pure souls.

With all this evidence it cannot be doubted that the extended ceremonial of the Eleusinia had a profound effect in stirring deeply the feelings of the *mystae*. They experi-

[1] Plutarch *De profectus in virtute* 10.

[2] *De facie in orbe lunae* 28.

enced the whole gamut of emotions from doubt and fear to hope and joy.

Furthermore, the Eleusinian rites were so ordered as to enable the worshiper to enact the legendary experiences of his goddess, and feel as she had felt of old. There was, first of all, the careful mental and physical preparation, the purification of body, and the disposition of mind, which Epictetus stressed, without which, he said, the mysteries could bring no benefit.[1] It was a long preparation beginning at Agrae six months before the initiation proper. At the opening of the greater mysteries the candidates prepared themselves for approach to divinity by fasting and lustrations. They marched in solemn procession along the Sacred Way from Athens to Eleusis, stopping at holy places redolent with memories of their goddess. After all these preliminaries, they were impressionable and psychologically prepared to share intensely in the emotional experiences of the Great Goddess. When in the passion play of the *telestērion* they witnessed the abduction of Persephone they were sensitive to the grief of the mother. They assisted her in her frenzied search for her lost daughter, and at the reunion of the goddesses they participated in the joy of the occasion. Like Demeter herself they broke their fast by drinking of the barley drink. As completely as possible the devotees of Demeter reproduced her experiences, shared her feelings, and thereby established a sense of mystical fellowship with their goddess. This was the great experience of their religion.

It was not, however, a mere matter of temporary emotional satisfaction to the initiates; for the rites of Eleusis gave positive assurance for the future as well. The mystical communion established by initiation was a lasting one. Sharing in the other experiences of the goddess, the *mystae* believed they would share also in her triumph over death.

[1] Epictetus *Discourses* iii. 21.

According to Farnell, it was their sense of present fellow-ship that led directly to this conviction concerning the future.

> These deities, the mother and the daughter and the dark god in the background, were the powers that governed the world beyond the grave: those who had won their friendship by initiation in this life would by the simple logic of faith regard themselves as certain to win blessing at their hands in the next. And this, as far as we can discern, was the ground on which flourished the Eleusinian hope.[1]

Nothing is clearer than that the devotees of Demeter enjoyed the anticipation of a happy future life. It was not merely the vague promise of a future existence, it was the definite assurance of a *blissful* future that the mysteries of Eleusis offered to seekers for salvation. In classical antiquity this Eleusinian assurance was generally known and appreciated. The Homeric Hymn declared, "Happy is he among deathly men who has seen these things! But he who is uninitiated, and has no lot in them, will never have equal lot in death beneath the murky gloom." Pindar and Sophocles re-echoed the same thought. "Thrice happy they who go to the world below, having seen these mysteries; to them alone is life there, to all others is misery."[2] Among the orators, Isocrates declared, "Those who share this initiation have sweet hopes for the end of life and for all future time."[3] Plato also gave recognition to this conviction when he said that the mysteries taught enigmatically "that he who passes unsanctified and uninitiated into the world below will lie in a slough, but he who arrives there after initiation and purification will dwell with the gods."[4] At the beginning of the Christian era, this was still the strong hope that the mysteries of Eleusis guaranteed.

---

[1] *Cults of the Greek States*, III, 197.

[2] Sophocles *Fragmenta* 719; Pindar *Fragmenta* 137 (102).

[3] Isocrates *Panegyricus* 28.

[4] Plato *Phaedo* 69C. Cf. *Gorgias* 493B.

Cicero said of them, "In the mysteries we learn not only to live happily but to die with fairer hope."[1] Thus, the mythical experiences of the Eleusinian goddesses in breaking the power of death became the basis for a definite assurance of a happy life beyond the grave. Precisely what the relationship was between the mythological experiences of the Great Goddess and the hopes of her devotees is, indeed, unclear, but that the relationship existed is certain and that the mysteries gave prized assurance of immortality is indubitable.

Not only did the experience of initiation result in a temporary emotional exaltation and a lasting guaranty of future bliss, but it eventuated also in a purification and elevation of the present life of men as well. It is true that the Eleusinian mysteries were criticized at exactly this point. Diogenes of Sinope, for example, sarcastically declared, "It will be an absurd thing if Aegesilaus and Epaminondas are to live in the mire and some miserable wretches who have been initiated are to be in the island of the blest."[2] Undoubtedly there was reason enough for his criticism. Nevertheless, the general testimony of the ancients was on the other side of the case. Andocides, on trial for impiety before a jury of *mystae*, assumed that those who had been initiated would be more ready to punish the impious and save the righteous than others would be, and that sin was the more heinous in one who was consecrated to the service of the mother and daughter.[3] At the close of one of his beautiful odes, Aristophanes had the happy initiated sing, "To us alone is there joyous light after death, who have been initiated and who lived in pious fashion as touching our duty to strangers and private

[1] Cicero *De legibus* ii. 14.

[2] Diogenes Laertius vi. 39.

[3] Andocides *De Mysteriis* 125.

people.''[1] Cicero stated as his conviction that in the mysteries we perceive the real principles of life.[2] Even such a stern moralist as Epictetus encouraged reverence for the mysteries, recognized their benefits, and asserted that they "were established by those of old for our education and the amendment of life."[3] In face of such an imposing array of evidence, the modern student cannot avoid the conclusion that the Eleusinian mysteries did exert an elevating influence on the moral life.

Here again, the precise relationship between the Eleusinian ritual and its moral effect is exceedingly unclear. We do not know what was the basis for the Eleusinian ethic. There may have been no exhortation to the *mystae* to lead pure and good lives. Indeed, the immediate and conscious aim of the rites may not have been an ethical one at all. Nevertheless, it is undeniable that the mysteries of Demeter did exercise a salutary influence in the matter of practical living. Not only a temporary stimulation of the emotions, not only a positive guaranty of future happiness, but also a lasting elevation of moral standards was a result of initiation into the mysteries at Eleusis.

V

For the devotees of Demeter initiation into her cult marked the beginning of a new kind of life more divine than they had known before. It was virtually for them the experience of a new birth. True, the exact word *palingenesia* does not occur on any of the Eleusinian monuments, but Tertullian attests that the *mystae* applied this very figure of speech to their initiation experiences and to baptism especially. Tertullian himself did not question the applicability of the term, though as a Christian he naturally

[1] Aristophanes *Ranae* 455 ff.

[2] Cicero *De legibus* ii. 14.   [3] Epictetus *Discourses* iii. 21.

insisted on the superior validity of the Christian rite and experience.[1] He argued thus:

> If the mere nature of water, in that it is the appropriate material for washing away, leads men to flatter themselves with a belief in the omens of purification, how much more truly will waters render that service through the authority of God, by whom all their matter has been constituted.

In other words, Christian baptism according to Tertullian was a potent agency for spiritual regeneration, while Eleusinian baptism was not, though the Christian lawyer admitted that pagan religionists claimed regenerative power for their rite.

In the Eleusinian ritual itself there was much besides baptism to suggest and realistically induce a new birth experience. The mythical background of Eleusinian thought distinctly picturized the recurrent revival of life in nature with each successive year. It represented this fact of common experience in the mythological terms of a goddess who was carried off to Hades but later returned to the upper air. The lesser mysteries, celebrated at Agrae in the springtime, were probably especially suggestive of this renewal of life in nature. The ritual of purification and the long period of fasting preliminary to the great mysteries were intended to wash away the stains of the old life so that the purified candidates might approach the two goddesses prepared for personal renewal. If a ritual marriage formed a part of the mysteries, then the initiates realized a real *unio mystica* with the divine, in itself a completely transforming process. If the sacred marriage was followed by a holy birth, then the idea of a new life "spiritual, heavenly, and from above," was further accentuated. With the exhibition of sacred relics the initiates were brought very close to things divine, and the most sacred

[1] Tertullian *De Baptismo* 5.

of these objects, the corn token, was itself a symbol of regeneration. Furthermore, in a realistic sacrament of eating and drinking, the neophytes assimilated food charged with such divine potency that it could transmute human nature into immortal essence. Thus, by realistic union as well as by sympathetic communion, the individual neophyte came to realize a new life by means of initiation.

The type of life which was thus induced by the Eleusinian ritual has been sufficiently characterized. From a purely descriptive standpoint the new birth experience of Eleusis was temporarily a matter of the feelings—the arousal of deep emotions by participation in an ancient and well-ordered ritual. But it resulted in more than a temporary satisfaction of the emotions merely. It eventuated in an amended moral life and the ultimate assurance of future happiness. These were the permanent effects of Eleusinian regeneration.

BIBLIOGRAPHY

BRILLANT, M., *Les Mystères d'Éleusis*. Paris, 1920.

D'ALVIELLA, E. G., *Eleusinia*. Paris, 1893.

DYER, LOUIS, *Studies of the Gods in Greece* (New York, 1894), pp. 46–218.

FARNELL, LEWIS R., *Cults of the Greek States* (Oxford, 1907), III, 127–278.

FOUCART, PAUL, *Les Mystères d'Éleusis*. Paris, 1914.

HATCH, EDWIN, *Influence of Greek Ideas and Usages on the Christian Church* (London, 1897), pp. 283–92.

JEVONS, FRANK BYRON, *Introduction to the History of Religion* (London, 1896), pp. 358–81.

LOBECK, C. A., *Aglaophamus* (Königsburg, 1829), I, 1–228.

LOISY, ALFRED, *Les Mystères païens et le Mystère chrétien* (Paris, 1919), pp. 51–83.

MOMMSEN, A., *Feste der Stadt Athen* (Leipzig, 1898), pp. 204–77.

NOACK, FERDINAND, *Eleusis, die Baugeschichtliche Entwicklung des Heiligtumes*. Leipzig, 1927.

PHILIOS, D., *Éleusis, ses Mystères, ses Ruines, et son Musée*. Paris, 1896. English translation by Hamilton Gatliff. London, 1906.

CHAPTER III

DIONYSIAN EXCESSES

IN A characteristic passage in the *Bacchae*, Euripides, "the Rationalist," speaks of Demeter and Dionysus as the greatest of the gods. He puts into the mouth of the aged prophet Teiresias this preachment for the instruction of the honest but irreconcilable Pentheus:

> Two chiefest powers,
> Prince, among men there are: Divine Demeter—
> Earth is she, name her by which name you will.
> She upon dry food nurtures mortal men;
> Then follows Semele's son, to match her gift
> The cluster's flowing draught he found and gave
> To mortals, which gives rest from grief to men,

So that through him do men obtain good things.[1]

This juxtaposition of Demeter and Dionysus is not at all surprising; for among the friendly rivals of the Eleusinian mysteries in Greece the most vigorous, the most distinctive, and the most widespread was the worship of Dionysus. Three centuries before Alexander made his conquest of the Orient, Dionysus had made his conquest of Greece. Coming as an immigrant from Thrace, attended by a wild crew of satyrs and maenads, he took Greece by storm, and sometime between Homer and Phidias, he won a place for himself on Olympus and the patronage of the most dignified city-states in Greece. The type of religious experience exemplified by his cult is of exceptional interest to the student of personal religion. In order to understand the Dionysian experience, however, it is necessary to know who Dionysus himself was.

[1] Euripides *Bacchae* 274–85.

I

Notwithstanding his elevation to Olympus, Dionysus was anything but an aristocratic sky-god. He was rather an earth-deity, a god of the peasantry. Though his father was Zeus, the sky- and rain-god, his mother was of the earth earthy. Dionysian mythology named her Semele, the daughter of Cadmus, founder of Thebes, and this name betrays her real significance as a personification of the earth (cf. *Nova Zembla*, "new earth").[1] In the Hope collection there is a vase painting representing the youthful Dionysus rising out of an earth mound—the vase-painter thus emphasizing the earth-born nature of the god.[2]

But Semele, the god's earth-mother, was not only the fertile earth of springtime absorbing the warm showers of the sky and naturally productive; in local legend at Thebes she was represented as the thunder-smitten earth also. For Hera in her jealousy had craftily persuaded Semele to ask her lover to prove his deity by appearing in all his power and glory as god of heaven. Zeus acceded to her request and, appearing to her armed with all his terrors, destroyed her with his lightnings. Even as the mother was dying, however, Zeus rescued their unborn child from her tortured body.

> In birth-bowers new did Zeus Cronion
> Receive his scion;
> For hid in a cleft of his thigh,
> By the gold clasps knit, did he lie
> Safe hidden from Hera's eye
> Till the Fates' day came.[3]

Lucian, in his usual satirical vein, made the most of his opportunity to parody this mythological theme.[4] Thus, in

---

[1] See Harrison, *Prolegomena to the Study of Greek Religion*, pp. 404 f.

[2] Tischbein, *Greek Vases*, I, 39.

[3] Euripides *op. cit.* 94–100.   [4] Lucian *Deorum Dialogi* ix.

popular legend the earth-born Dionysus, the son of Semele, was himself represented as a twice-born deity. He was *dithyrambus*, which for the Greeks meant "he who entered life by a double door." In this peculiarly artificial sense he was Dionysus, the son of Zeus, as his name suggests.

Quite naturally this son of earth and sky functioned as the personification of vegetable life. As such he was a yearly divinity, who came and went with the seasons. His experience in relation to men was characterized by recurrent theophanies and recessions as the life of nature died and revived year after year. Plutarch noted among various peoples this characteristic conception of Dionysus:

The Phrygians think that the god is asleep in the winter and is awake in summer, and at one season they celebrate with Bacchic rites his goings to bed and at the other his risings up. And the Paphlagonians allege that in the winter he is bound down and imprisoned and in the spring he is stirred up and let loose.[1]

In the popular phrases of his worship, Dionysus was apprehended in very concrete terms. He was, on the one side, the god of vegetation in general and the vine-god in particular. Thus he made his chief impression on the Greeks. It may be, as Miss Harrison has suggested,[2] that in his native Thracian home he functioned as a beer-god, Sabazius or Bromius, the god of a cereal intoxicant; but certainly he came to Greece and won his signal triumph there as the wine-god. Even as the olive was constantly associated with Athena, so the vine was characteristically associated with Dionysus. Other familiar symbols of Dionysus were the grape cluster and a two-handled drinking cup. By these accessories the god may easily be identified in Greek vase paintings and on cult monuments. The various cult appellatives emphasizing this aspect of Dionysus

[1] Plutarch *De Iside et Osiride* 69.

[2] Harrison, *op. cit.*, pp. 416–21.

are far too numerous to be listed.[1] Greek literature, too, rang with the praises of the god who "made grow for men the clustered vine,"[2] but the fact is so familiar that it does not demand special citation.

What is particularly noteworthy is this, that the relation of the god to the drink was not merely that of creator to the thing created. Many times the relationship expressed was that of identification even. The god was in the wine; he was the wine, even. He was not merely the god of libation. To quote Euripides' statement, he was the libation, "The god who himself is offered in libation to the other gods."[3] In this passage the identification of the god with the wine is as absolute as the identification of Christ in Catholic thought with the consecrated wine of the mass, or, to cite an illustration from the far away religious system of the Vedas, the identification of the god Soma with the soma drink. It is not surprising, therefore, to find in Attica the festival of the *theoinia* or the "god wine," celebrated by those families who were believed to be the direct descendants of Dionysus' original followers, in whose vineyards grew vines which were offshoots from the vine spray that the god himself had given them. Under such circumstances the devotees of Dionysus would be sure of the presence of the very god himself in the consecrated wine made from the sacred grapes. That this realistic identification of the deity and the fruit of the vine was not merely a primitive conception is proved by the existence at Philippi in Paul's time of a religious brotherhood dedicated to Dionysus *Botreus* ("Dionysus the Vine Cluster").

Dionysus was the god of animal life as well as of vegetable life. As such he was variously represented in different animal forms. It was inevitable that these animal

[1] See Farnell, *Cults of the Greek States*, V, 287.

[2] Euripides *op. cit.* 651.　　　　[3] *Op. cit.* 284.

embodiments should be varied in different localities. In a goat-raising country the normal representation of the power of life and generation would be the goat. Similarly, in a cattle-raising country the embodiment of the divine power in the form of a bull was to be expected. And so we have various animal theophanies of Dionysus recorded in Greek literature. Euripides' chorus of Bacchanals, for example, thus variously invoke their god in their moment of supreme anxiety:

> Appear, appear, whatso thy shape or name
> O Mountain Bull, Snake of the Hundred Heads,
> Lion of the Burning Flame!
> O God, Beast, Mystery, come![1]

Of the less frequent animal forms under which Dionysus was revered, that of the goat should especially be noted. What makes this conception of Dionysus peculiarly important is the fact that as a goat-god he was involved in the obscure beginnings of Attic tragedy, and thereafter he remained the patron deity of this highly artistic literary form (*trag-odia*, goat-song). Another less familiar animal embodiment of Dionysus was that of a kid. There was a common legend that Zeus, in order to save his son from the jealous wrath of Hera, transformed him into a kid.[2] A mystic expression *nebrizein*, "to play the fawn," was common in the Dionysus cult. While it is an expression of doubtful import, yet it is clearly reminiscent of another primitive conception of Dionysus as a fawn.

By far the most generally accepted and most significant of the animal embodiments of the god, however, was that of a bull. There were a multitude of cult appellatives emphasizing this conception of Dionysus. He was variously addressed as the "horned child," the "horned deity,"

[1] Euripides *op. cit.* 1017–19.

[2] Apollodorus *Bibliotheke* iii. 4. 3.

the "bull-horned," and the "bull-browed."[1] The Argives
worshiped him as "the son of a cow" or "bull-born," and
an ancient Elean chant addressed him directly as a bull.
"Come, hero Dionysus, come with the Graces to thy house
by the shores of the sea; hasten with thy bull-foot." So
ran the hymn itself, while the chorus repeated "goodly bull,
goodly bull."[2] One readily recalls, also, that the residence
of the king-archon at Athens, where the sacred marriage
between Dionysus and the *basilinna* was celebrated, was
called the *boukolion*, or "ox stall."

With all this background of realistic thought, it is
strange that we do not have a representation of the bull-
Dionysus in Greek vase paintings. Plutarch, however,
states that the Greeks not infrequently imaged the god in
bull form in sculpture, and in classical literature this representation of the god was a stock one. Thus the *Bacchae*
of Euripides is permeated with the conception of Dionysus
as a bull-god. Of Dionysus' second birth it is said:

> Then a God bull-horned Zeus bare,
> And with serpents entwined his hair.

When Pentheus attempted to imprison Dionysus, "a bull
beside the stalls he found." And finally when the god led
the king in a hypnotized state out to his doom, Pentheus
seemed to see a bull going before him. In his hallucination
the king exclaimed:

> A bull you seem that leads on before;
> And horns have sprouted upon your head.
> How, were you a brute?—Truly you are a bull now![3]

These passages reflect perfectly the realism of primitive
thought about the god. Far more than being represented

[1] Clement of Alexandria *Protrepticus* ii. 16–18; Athenaeus ix. 476A; Nonnus
vi. 264.

[2] Plutarch *Quaestiones Graecae* 36.

[3] Euripides *op. cit.* 100–102, 618, 920–22.

by the bull, Dionysus was thought of as being actually embodied in the bull, so that the animal, like the wine, was the god.

II

With these primitive conceptions of Dionysus in mind, it is possible for the modern student, even, to appreciate something of the vivid, central experience of the god's devotees. Wine played a prominent part in Dionysian worship. Bacchic literature reeks with wine and rings with the joys of intoxication. The chorus in Euripides' *Bacchae* sings:

> The cluster's flowing draught . . . .
> . . . . gives rest from grief to men
> Woe-worn, soon as the vine's stream fills them
> And sleep, the oblivion of our daily ills,—
> There is none other balm for toils.

This Bacchic joy puts an end to woe.

> When blent with the flute light laughters awaken,
> And the children of care have forgotten to weep
> Whensoever is revealed the cluster's splendour
> In the banquet that men to the high Gods tender
> And o'er ivy-wreathed revellers drinking deep
> The wine bowl drops the mantle of sleep.[1]

The truth is that sheer physical intoxication from the drinking of wine was the essence of Dionysian religion. In the service of their god the Bacchanals drank wine until they were intoxicated. There was indeed point to Plato's criticism that an immortality of drunkenness seemed to be considered the Dionysian reward of virtue. For the Bacchanals themselves, however, the experience was something more and higher than drunkenness. It was spiritual ecstasy, not mere physical intoxication. The wine they drank was for them potent with divine power—it was the

---

[1] Euripides *op. cit.* 280-83, 380-85.

god himself, and the very quintessence of divine life was resident in the juice of the grape. This the devotees of Bacchus knew as a matter of personal experience when, after drinking the wine, they felt a strange new life within themselves. That was the life and power of their god. Their enthusiasm was quite literally a matter of having the god within themselves, of being full of and completely possessed by the god. So they themselves described it in their own language (*entheos*, hence enthusiasm). They might be intoxicated; but they felt themselves possessed by the god. The drinking of wine in the service of Dionysus was for them a religious sacrament. Even Plato, who had few kind words to say for intoxication, made one exception to his usual rule that it was unfitting for a man to drink to the point of drunkenness. That one exception was "on the occasions of festivals of the god of wine."[1] At such times drunkenness was a matter of communion with the god. So Euripides could say that he who knows the Dionysian mysteries "is pure in life, and revelling on the mountains, has the Bacchic communion in his soul."[2]

The devotees of Dionysus had other realistic means of attaining to communion with their god. They had a sacrament of eating as well as a sacrament of drinking. This rite was the "feast of raw flesh." To be an initiate into the mysteries of Dionysus one must be able to avow

> I have . . . .
> Fulfilled his red and bleeding feasts.[3]

The victim varied. Sometimes it was a goat, as was probably the custom in Thrace. The Bacchanals of Euripides follow this practice and know

> The joy of the red quick fountain
> The blood of the hill-goat torn.

---

[1] Plato *Leges* 775.　　　[2] Euripides *op. cit.* 72 ff.

[3] Euripides *Fragmenta* 475, quoted from Porphyry *De Abstinentia* iv. 19.

They

> Quaff the goat's delicious blood,
> A strange, a rich, a savage food.[1]

Sometimes the victim was a fawn, and the sacred fawn-skins with which the maenads were clothed were the skins torn from these luckless animals. One of the familiar depictions of the maenads on Greek vases was to show them carrying a fawn in their arms or tearing it to pieces in frenzy. More frequently, however, the Dionysian victim was a bull. This was particularly the case in Crete where, to quote Firmicus Maternus, "the Cretans rend a living bull with their teeth, and they simulate madness of soul as they shriek through the secret places of the forest with discordant clamors."[2]

This quotation well suggests the orgiastic character of the feast of raw flesh. The devotees tore asunder the slain beast and devoured the dripping flesh in order to assimilate the life of the god resident in it. Raw flesh was living flesh, and haste had to be made lest the divine life within the animal should escape. So the feast became a wild, barbaric, frenzied affair. In the *Bacchae* one of the herdsmen describes to Pentheus an attack of the maenads upon the royal herd. Doubtless the description gives an adequate impression of one of the Bacchic feasts.

> Down swooped they then
> Upon our pasturing kine with swordless hand,
> Then had you seen your mother with her hands
> Rend a deep uddered heifer bellowing loud:
> And others tore the calves in crimson shreds.
> Ribs had you seen and cloven hoofs far hurled
> This way and that, and flakes of flesh that hung
> And dripped all blood bedabbled, 'neath the pines.
> Bulls chafing, lowering fiercely along the horn
> Erewhile, were tripped and hurled upon the earth

---

[1] Euripides *Bacchae* 140.

[2] Firmicus Maternus *De Errore Profanarum Religionum* vi. 5.

Dragged down by countless clutching maiden hands
More swiftly was the flesh that lapped their bones
Stripped, than you could have closed your kingly eyes.[1]

This orgiastic rite furnished the Fathers of the early
church with just the material for which they were looking
to use in discrediting paganism. With genuine satisfaction
they described the barbarous ceremonial in all its revolting
detail. Clement of Alexandria said:

I will not dance out your mysteries as they say Alcibiades did, but I
will strip them naked, and bring them out on the open stage of life, in
view of those who are spectators at the drama of truth. The Bacchi
hold orgies in honor of a mad Dionysus. They celebrate a divine madness by the eating of raw flesh. The final accomplishment of their rite
is the distribution of the flesh of butchered victims. They are crowned
with snakes, and shriek out the name of Eva, that Eve through whom
sin came into the world, and the symbol of their Bacchic orgies is the
consecrated serpent.[2]

In a similar vein, Arnobius wrote of the "feasts of raw
flesh in which with feigned frenzy and loss of a sane mind
you twine snakes about you, and to show yourselves full
of the divinity and majesty of the god, you demolish with
gory mouths the entrails of goats bleating for mercy."[3]

The fact should not be blinked that in its primitive
form this rite probably involved the sacrifice of a human
victim. Porphyry knew a tradition that in Chios a man
was torn to pieces in the worship of Dionysus *Omadius*, the
"Raw One."[4] At Potniae, according to Pausanias, a priest
of Dionysus was once slain by the inhabitants and a plague
was sent upon them in punishment. They sought relief,
and the Delphian oracle told them that a beautiful boy
must be sacrificed to the deity. Immediately afterward,
however, Dionysus let it be known that he would accept

---

[1] Euripides *op. cit.* 736–47.

[2] Clement of Alexandria *Protrepticus* ii. 12.

[3] Arnobius v. 19. [4] Porphyry *De Abstinentia* ii. 55.

a goat as a substitute.[1] This story records the ancient tran-
sition in cult practice from the cannibal to the animal
feast. Also in the fearful fate that met Pentheus at the
hands of his own mother, as recorded by Euripides, there
is a late literary echo of the primitive cannibalistic ritual.

To focus attention on these savage features, however,
is to miss entirely the significance of the crude ceremonial.
The real meaning of the orgy was that it enabled the devotee to partake of a divine substance and so to enter into
direct and realistic communion with his god. The warm
blood of the slain goat was "sacred blood," according to
Lactantius Placidus.[2] The god Dionysus was believed to
be resident temporarily in the animal victim. One of the
most remarkable illustrations of this ritual incarnation of
the god was described by Aelian. Of the people of Tenedos,
he said: "In ancient days they used to keep a cow with
calf, the best they had, for Dionysus, and when she calved,
they tended her like a woman in childbirth. But they sacrificed the newborn calf, having put *cothurni* on its feet."[3]
The use of the tragic buskins symbolized the conviction
that the god was temporarily incarnate in the calf—pious
opinion did not doubt that. Primitive logic easily persuaded men that the easiest way to charge oneself with divine
power was to eat the quivering flesh and drink the warm
blood of the sacred animal. Some went farther and sought
to assimilate themselves to deity by wearing the skin of
the animal. The central meaning of the celebration was
that it enabled the devotee to enter into direct and realistic
communion with his god.

Another means of inducing the divine possession, and
the usual concomitant of the sacraments of eating and
drinking just described, was the vertigo of the sacred

---

[1] Pausanias ix. 8. 2.   [2] *Thebais* v. 159.

[3] Aelian *De Natura Animalium* xii. 34.

dance. In preparation for the Bacchic revel, the devotees of the god properly equipped themselves with the gear of Dionysus. Like him they carried the thyrsus, a wand tipped with a pine cone and usually entwined with ivy. In their hair serpents were twisted and over their shoulders was thrown the sacred fawn-skin. Sometimes they wore horns on their foreheads. In clothing and equipment they were as like their god as possible.

The dances in honor of Dionysus were usually held at night time by torchlight and were preceded by fasting. They were accompanied by the weird music of wind instruments and the clashing of tambourines. Mingled with this strange music were the shouts of the Bacchanals themselves as they waved their torches in the darkness, thus giving to the scene an unearthly light. The dances were wild and irregular and were characterized by a tossing of the head and a violent, whirling bodily motion. Thus, by the very movements of the dance a physical frenzy was quickly induced, quite as the "dancing dervishes" of Mohammedanism lose control of themselves in the delirium of their ritual. It was for this ecstatic experience that the *Bacchae* of Euripides were yearning when they sang together:

> Ah, shall my white feet in the dances gleam
> The livelong night again? Ah, shall I there
> Float through the Bacchanal's ecstatic dream,
> Tossing my neck in the dewy air?[1]

Significant of the maddening experience of the sacred dance were the names applied to the female followers of Dionysus. They were the maenads or "mad ones," and the thyiads or "rushing distraught ones." These epithets were but different ways of describing the female devotees who were under the influence of and possessed by their god. A more frequent designation was the more intimate

---

[1] Euripides *op. cit.* 862-65.

one which called the devotees after the name of the god himself. The women who shared in the frenzied rites of Bacchus were themselves called *Bacchae* even as the men were *Bacchi*. Each one, without distinction of sex, by the very experience of divine possession became a personification of the god. Their delirium, induced by purely physical means, was for them a spiritual experience, and eventuated in the conviction, deep and strong, that they had their god within themselves. Plutarch connected the Dionysian frenzy with the Bacchic custom of chewing ivy leaves during this ceremonial, and affirmed that thus "the violent spirits which caused their enthusiasm entered into them."[1] Dionysus was god of the ivy quite as much as god of the vine. By the realistic ritual act of chewing ivy, then, the maenads of Dionysus incorporated his spirit within themselves. Herodotus, in speaking of the initiation of the Scythian king, Scyles, cited a particular and notable instance of Dionysian possession. The historian said of the king that "the god took possession" of him so that "he was maddened by the god and played the part of Bacchus."[2] Thus, in the frenzy of the ritualistic revel, as in the orgy of eating raw flesh and drinking wine, the Bacchanals experienced communion with their god.

Apparently, in later times, at least, a sharp distinction was drawn between those who merely indulged in the physical excitement of the Bacchic revel and those who really shared in the spiritual experiences of the cult. At least we are acquainted with a familiar proverb, quoted by Plato, to the effect that "many are the bearers of the thyrsus, but the Bacchanals are few."[3] Unless the initiate himself was conscious of contact with the divine he had not shared in the genuine Bacchic experience.

[1] Plutarch *Quaestiones Romanae* 112.

[2] Herodotus iv. 78 f.

[3] Plato *Phaedo* 69C.

III

This predominantly emotional experience, whether induced by the dizziness of dancing or the crude sacraments of wine and raw flesh, marked for the Bacchanal the beginning of a new life. In a very real sense it was a new birth for the individual who experienced it. Hitherto he had been a man merely. Now he was something more; he was man plus god, a divinized human. Certain aspects of his new divine life deserve to be noted in order to emphasize the contrast with life as it was lived at the ordinary levels of human experience.

In its temporary emotional aspect it was characterized by excessive indulgence as contrasted with the reasoned moderation that was typical of Greek life generally. For the Greek self-control was one of the four cardinal virtues and "nothing in excess" was a fundamental Hellenic principle of life. The Bacchic experience, however, cut sheer across this principle. In the *Bacchae*, Euripides said of Dionysus, "By halves he cares not to be magnified."[1] And even Plato admitted that "madness sent by god is better than the moderation of men." Such was clearly the conviction of the followers of Dionysus.

Bacchic experience also caused a break with the customs and conventions of ordinary life and a return to the freedom of nature. The devotees of Dionysus deserted their homes temporarily, wandered free on the mountains, and indulged in certain wild, primitive, half-animal passions. Euripides gave a picture of the matrons of Thebes leaving their homes, their work, their babies even, to wander and revel in the mountains. They dressed themselves in fawnskins and wound snakes around their bodies.

> Some cradling fawns or wolf cubs in their arms
> Gave to the wild things of their own white milk—
> Young mothers they, who had left their babies.[2]

[1] Euripides *op. cit.* 209.   [2] *Op. cit.* 699 ff.

With this return to the life of nature there was mingled a recrudescence of certain very primitive impulses. There was a lust for hot blood and a certain ferocious cruelty in the tearing to pieces of hapless victims.

The Bacchic revel also caused the joy and abandon of self-forgetfulness. The Bacchanals were no longer themselves, and this very fact brought a sense of freedom from former limitations and restraints. To what ridiculous extremes this self-abandon might be carried Euripides gave illustration when he represented aged Cadmus and blind Teiresias clad in fawnskins and gamboling off to join the Bacchic revel. The ancient founder of Thebes gleefully affirms:

> I shall not weary, nor by night nor day
> Smiting on earth the Thyrsus. We forget
> In joy our age.[1]

Again, in a beautiful strophe by the chorus, Euripides glimpsed in more serious and appreciative fashion the sense of freedom which characterized the Bacchanal's experience. The simile he used was appropriately that of the faun escaping nets and huntsmen:

> Till sheltering arms of trees around her close
> The twilight of the tresses of the woods;—
> O happy ransomed one, safe hid from foes
> Where no man tracks the forest solitudes![2]

Altogether, therefore, the new Bacchic life was one of joyful self-abandon, of freedom from the complexities and restraints of civilization, of return to the direct simplicities of nature.

More than all this it was a life of miraculous power; for by the very fact of divine possession the Bacchanal believed himself to have acquired the power of the god. Hence, he could heal diseases, control the forces of nature, and even

---

[1] *Op. cit.* 187 ff.　　　[2] *Op. cit.* 862 ff.

prophesy. Plato reflected the popular conviction that the Bacchae could work miracles in his famous comparison of the lyric poets to the maenads. He said:

> Lyric poets are not in their right minds when they are composing their beautiful strains; but when falling under the power of music and meter they are inspired and possessed; like Bacchic maidens who draw milk and honey from rivers when they are under the influence of Dionysus but not when they are in their right mind.[1]

The *Bacchae* of Euripides literally teems with miracles.[2] There

> flows with milk the plain,
> and flows with wine,
> Flows with the wild bees' nectar dews divine.

The credulous herdsman of Pentheus tells of particular wonders wrought by the maenads:

> One grasped her thyrsus staff, and smote the rock,
> And forth upleapt a fountain's showry spray:
> One in earth's bosom planted her reed-wand,
> And up there through the god a wine-fount sent:
> And whoso fain would drink white-foaming draughts
> Scarred with their finger tips the breast of earth,
> And milk gushed forth unstinted: dripped the while
> Sweet streams of honey from their ivy staves.

In the battle between the Theban folk and the Bacchae, later narrated, this strange portent occurred: the javelins of the townspeople drew no blood while the wands of the maenads caused wound after wound. The same drama of Euripides also tells of the prophetic power of one who was possessed by Dionysus. Again it is Teiresias, himself a professional prophet, who thus testifies of Bacchus:

> A prophet is this god, the Bacchic frenzy
> And ecstasy are full fraught with prophecy:
> For, in his fullness when he floods our frame
> He makes his maddened votaries tell the future.

[1] Plato *Ion* 534A.　　　　[2] *Op. cit.* 145 f., 704 ff., 761 ff., 298 ff.

The life of the Bacchant was, therefore, a dynamic life in which the peculiar power of the deity operated to perform wonderful deeds through men.

Most important of all, the new Bacchic life in its emotional and dynamic aspects was viewed as but the foretaste of a happy existence in the future. The Thracians, among whom the Dionysian cult originated, seem to have early attained the belief in a blessed future life with the gods. In speaking of the Getae, a tribe of the Thracians, Herodotus affirmed, "They were the most valiant and most just of the Thracians," and then he added in explanation of these characteristics that "they believe themselves immortal; they think that they do not die, but that the dead go to join their god Zalmoxis."[1] Pomponious Mela, a Latin geographer of the early imperial period, repeated a similar testimony concerning the Getae, only more in detail.[2] There is considerable probability that this Zalmoxis was an indigenous Getan divinity, and was related to Sabazius, the Thracian prototype of the Greek Dionysus. Whatever may have been the relationship, it is clear that Dionysus functioned in Hellenistic cults as god of the underworld, and his devotees had the same expectation in relation to him that the ancient Getae had concerning Zalmoxis.

Being a yearly divinity Dionysus was a natural candidate for this function. His experience in nature was characterized by a constant dying and rising again. Yet it was only by proxy that Dionysus passed through these experiences; just as he was immolated by proxy in the rending of the sacred victim. The real Dionysus was the permanent spirit back of the phenomena of nature which caused the recurrent revival of life. He was a god, and immortality was one of the distinguishing characteristics of godhead.

[1] Herodotus iv. 93 f.

[2] Pomponius Mela *De Situ orbis* ii. 2.

Immortality and divinity were all but interchangeable
terms in primitive Greek thought.

Thus when the Bacchanals by the sacraments of eating
and drinking entered into direct communion with their
god, they became partakers of his immortality. In assimi-
lating the raw flesh wherein the god was temporarily incarnate and in drinking the juice of the grape, they received into their bodies an undying substance. In life mystically united with their god, in death they could not be
divided, and when the time came for them to go to the
invisible world, they were sure of sharing the blessed life
of their god. So the unusual emotional experiences fostered
by the Dionysian rites, the intoxication of wine or of the
dance, the frenzy of the orgy, the divine gift of foresight
or miracle-working power—these were more than merely
proofs of divine possession. They were a definite foretaste
and assurance of a blessed future life. In the crude physical
emotionalism of Bacchic ecstasy, therefore, the devotees of
the wine-god found a new birth experience which guaranteed them a happy immortality.

IV

The question of the influence of the Dionysian type of
experience in the Graeco-Roman world remains to be discussed. As early as the seventh century before the Christian
era the state religions of the serene and placid Olympians
were failing to satisfy the religious needs of great masses of
the common people in Greece. In their dissatisfaction they
turned to the more intimate gods of the earth who had to do
with the common things of life: to Demeter, the goddess of
grain, and to Dionysus, the god of the vine. These were
divinities who suffered with men in their toil and who gave
them joy at harvest time. The cult of Dionysus coming from
the northland spread in a great wave of religious enthusiasm

over Greece proper, over the island states of the Aegean, and across to the mainland of Asia Minor. At first it met with violent opposition, as the legends of Lycurgus and Pentheus prove. In those early days rarely was the god graciously received as he was, for example, by Icarus in Attica. In spite of opposition, however, the contagious enthusiasm of the wine-god spread with unusual rapidity throughout Greece. In order to restrain Bacchic excesses the city-states of Greece had no other alternative than to adopt the cult, bring it under state patronage, and by official regulation temper its enthusiasm somewhat. At Delphi Dionysus was associated with Apollo, and there the sacred maidens went mad in the service of the two gods. In Athens he entered into civic partnership with Athena and yearly wedded the *Basilinna*. At Eleusis he was brought into relation with Demeter and led the march of the candidates along the Sacred Way from Athens. In Teos and Naxos he even became the paramount state deity, the "god of the city" and "protector of the most holy state."

It was as a private cult, rather than as a state religion, however, that the worship of Dionysus made its deepest impression on both Hellenic and Hellenistic life. In the private brotherhoods, the natural emotions aroused by the cult practices were allowed free play and the guaranties offered to initiates were of a very realistic order; hence the appeal of the cult was strong, particularly to the masses and to women generally. At the beginning of Aristophanes' comedy, Lysistrate, impatient with waiting, complains that if the women had been invited to the shrine of Bacchus "there would be no getting along for the crowd of timbrels." Indeed, the prominence of women in the worship of Dionysus is one of the most striking features of the cult.

Such a religion as this, which overflowed the political boundaries of states and appealed not to local interests but to certain elemental human desires and emotions, had a great opportunity in the Hellenistic period. With the conquests of Alexander the eastern Mediterranean world was thrown open to Dionysian influence. It is difficult, however, to trace the independent existence and influence of Bacchic mysteries for the simple reason that they fused so readily with similar cults all over the Mediterranean area. The religion of Dionysus lived on in altered form in Orphism. In Asia Minor it merged with the cults of Attis and Sabazius. Plutarch noted the affinity between the rites and legends of Adonis and their Dionysian counterparts,[1] while Tibullus, in one of his elegies, clearly recorded the identification of Dionysus and Osiris.[2]

Notwithstanding this widespread syncretism, the literature of the Hellenistic and Graeco-Roman periods is full of references which show the strength and extent of peculiarly Dionysian influences. At the very beginning of the Hellenistic period stands the classical instance of the estrangement of Philip of Macedon and his queen Olympias. Plutarch was of the opinion that Bacchic orgies had much to do with this unfortunate situation. He said that Olympias was more zealous than all the rest of the women of that country in her devotion to Dionysian orgies and

carried out these rites of possession and ecstasy in very barbarous fashion. She introduced huge tame serpents into the Bacchic assemblies, and these kept creeping out of the ivy and mystic *likna* and twining themselves around the thyrsi of the women and their garlands and frightening the men out of their senses.[3]

Philip was jealous and suspicious of his queen's exclusive devotion to the Dionysus cult. In Italy, at the beginning of the second century B.C., Dionysus worship spread with such rapidity and created such a disturbance in society

[1] Plutarch *Quaestionum Convivalium* 671B.

[2] Tibullus i. 7. [3] Plutarch *Alexander* 2.

that the Senate, as a result of reported excesses, took strenuous measures for the suppression of the cult. The affair ended with the promulgation of rigid regulations governing the conditions under which meetings of the brotherhood might be held.[1] The Sicilian Diodorus, writing in the Augustan age, said, "In many of the Hellenic states every other year, Bacchic bands of women collect, and it is lawful for maidens to carry the thyrsus and join in the enthusiasm; while the women forming in groups, offer sacrifices to the god, and revel, celebrating with hymns the presence of Dionysus."[2] Plutarch, in his writing, made many references to Dionysian practices and told strange tales concerning the Bacchantes of Delphi especially. Once when the thyiades on Parnassus were overtaken by a violent snowstorm, the good people of Delphi went out to rescue them, and their coats actually crumbled to pieces they were frozen so hard.[3] Again, during a sacred war between Phocis and Delphi, the thyiades lost their way and came to Amphissa without realizing where they were. Here they threw themselves down in the agora and fell asleep from sheer exhaustion. The women of the city guarded them so long as they were asleep, refreshed them when they awakened, and set them on their homeward way in safety.[4] These tales are recalled in order to show the reverence with which the devotees of Dionysus were held in the first Christian century. Pliny told of the popularity of the Dionysian cult in Thrace even in his day,[5] while Pausanias referred to the worship of the god in many widely scattered localities.[6] Even in the later days of paganism, Firmicus Mater-

---

[1] Livy xxxix. 8–20.

[2] Diodorus Siculus iv. 3.

[3] Plutarch *De Primo Frigido* 18.

[4] Plutarch *De mulierum virtutibus* 13.

[5] Pliny *Historia Naturalis* xvi. 62.

[6] See "Geographical Register" in Farnell, *Cults of the Greek States*, V, 324 ff.

nus said that the Cretans still practiced their orgiastic rites in honor of Dionysus.[1]

These are but samples of an array of evidence which might be assembled to prove the widespread influence of the Bacchic type of experience with all of its excessive emotionalism in the first-century Graeco-Roman world. People in general were thoroughly familiar with it, as contemporary literature fully proves. Accordingly, in reckoning up the satisfactions offered by pagan religions to the seekers for salvation in the day of Jesus and Paul, the emotional rebirth experience in the Dionysian cult must be counted as significant.

BIBLIOGRAPHY

DAVIS, GLADYS M. N., *The Asiatic Dionysos*. London, 1914.

DYER, LOUIS, *Studies of the Gods in Greece* (New York, 1894), pp. 75–173.

ELDERKIN, GEORGE W., *Kantharos*. Princeton, 1924.

EURIPIDES, *The Bacchanals*. Translated by Arthur S. Way. "Loeb Classical Library" (New York, 1912), III, 1–123.

FARNELL, LEWIS R., *Cults of the Greek States* (Oxford, 1909), V, 85–344.

FOUCART, PAUL, *Le culte de Dionysos en Attique*. Paris, 1904.

HARRISON, JANE ELLEN, *Prolegomena to the Study of Greek Religion* (Cambridge, 1903), pp. 364–572.

LOISY, ALFRED, *Les Mystères païens et le Mystère chrétien* (Paris, 1919), pp. 51–83.

NILSSON, M. P., *Studia de Dionysiis Atticis*. Linden, 1900.

QUANDT, W., *De Baccho ab Alexandri aetate in Asia Minore culto* (Halle, 1913), XXI, 108–279.

ROHDE, ERWIN, *Psyche* (Tübingen, 1924), Vol. II. English translation by W. B. Hillis. London, 1925.

WHEELER, BENJAMIN IDE, *Dionysus and Immortality*. Boston, 1899.

---

[1] Firmicus Maternus *De Errore Profanarum Religonum* vi. 5.

CHAPTER IV

ORPHIC REFORM

HISTORICALLY the cult most nearly related to that of Dionysus was the philosophico-religious system bearing the name of Orpheus. It is not possible to pronounce with certainty whether such a man as Orpheus ever really existed or not. He may have been a purely mythical figure. If he was a real man he was a religious leader of mark and deserving of admiration: a prophet, reformer, and martyr. Whether mythical or real, Orpheus was the antitype of the flushed and maddening wine-god Dionysus. He was a sober and gentle musician who charmed savage men and beasts with his music, an exact theologian, the prophet of reform in religion, who was martyred for his efforts.

The difference between Dionysus and Orpheus was the difference between the two religious systems which bore their names. The cult of Dionysus was more simple, primitive, elemental, spontaneous, and emotional. That of Orpheus was more elaborate, developed, controlled, and intellectualistic. Still, when all is said, the two systems had much in common. Both centered in the same god, Dionysus. Both aimed at the same goal, immortality through divinity. Both sought to attain that goal by prescribed rites and ceremonies. Both made a strictly individualistic appeal and were highly developed along the lines of personal experience. But Orphism fostered an ascetic rule of life that was the exact opposite of Dionysian license, and developed an elaborate theology of a highly speculative character. In brief, Orphism represented a reformed Dio-

nysianism, and the practices it could not or did not reform
it sought to explain and justify by its mythology.

I

Our sources of information concerning the Orphic
movement are unusually authoritative and accessible.
They include chiefly a reputable group of classical writers
together with a singular collection of Orphic tablets found
in south Italy and Crete. The list of classical witnesses to
the Orphic cult is headed by the name of Pindar. In his
"Dirges," or choral lyrics intended to be chanted at
funerals, he offered consolation to mourners by telling
them of the Orphic promise of immortality.[1] He further
detailed the Orphic doctrine of reincarnation which he
represented as a scheme of preliminary purgation by means
of triple earthly lives, preceding the final bliss.[2] Again he
described with pleasing detail the delights of the Elysian
land where the final beatification was to be realized, and
in the second *Olympian Ode* he told of the future of the
wicked as well as of the pure.[3] Another important classical
witness to Orphism was Plato. Though affecting to despise
the system, he was actually much influenced by it. In
Cratylus, for example, he made use of the characteristic
Orphic idea of the body as a prison house of the soul (*sōma-
sēma*).[4] In the *Republic* he described the missionary methods of the Orphics in terms that were not complimentary,
yet revealed the vigor of the movement. He told of zealous
propagandists who besieged the doors of the rich and
persuaded them by a parade of Orphic scriptures that they
could provide deliverance and purgation from sin, both for

[1] Pindar *Threnodies* 131.

[2] *Op. cit.* 133.

[3] *Op. cit.* 129, 130; also *Olympian Ode* ii. 56–75.

[4] Plato *Cratylus* 400C. Cf. *Georgias* 493

the living and the dead, by means of initiation.[1] Plato also
made reference to the idea of the transmigration of souls
and to the Orphic rule of life.[2] The dramatist Euripides
included an all-important Orphic confessional in his *Cretans*, and in his admirable *Hippolytus* he drew a character
sketch of a typical and consistent Orphic.[3] Even the co-
median Aristophanes bore favorable testimony to the influence of the Orphic mysteries. He had the glorified
Aeschylus, the "grand old man" of Attic tragedy, commend Orpheus for teaching mystic rites to mortal men.[4]
This torch of reverence, however, did not prevent Aristophanes from giving a lively parody of Orphanic initiation in
telling of old Strepsiades' visit to Socrates' "thinking
shop."[5] These four names, Aristophanes, Euripides, Plato,
and Pindar, include the bulk of classical *testimonia* to the
Orphic mysteries.

Quite as revealing as these literary references, however,
are the so-called Orphic tablets from tombs in southern
Italy and Crete.[6] They are eight in number and are all of
very thin gold. According to a consensus of scholarly opinion, they contain the mutilated fragments of a ritual hymn
composed for members of the Orphic sect as early as the
fifth century B.C. In their present form they may be dated
roughly from the fourth century B.C. to the second century
of our era. Their purpose is self-evident. Buried with the
dead they were intended to give instructions concerning
conduct in the next world, formularies and confessionals

[1] Plato *Republic* 364C.

[2] Plato *Phaedo* 70C; *Laws* vi. 782C.

[3] Euripides *Fragmenta* 475 (from Porphyry *De Abstinentia* xiv. 19), also
Hippolytus 952 ff.

[4] Aristophanes *Ranae* 972.   [5] Aristophanes *Nubes* 223 ff.

[6] See Harrison, *Prolegomena*, pp. 572 ff.; pp. 659 ff.; also A. Dieterich,
Nekuia, pp. 84 ff., and *De Hymnis Orphicis*, pp. 31 ff.

to be repeated, and directions as to postmortem ceremonial observances. Their ritualistic character and the tone of conviction that pervades them give them peculiar value as sources of information concerning Orphic experience and practice. These remarkable tablets, though they are few in number, constitute our most valuable source materials for the Orphic cult.

For an expansive expression of Orphic theology, however, one must turn to the corpus of so-called Orphic literature. We know that as early as the time of the Pisistratidae there were in existence at Athens various poems attributed to Orpheus. They were quoted by Plato and later writers, but their genuineness was challenged by Aristotle and Herodotus. Under the hands of the Orphics a vast literature grew up around this nucleus, but for our purpose the hymns only are of special importance.[1] They are of late compilation and uncertain date, although Professor Dieterich would locate their original composition between 200 B.C. and the beginning of the Christian era.[2] In their present form they represent the developed state of Orphic theology, their general tone being that of mystical monotheism. Of the eighty and more extant hymns, all but nine carry in their headings specifications concerning the particular perfume to be burned while they were being sung. Most of them also conclude with an invocation to the deity addressed to bless the mystics in the fulfilment of their rites:

> The sacred rites benevolent attend
> And grant a blameless life, a blessed end.
> Propitious to thy mystics' works incline
> Rejoicing come, for holy rites are thine.

[1] See Abel, *Orphica* (Leipzig, 1885). For a translation of the hymns consult Taylor, *The Mystical Hymns of Orpheus* (London, 1896).

[2] Dieterich, *De Hymnis Orphicis* (Marburg, 1891).

So runs the slightly varied refrain at the conclusion of almost every hymn. These formulas make it practically certain that this collection of hymns was made for liturgical use in Orphic brotherhoods.

In comparison with these major sources of information, classical writers, Orphic tablets, and Orphic hymns, other sources are distinctly of less significance. For the sake of completeness, however, there should be mentioned the "Apulian" vase paintings which depict the blessed dead in the society of the gods. These paintings are particularly significant in that they show the influence of Orphic ideas in Magna Graecia, south Italy especially, during the Hellenic era. Similarly, Greek sepulchral art and grave inscriptions of the Hellenistic and Roman periods are important. There are also casual references to Orphism in later pagan writers, Strabo, Pausanias, and Plutarch, which prove the vigorous persistence of Orphic ideas and practices through the early imperial period. Later Christian notices of Orphism are distinctly secondary to these pagan sources and are chiefly valuable in showing the later persistence of Orphism and its active competition with Christianity.

II

One of these Christian sources, however, deserves specific citation because it preserves in convenient mythological form a bit of fundamental Orphic theology. The passage in question is found in the "Exhortation to the Greeks" by Clement of Alexandria, and it includes a detailed narration of the myth of Dionysus Zagreus.[1] Undoubtedly Clement's rendering of the legend was based upon a lost Orphic poem or poems—at least in the passage itself Clement made two quotations from Orphic literature. Ac-

---

[1] Clement of Alexandria *Protrepticus* ii. 14 ff. Other scattered sources of this myth are cited in Abel, *Orphica*, pp. 230 ff.

cording to his version of the myth, Persephone bore to
Zeus a son "who had the form of a bull." To quote "a
certain mythological poet":

> The bull begets a snake, the snake a bull.

This divine son was Dionysus Zagreus, or "the hunter."
He was the favorite of his father, and Zeus destined him
to become the ruler of the universe. Even while he was
a child, the father of gods and men entrusted him with
thunderbolts and allowed him to sit on his throne. But the
malignant Titans, stung by jealousy and urged on by the
vengeful Hera, sought the young child's life. Though he
was carefully guarded by the warlike Curetes, the Titans
succeeded in luring him away with childish toys, which
were carefully enumerated in a quotation from "Orpheus
of Thrace, the poet of the initiation." Having gained possession of the divine child, the Titans savagely tore him to
pieces, and cooked and ate the pieces. Athena, however,
preserved the heart of Zagreus and carried it away to Zeus
who, in his anger, blasted the savage Titans with his
thunderbolts. Clement omitted one item of the myth
which formed an interesting connection with the Theban
legend of Dionysus. Zeus, having received the heart of
Zagreus from Athena, swallowed it. So when Semele bore
Dionysus to Zeus the new god was but Zagreus reborn.

The Cretan provenance of the Zagreus legend was ex-
pressly stated by Diodorus. In his account of the various
forms assumed by Dionysus, he said: "They allege that
the god (Zagreus) was born of Zeus and Persephone in
Crete, and Orpheus in the mysteries represents him as torn
to pieces by the Titans."[1] The relationship of this legend
to the Cretan rite of eating raw flesh already described in
connection with the Dionysus cult is obvious. It was an

---

[1] Diodorus Siculus v. 4. 75.

aetiological myth through and through. The worshipers of Dionysus were familiar with the ritual fact that a sacrificial animal, which in a sense embodied the god, was torn to pieces and eaten. They sought the sanction of antiquity and divinity for their ritual and posited the dismemberment of their god by the ancient Titans. Shocked at the thought of the brutal murder of a god, they had the bad Titans blasted by Zeus for their wickedness. Thus from the ritual fact of a feast of raw flesh, there grew up the myth of Dionysus Zagreus, the god on whom the Orphic cult was focused.

The importance of this myth lies in the fact that in Orphic thought it was connected with a peculiar theory concerning the origin and nature of man, and so ultimately with the thought of man's eternal destiny. From the ashes of the blasted Titans, the Orphic said, man was created. But these Titans had already consumed the god Dionysus, and their ashes contained the vitality of a divine being. Hence man by his very constitution was believed to be a compound of two natures, one Dionysian and immortal, the other Titanic and mortal. His soul was divine, but while in the body it was confined in a charnel house. Plato made full use of this Orphic conception, and in his *Gorgias* he quoted "a certain philosopher," who said, "We are dead and the body is a tomb."[1] Pindar earlier stressed the divine origin and nature of the human soul in contradistinction to the mortality of the human body. "While the body of all men is subject to over-mastering death, an image of life remains alive, for it alone comes from the gods," he affirmed.[2] This sharp dualism of soul and body appears again and again in the Orphic tablets, though it is not always clear that the myth of the origin of man from the ashes

---

[1] Plato *Gorgias* 493; see also *Cratylus* 400C.

[2] Pindar *Threnodies* 131.

of the Titans was in mind. On the Petelian tablet (south Italy, third century B.C.) the soul is represented as asserting its divine nature thus:

> I am a child of Earth and of Starry Heaven;
> But my race is of Heaven.[1]

Similarly, on three Cretan tablets the soul answers the challenge "Whence are you?" with a reiterated declaration of its dual origin, "I am son of Earth and of Starry Heaven."[2] On the Compagno tablets found near Sybaris the soul makes a like affirmation to the "Pure Queen of Them Below . . . . ," "I avow me that I am of your blessed race."[3] The dualism thus fixed between body and soul was fundamental in Orphic theology. Though the body was an evil thing, the soul was divine and immortal.

In its first analysis, therefore, the Orphic process of salvation was a process of purification from bodily taint. The problem, however, was not such a simple one as these words would indicate. It was not merely from the evils of a single existence that the Orphic sought deliverance, but from the evils of a long series of bodily existences. The Orphic first, and the Pythagorean later, believed in the transmigration of souls from body to body. On leaving the corpse at death, the soul was normally doomed to inhabit the bodies of other men or of animals even, passing on through a chain of physical existences until finally purified. An Orphic fragment preserved by Proclus reads: "Therefore the soul of man changing in the cycles of time enters into various creatures; now it enters a horse, again it becomes a sheep . . . . or as one of the tribe of chill serpents creeps on the sacred ground." Reincarnation, like dualism, was an important item in Orphic theology.

---

[1] Kaibel, *Inscriptiones Graecae Sicilae et Italiae*, No. 638.

[2] *Bulletin de correspondance hellénique*, XVII (1893), 122.

[3] Kaibel, *Inscriptiones Graecae Sicilae et Italiae*, No. 641.

What the Orphic did with the idea of transmigration was to moralize it into a cycle of purgations intended to free the soul from bodily taint and leave it in the end a pure heavenly essence. According to Pindar, the soul had to undergo three such periods of purification in as many different incarnations before the process would be complete. Only those who "thrice had been courageous in keeping their souls pure from all deeds of wrong" could "pass by the highway of Zeus into the tower of Cronus where the ocean breezes blow around the Islands of the Blest."[1] In Plato the series of three incarnations was magnified to three periods of a thousand years each, during which the process of purgation might be completed. At the close of each thousand-year period, the souls drew lots, thus choosing the manner of their next incarnation.[2] One of the most striking scenes depicted in any of Plato's writings was the eschatological vision of Er, son of Armenius, recounted in the tenth book of the *Republic*. At the place of judgment, Er saw mortal souls allotted to a new cycle of life choosing their several destinies.

> He saw the soul which had once been Orpheus choosing the life of a swan out of enmity to the race of woman. . . . . He beheld also the soul of Thamyras choosing the life of a nightingale. Birds on the other hand, like the swan and other musicians, wanting to be men. . . . . After making choice and drinking of the waters of Lethe, these souls shoot away like stars, to birth.[3]

Empedocles announced three transmigration periods of ten thousand years each ere the soul could be considered eligible for heavenly bliss.

The technical Orphic expression for the transmigration of souls and their reappearance in human bodies was "re-

---

[1] Pindar *Olympian Ode* ii. 68 ff.

[2] Plato *Phaedrus* 249.

[3] Plato *Republic* x. 614 ff.

birth" (*palingenesia*).[1] These physical rebirths, however, were what the Orphic least desired, and to escape this weary round of reincarnation was the goal of all his endeavor. According to Proclus, the salvation offered by this system was the freeing of the spirit from the wheel of physical rebirths. In his commentary on Plato's *Timaeus*, he said, "This is what those who are initiated by Orpheus to Dionysus and Kore pray that they may attain:

'To cease from the wheel and breathe again from ill.' "[2]

Undoubtedly this was an Orphic formula for the salvation process. By Simplicius it was attributed to Orpheus himself.[3] Appropriately, therefore, the purified Orphic soul was represented on the Campagno tablets as having escaped from the cycle of necessity and attained to the seats of the hallowed. Its joyful affirmation to the "Pure Queen of Them Below" was:

I have flown out of the sorrowful weary Wheel;
I have passed with eager feet to the Circle desired.[4]

Thus, while the view of human existence fostered by Orphism was essentially pessimistic in its dualism and its theory of successive reincarnations, it did hold out the possibility of escape to weary mortals. It posited one great spiritual rebirth at the time of death which should put an end once for all to the series of physical rebirths that were so much dreaded. The question remains, How was this great deliverance from the cycle of physical existences to be accomplished?

[1] Plutarch *De Ei apud Delphos* 9, *De Defectu Oraculorum* 51, *De Esu Carnium* i. 7, ii. 6.

[2] Proclus on Plato *Timaeus* v. 330.

[3] Simplicius on Aristotle *De Caelo* ii. 168.

[4] Kaibel, *Inscriptiones Graecae Sicilae et Italiae*, No. 641.

III

The Orphic answer to this problem was, in the first instance, by participation in certain prescribed rites of initiation. Orphism came to the seekers for salvation in the Greek world not merely as a philosophy of life but as a religious cult with divinely authenticated rites which must be fulfilled, else there could be no guaranty of deliverance. To those only who had "by happy fortune culled the fruit of the rite that releases from toil,"[1] was there assurance of salvation, the rite in this instance being initiation into the Orphic mysteries. The mendicants who, according to Plato, harassed the rich, exhibiting scriptures by Orpheus, sought to persuade people that they might obtain purification in life and release from suffering after death by the observance of their ritual.[2] Initiation into an Orphic cult was the first step toward deliverance.

In general the prescribed Orphic ritual was a modification of the rude Bacchic rites we have already examined. The persistent representation of Orpheus in antiquity was that of a reformer of Dionysiac rites. Diodorus affirmed that "Orpheus being a man highly gifted by nature and highly trained above all others, made many modifications in the orgiastic rites; hence they call Orphic those rites that took their rise from Dionysus."[3] From the standpoint of ritualistic observance, therefore, there was much in common between Dionysian and Orphic practices. On the very threshold to the Orphic cult stood the omophagy, or feast of raw flesh, which was so prominent a Dionysian rite. In the remaining fragment of Euripides' *Cretans* an initiate tells of certain ritual acts which he performed in the process of becoming a "Bacchus" and the one he stresses particularly is the eating of raw flesh.[4]

[1] Pindar *Threnodies* 131.

[2] Plato *Republic* 364B.   [3] Diodorus Siculus iii. 4. 65.

[4] Euripides *Fragmenta* 475, from Porphyry *De Abstinentia* iv. 19.

For the Orphic this "red and bleeding feast" had two important meanings. It was, first of all, a communion service. Already he had within himself the spark of divinity which came from the ashes of the Titans. This divine life within him, however, was weak, very weak. It needed nourishment. In the sacrificial bull his god Zagreus was ritualistically incarnate; hence, in eating the raw flesh of the torn bull, he partook of a divine substance that nourished and strengthened the immortal life within himself. Just as the life of Zagreus entered the devotee physically when he partook of the flesh of the bull, so the man's soul entered more fully into the spiritual life of Zagreus by this very physical process. In a mystical sense God and man became one by the communion.

But the feast of raw flesh was also a memorial service to the Orphics. With the legend of the divine child Zagreus in mind, they looked upon their own ritual as a re-enactment of the ancient tragedy in which their god was done to death by the Titans. Just as they tore to pieces the flesh of the sacrificial bull and ate it, so the Titans of old had dismembered the child Zagreus. According to Nonnus, it was customary for Orphic initiates to daub themselves with white clay or gypsum as the Titans did in order to conceal their identity.[1] One of the technical expressions for the ritual act of bedaubing with clay was *apomattein* (literally, "to smear off"). Harpocration has the following note on this word:

Others use it in a more special sense, as for example when they speak of putting a coat of clay or pitch on those who are being initiated. In this ceremony they were mimetically enacting the myth told by some persons, in which the Titans, when they mutilated Dionysus, wore a coating of gypsum in order not to be identified.[2]

In this comment the mimetic character of the Orphic ritual is definitely asserted.

[1] Nonnus *Dionysiaca* xxvii. 204, 228.   [2] Harpocration *s.v.*

The real inwardness of this act of daubing with gypsum, however, lay in another direction. It was an act of purification—strange as it may seem. The terms *perimattein* and *apomattein* ("to besmear" and "to smear off") were used interchangeably to mean "to purify." In the Orphic rite of initiation, just as in the Sabazian rite at which Aeschines assisted, the candidates for initiation were "purified and wiped clean with mud and pitch."[1] They were not purified *from* mud and pitch but rather *with* mud and pitch. Since it was not a physical cleansing that was sought but rather a spiritual cleansing, clay and pitch served the purpose quite as well as water. Yet Plutarch, with all his sympathy for Orphism, protested vigorously against purifications in this manner, calling them "unclean purifications, filthy cleansings and bemirings."[2] Orphic initiation, then, in addition to the rite of communion, featured a strange ceremonial of cleansing intended to rid the candidate of the stains inherent in his physical nature.

For the Orphic, however, mere initiation with its prescribed rites, its mysticizing of crude Dionysian ritual, its communion service, and its purifications, was not sufficient as a guaranty of salvation. Initiation, while it was the beginning of a process that eventuated in complete salvation, was but the beginning. The salvation process itself continued as an arduous self-discipline and it lasted a lifetime. The initial sacraments of communion and purgation were supplemented by the austerities of the "Orphic life"—an expression that became proverbial. So the "Bacchus of the Mailed Priests" in Euripides' *Cretans* ends his confession thus:

> Robed in pure white I have borne me clean
> From man's vile birth and coffined clay,

[1] Demosthenes *De Corona* 313.

[2] Plutarch *De Superstitione* 12.

> And exiled from my lips alway
> Touch of all meat where life has been.[1]

In general the disciplinary prescriptions of Orphism were almost identical with those of Pythagoreanism. Herodotus characterized the Orphic way of life as at once Egyptian and Pythagorean.[2] Diogenes Laertius, in his life of Pythagoras, has given a convenient and comprehensive statement of the main items in the Pythagorean *ascesis*. His list of prescriptions is as follows:

> Purification is by means of cleansings, and baths and aspersions. A man must also keep himself from funerals and marriages and every kind of physical pollution, and abstain from all food that is dead or has been killed, and from mullet, and from the fish melanurus, and from eggs, and from animals that lay eggs, and from beans, and from the other things that are forbidden for those who accomplish the holy rites of initiation.[3]

The Orphic, like the Pythagorean, lived a life of ceremonial cleanliness and holiness. By washing and aspersions, at once symbolic and sacramental in character, he sought to purge away the taint of his bodily nature, the "ancient woe" inherited from the Titans. He kept himself rigorously from all defilement of physical contacts with human or animal bodies, from human births especially, and from dead bodies; for in a corpse the evil Titanic matter was left without any vital Dionysian element. Both in life and in death certain clothing regulations were strictly observed. In life the Orphic wore garments of pure white. In death the initiated were never buried in woolen wrappings.

Not only were rules concerning cleanliness and clothing strictly adhered to, but certain food regulations were also carefully followed. Having once partaken of the sacrament

---

[1] Euripides *Fragmenta* 475.

[2] Herodotus ii. 81.   [3] Diogenes Laertius viii. 33.

of raw flesh, the Orphic fasted forever thereafter from animal food. This was the most familiar of all the prohibitions
observed by the Orphics, and Plato defined the Orphic
manner of living in terms of this observance. "Orphic lives,
as they are called," he said, "were led by those of our race
who adhered to the use of all inanimate things, but ab-
stained from every thing wherein is life."[1] This abstinence
from animal food was a main item in the discipline of the
tragic Orphic Hippolytus, whose asceticism was the object
of Theseus' bitter invective in Euripides' drama. In his
rage the old king cried out against his own son:

> Now vaunt, ay now!—set out your paltry wares
> Of lifeless food: . . . .
> . . . . I warn all men to shun
> Such hypocrits as you.[2]

These words, from the mouth of a sadly mistaken father,
should not be taken as proof of priggishness on the part of
the Orphics, but at least they serve to emphasize the rigor
of the Orphic discipline in the matter of abstinence from
animal foods. By fasting and purifications, the disciple of
Orpheus sought to purge away the evil which he had inherited with his physical nature. Only after a whole lifetime of such purgation could he affirm, in the terminology
of the Compagno and Caecilia Secundina tablets,

> Out of the pure I come, Pure Queen of Them Below.

The question naturally suggests itself, whether or not
the Orphic ideal made any moral demands on these who
were initiated. Since personal purity, even though it was
of a ceremonial and ritualistic character, stood at the very
center of Orphism, the way was open for the development
of morality. The very will to observe its rigid prescriptions
was itself a moral attitude. Moreover, there is valuable tes-

---

[1] Plato *Laws* 782C.   [2] Euripides *Hippolytus* 952 ff.

timony among ancient writers to show that Orphism did
have an elevating effect on the moral life. Pindar, for example, based his Orphic eschatology on moral conditions
and assumed that knowledge of the lore of Orphism would
help men lead good lives.[1] Aristophanes, who did not hesitate to poke fun at Orphism, paid a serious tribute to it
in *The Frogs* when the tragedian Aeschylus said of the poet
Orpheus: "He made known to us mystic rites, and to abstain from slaughter."[2] Certainly this last statement had
reference to something more than mere abstinence from
animal food. At the very least it meant that Orphic ritual
laid stress on the necessity of purification from blood, and at
most it meant that Orphism came with a gospel of absten-
tion from murder and of peace on earth. Horace doubtless
had much the same thought in mind when he declared that
Orpheus not only tamed fierce animals but savage men as
well.[3] The author of the speech against Aristogeiton also
spoke reverentially of Orpheus "who instituted for us the
most holy mysteries and declared that Justice is seated on
the throne of God watching all the actions of mankind."[4]

At one point especially the moral influence of Orphism
was clear and indubitable: that was in its protest against
suicide. Since the body was the soul's place of penance a
man had no right to take his own life. If he did he was a
fugitive prisoner trying to escape before God had released
him. Here Plato found Orphic thought peculiarly con-
genial to his own. In the *Phaedo* he represented Socrates
as saying, shortly before his death, "There is a doctrine
whispered in secret that a man is a prisoner who has no
right to open the door and run away; this is a great mystery which I do not quite understand. Yet I too believe
that the gods are our guardians and that we are a posses-

---

[1] Pindar *Olympian Odes* ii.   [3] Horace *Ars Poetica* 391.

[2] Aristophanes *Ranae* 1032.   [4] (Demosthenes) *Aristogeiton* 11.

sion of theirs."[1] In view of all this array of literary evidence, certain moral obligations must be added to the ritualistic requirements which characterized the Orphic life.

But participation in rites of initiation and a life of ascetic observance, even, were not sufficient to guarantee full and final salvation for the Orphic. There were certain postmortem rules of conduct to be observed as well. The Orphic tablets bring this out most clearly. They chart the geography of the next world for the initiate, acquaint him with the divine beings who have the determination of future weal or woe, prescribe certain ritual acts to be observed, and instruct him in formularies and confessions to be repeated under certain circumstances.

The Petelia tablet told of a nameless well-spring situated at the left of the House of Hades.[2] This the soul must avoid. Since it was contrasted specifically with the Well of Memory in the following verses, the forbidden spring was probably Lethe, or Forgetfulness. Because the Orphic had spent a lifetime in purification he had no need of forgetfulness. The well-spring of which he must drink was the one flowing from the Lake of Memory. This was the Orphic counterpart of the "well of water springing up unto everlasting life." The Petelia tablet also served to inform the soul what formula to use in asking for a drink from the Well of Memory. It was an avowal of divine origin: "I am a child of Earth and Starry Heaven." According to the tablet, this declaration would be sufficient to gain the boon desired from the guardians of the Lake of Memory.

> Of themselves they will give you to drink,
>> From the holy Well-spring,
> And thereafter among the other Heroes,
>> You shall have lordship.

[1] Plato *Phaedo* 62B.

[2] Kaibel, *Inscriptiones Graecae Sicilae et Italiae*, No. 638.

The Eleuthernae tablets represented much the same situation in the lively form of a dialogue between the soul and the well itself.

On the Compagno tablets[1] certain additional declarations were placed in the mouth of the initiate. Here the soul came as a suppliant to the holy Persephone herself, and the prescribed words were addressed to her as the "Pure Queen of Them Below." As in the other tablets, there was the assertion of divine origin. "I avow me that I am of your blessed race." In addition, however, there was the further declaration of purity attained by the observance of Orphic practices.

> Out of the pure I come. . . . .
> I have flown out of the sorrowful weary wheel,
> I have passed with eager feet to the circle desired.

These affirmations on the part of the soul were an "open sesame" to immortal bliss for they brought the final assurance, "Happy and Blessed One, you shall be God instead of mortal." In this climactic fashion the postmortem ritual as recorded on the Orphic tablets was completed.

On the basis of Dionysian practice and experience, therefore, Orphism built up an elaborate theological construction with refined and extended ritualistic observances. Faced by the problem of the dual constitution of man, his soul Dionysian, divine and immortal, and his body Titanic, evil and mortal, Orphism found the solution of the antinomy in two very different directions. On the one hand, there was the prospect of a natural process of purification through a series of physical rebirths in animal or human form. This was a gloomy prospect, however—a remedy that was worse than the disease. On the other hand there was a way of salvation provided by the Orphic cult itself, an extended process of self-discipline ending in a spiritual

[1] *Ibid.*, No. 641.

regeneration that would break, once for all, the chain of successive physical births. It was a long and arduous process beginning with a rite of initiation which marked the formal entrance upon a new way of living. There were prayers to be repeated and sacrifices to be fulfilled. There were sacraments of communion and purification. Following the initiatory rites was the rigid discipline of a life-long asceticism that included purgations, fastings, and freedom from bodily contamination, as well as certain elementary moral requirements. All this, even, was not deemed sufficient. It had to be supplemented by a post-mortem ritual. The Orphic imagination pictured the future, charted the next world, and prescribed the formulas and confessions to be repeated under given circumstances. Thus the final goal of ultimate assimilation to deity was to be attained. Thus the initiated, having lived a life of Orphic purity, finally became "God from man."

Admittedly Orphic practice did not offer a new birth experience as a single catastrophic event to be realized in one's lifetime, unless initiation itself is considered that event in a proleptic way. But Orphism did furnish the possibility for a long regenerative process, beginning at initiation and ending after the death of the physical body— a development that eventuated in happy immortality. As an extended process, therefore, rather than as a single event, Orphism fostered the experience of regeneration.

IV

It is certainly pertinent to inquire whether or not the Orphic type of religious experience had real significance in the Graeco-Roman world at the beginning of the Christian era. Of the influence of Orphism in the Greek world during classical times, we have found ample testimony by writers of the highest repute. It is more difficult to trace the influence of Orphism as a distinct religious movement during the Hellenistic and later periods. Still the discovery of the important private Orpheum in the recently excavated Villa Item at Pompeii[1] leads one to anticipate similar finds elsewhere that may illustrate the distinctive functioning of the Orphic cult in first-century life. If when Pompeii was overwhelmed by the eruption of Vesuvius in 79 A.D. an Orphic brotherhood was operating under private patronage in this charming villa, similar groups were certainly to be found elsewhere in the Roman world maintaining their peculiar cult practices. Aside from such independent functioning, however, Orphism continued to influence the world through systems other than its own. Like Pythagoreanism in this as in much else, it merged readily with other movements. Its ideas were adopted by popular philosophies and its practices were taken over by popular religions. Orphism became very influential at ancient Eleusis particularly, and with the influx of foreign gods and goddesses into the Greek world it captivated them also. In these secondary forms the Orphic view of life and the Orphic way of living continued to influence thought and action even where Orphic brotherhoods as such had ceased to exist.

There is plenty of direct literary evidence as to the power of Orphic ideas and practices, however institutionalized, during the Hellenistic and Graeco-Roman periods. One of the *characteres* of Theophrastus, for example, was a man who every month repaired to the priests of the Orphic mysteries to partake of their rites. Usually he was accompanied by his wife. But if she was too busy, his children and their nurse went along with him.[2] Perhaps the most

[1] Macchioro, *Zagreus* (Bari, 1920). See also Rostovtzeff, *Mystic Italy* (New York, 1928), pp. 40 ff.

[2] Theophrastus *Characteres* 28.

notable example of a prominent man who shared the Orphic hope in the first Christian century was Plutarch. Both he and his wife were initiated into an Orphic *thiasus*. Though he strongly criticized certain Orphic practices, and refused to be frightened by the terrors of their Hell, and depreciated the morbid type of self-examination fostered by their manner of life, yet he and his wife found the Orphic hope a real consolation to themselves in the time of trouble.[1] Strabo and Pausanias, as well as Plutarch, made casual reference to Orphism as a feature of contemporary religion, while Lucian, in his irresponsible manner, reflected Orphic ideas here and there. The Latin poet Statius praised the widow of a certain Lucan for not deifying him as Bacchus and consecrating to him "a deceitful *thiasus*"[2] —a testimony that the Orphic practice of deifying the dead was not infrequent in the Graeco-Roman world.

Of more concrete significance is the archaeological evidence furnished by sepulchral art and grave inscriptions. According to the Orphic scheme of things, the soul entered upon the status of divinity after death. Among the monuments there are a number—quite apart from royal or imperial memorials—which actually represented the dead as gods. At Guthaeum, for example, a first-century (A.D.) statue representing a youth was found near a sarcophagus. It was obviously intended to be a portrait statue; but a panther stands by the side of the youth, a grape cluster is in his hand, and a vine crown is on his head. Here is a clear memorial of the process of apotheosizing a youth after death and of representing him as the god Dionysus.[3]

Among the grave inscriptions there are parallels to this sculptural representation of a deceased youth as a god.

[1] Plutarch *Consolatio ad Uxorem* 10.

[2] Statius *Silvae* ii. 7. 124.

[3] *Ephemeris Archaiologike* (1911), p. 118, pl. 5.

A priest of Thasos dedicated an inscription to his dead wife as "an incarnate goddess," and a man by the name of Lucius consecrated a monument to his child of four years with these words: "To my sweetest child and personal God who hearkens to my prayers."[1] More clearly reminiscent of certain characteristic Orphic ideas is a second-century (A.D.) inscription found in a Sabine village. "The soul is immortal for it came from God. The body is the garment of the soul. Honor the God in me."[2] This was good Orphic doctrine throughout.

Here and there also among grave inscriptions are to be heard the echoes of Orphic ritual. On a tombstone in Cnidus was engraved this affirmation, "I have not drunk of the water of Lethe that ends all things."[3] Immediately one is reminded of the Petelia tablet with its description of a nameless well-spring at the left of the House of Hades with a white cypress standing near—a well-spring by all means to be avoided. There are other inscriptions which recall the cool waters of Memory flowing from the well-spring on the right, from which the parched soul may drink and find new life for itself. Two epitaphs of the third century (A.D.) found at Rome contain prayers that are reminiscent of the Orphic tablets. "May Aidoneus, the king of the dead, give you the cold water" is the petition of one, while the second inscription repeats the same request in the first person, "May he give the cold water to my thirsting soul."[4] Most peculiar of the Orphic inscriptions is one from Abydos, dated roughly at the beginning of our era. It stood originally on the grave of a Lycian Greek buried near the reputed tomb of Osiris. The inscription expressed the conviction that since the tomb of the

---

[1] Kaibel, *Epigrammata Graeca*, No. 214.

[2] *Op. cit.*, No. 651.

[3] *Op. cit.*, No. 204.　　　　[4] *Op. cit.*, Nos. 658, 719.

god was near, the soul of the dead would escape Hades: "Hermes gathers me with the sons of the gods, and I have not drunk the water of Forgetfulness."[1] Here the Arcadian Hermes makes his appearance in the rôle of Psychopompos, as in classical mythology and the Hermetic literature, and the inscription as a whole memorializes the blending on Egyptian soil of Orphism, Hermetism, the Osiris cult, and local tradition.

Altogether, therefore, the grave monuments of Graeco-Roman times strongly reinforce the literary evidences that Orphic ideas were still very influential in the life of paganism when Christianity first emerged. Hence, among the new-birth experiences of paganism contemporary with early Christianity the extended Orphic process of regeneration must not be ignored.

BIBLIOGRAPHY

ABEL, EUGENE, *Orphica*. Leipzig, 1885.

BOUGLANGER, ANDRÉ, *Orphée*. Paris, 1925.

DIETERICH, ALBRECHT, *De Hymnis Orphicis*. Marburg, 1891.

EISLER, ROBERT, *Orphisch-Dionysische Mysterien-gedanken*. Leipzig, 1925.

FARNELL, LEWIS R., *Greek Hero Cults and Ideas of Immortality* (Oxford, 1921), pp. 373–402.

GRUPPE, OTTO, *Die griechischen Culte und Mythen* (Leipzig, 1887), I, 612–74.

HARRISON, JANE ELLEN, *Prolegomena to the Study of Greek Religion* (Cambridge, 1922³), pp. 454–673.

HAUCK, MAXIMILIAN, *De Hymnorum Orphicorum Aetate*. Breslau, 1911.

KERN, OTTO, *Orphicorum Fragmenta*. Berlin, 1922.

LOBECK, C. A., *Aglaophamus* (Regimonti, 1829), II, 233–1104.

LEGGE, F., *Forerunners and Rivals of Christianity* (Cambridge, 1915), I, 121–48.

MAAS, E. W., *Orpheus*. Munich, 1895.

MACCHIORO, V., *Zagreus*. Bari, 1920.

---

[1] *Bulletin de correspondance hellénique*, XXVI (1902), 440 ff.

MOORE, CLIFFORD HERSCHEL, "Greek and Roman Ascetic Tendencies," in *Harvard Essays on Classical Subjects* (New York, 1912), pp. 97–140.

ROSTOVTZEFF, M. I., *Mystic Italy*. New York, 1928.

ROHDE, E., *Psyche* (Tübingen, 1924[8]) Vol. II. English translation by W. B. Hillis. London, 1925.

TAYLOR, THOMAS, *The Mystical Hymns of Orpheus*. London, 1896.

CHAPTER V

THE REGENERATIVE RITES OF
THE GREAT MOTHER

FROM the Oriental as well as from the Hellenic world there emanated mystery religions that made their appeal and offered their satisfactions to the individual man. Like the Greek cults just described, they operated as private religious brotherhoods, though in occasional instances they were brought under state patronage and supervision. They came to the Graeco-Roman world with all the authority of a venerable past, with a theology developed in mythological forms, with a ritual, very crude perhaps, yet capable of lofty spiritual interpretation. Their appeal was primarily an emotional one, and it was addressed specifically to the individual; for all classes and all races, Greeks as well as barbarians, slaves as well as free men, were welcomed to their membership.

I

Of these Oriental mystery religions the first to invade the west was the cult of the Great Mother of the Gods, which came from central Asia Minor. The divine personage in whom this cult centered was the *Magna Mater Deum* who was conceived as the source of all life as well as the personification of all the powers of nature. This aspect of universal motherhood was the comprehensive feature of her character most frequently emphasized in the various cult titles applied to her. She was the "Great Mother" not only "of all the gods," but "of all men" as well. She was the "Mistress of All," the "All-Nourisher," and "All-Be-

getter," the "Mighty Mother," and the "Mother of Zeus
Himself."[1] "The winds, the sea, the earth, and the snowy
seat of Olympus are hers, and when from her mountains
she ascends into the great heavens, the son of Cronus himself gives way before her, and in like manner do also the
other immortal blest honor the dread goddess."[2] At Pessinus, the strongest center of her worship in Asia Minor,
she was from primitive times represented by a sacred stone,
said to have fallen from heaven. Indeed, the city itself,
according to one legend, was named from this very circumstance (*pesein*, "to fall").[3] Here all the vital forces of
mother earth were concentrated in "a stone not large,
which could be carried in a man's hand without pressure—
of a dusky and black color—not smooth, but having little
corners standing out."[4] This was the stone which was later
carried to Rome when the worship of the Great Mother was
officially introduced to the Occident. Ensconced in a silver
statue where the face ought to be, it became the center of
the Roman cult of the Great Mother—the whole life of
nature embodied in a small, rough stone.

The *Magna Mater* of all living creatures was especially
the goddess of the wilder aspects of nature. She was worshiped in the depths of virgin forests and on the tops of
mountains, and her cult titles named her the "Mountain
Mother," and the "Divinity of the Mountains," not to
mention such local appellations as "Dindymene,"[5] or the
"Idaean Mother."[6] Even Cybele, the familiar literary
designation of the Great Mother, was, according to Strabo

---

[1] Euripides *Bacchae* 78; Pindar *Fragmenta* 57; Apollonius *Argonautica* i.
1119, 1151, 1094; *Homeric Hymns* xiv; Aristophanes *Aves* 875; Sophocles
Philoctetes 392; *Orphic Hymns* xxx. 5.

[2] Apollonius *Argonautica* i. 1098 ff.

[3] Herodian i. 11.   [5] Herodotus i. 80.

[4] Arnobius vii. 49.   [6] Euripides *Orestes* 1453.

and Diodorus, derived from a mountain or range of mountains.[1] "A grove I had upon the mountains' crest, whither men brought me offerings," said the goddess herself in describing one of her favorite haunts, "a pine forest beloved for many years, dim with dusky firs and trunks of maple."[2] Anacharsis the Scythian was a typical devotee of the *Magna Mater*, for he worshiped her in a place "full of trees."[3] She was also the "Mistress of Wild Beasts," and lions were her constant companions in literature and in art. The author of the fourteenth Homeric Hymn addressed the Mother of the Gods as one who "is glad in the cry of wolves and fiery-eyed lions, and in echoing hills, and woodland haunts." Thus she appeared as the goddess of all natural life, particularly in its wild and untamed aspects.

With her was associated a hero-divinity called Attis who personified the life of the vegetable world particularly. The pine tree was peculiarly his own and played a prominent part in his annual ritual. His priests were tattooed with an ivy-leaf pattern. Statues represented him crowned with fruits and holding ears of corn in his hand. He was himself addressed as the "reaped green (or yellow) ear of corn" in the hymn of Hippolytus,[4] and the myth of his sufferings was interpreted now as the harvesting of ripened grain[5] or again as the fading of spring flowers.[6] His devotees in their feasts, while they might eat the stalks and upper parts of plants, were forbidden to eat seeds and the roots of vegetables,[7] for in these the divine life of their god was especially manifested. Above all, the great festival

---

[1] Strabo 469, 470, 567; Diodorus Siculus iii. 58.

[2] Vergil *Aeneid* ix. 85 ff.

[3] Herodotus iv. 76.   [4] *Philosophoumena* v. 1. 9.

[5] Firmicus Maternus *De errore profanarum religionum* 3.

[6] Augustine *De Civitate Dei* vii. 25.   [7] Julian *Orationes* v. 175 ff.

of Attis, held at the time of the vernal equinox, took the form of a mystery drama which obviously represented the reviving of the vegetable world at that season of the year.

Around these two divinities, the Great Mother and the god of vegetation, there grew up a confused tangle of myths in explanation of their cult rites. Various writers, pagan and Christian, gave different versions of the Cybele-Attis myth. Pausanias recounted two very different renderings of the legend.[1] One of these was repeated by the Christian writer Arnobius, on the authority of a certain Timotheus.[2] In detail the final edition was much more elaborate than the earlier rendition by Pausanias. Diodorus also recounted the Cybele-Attis myth with one or two singular omissions,[3] while Firmicus Maternus gave a markedly euhemeristic interpretation of the legend.[4] The accounts by Ovid, by the philosopher Sallust, and by the Emperor Julian were similar to each other at points, yet differed in important respects from the other renderings of the legend.

The specific variations in all these diverse statements do not concern us, for certain significant elements were common to all the various versions. In each instance the relationship of Cybele and Attis was essentially the same, and their experiences were much the same throughout. According to the myth, the goddess-mother loved the youthful, virgin-born shepherd Attis with a pure love. But Attis died, either slain by another or by his own hand. In the latter instance, he was unfaithful to the Great Mother and in a frenzy of regret he emasculated himself and died. The goddess-mother mourned her dead lover and finally effected his restoration. Thus, in the end, the mortal Attis became deified and immortal. These were the main elements in the developed myth which bulked largest in the

[1] Pausanias vii. 17. 9–12.   [3] Diodorus Siculus iii. 4. 58 f.

[2] Arnobius v. 5–8.   [4] Firmicus Maternus *De Errore* 3.

mind of the devotee as he participated in the rites of the cult.

The whole myth was palpably transparent. Attis, the god of vegetation grown to youthful beauty, is loved by Mother Earth. But the flowers of springtime fade and the fruits of summer are harvested. Nature is despoiled of her vegetation. Attis dies. Then the Mother mourns her dead plant life and remains in sorrow during autumn and winter. But with returning springtime vegetation revives and the youthful god Attis is restored to life. These familiar natural phenomena, dramatized in the ritual of the Cybele-Attis cult, became the basis on which the devotees of the *Magna Mater* developed their personal religious experiences.

II

The primitive *locus* of this nature worship was in the uplands of Anatolia. In a general way legends agree in locating the rise of the Cybele-Attis cult in the area covered by Galatia, Phrygia, and Lydia.[1] As M. Cumont has properly emphasized, the development of a highly emotional cult was natural in this vicinity.[2] Here the climate went to extremes, cold and bleak in winter, hot and even scorching in summer. These climatic contrasts made themselves felt on the character of the inhabitants. Men were responsive to the varying moods of nature with the changing seasons. During the winter months they shared the sorrow of nature at the loss of her vegetation; but with the returning verdure of springtime they hailed with joy the revival of nature. Thus there developed in the uplands north of Paul's birthplace a cult distinguished for its excessive emotionalism.

[1] Diodorus Siculus iii. 4. 58; Pausanias vii. 17, 10 ff.; Arnobius v. 5; Firmicus Maternus *De Errore* 3; Ovid *Fasti* iv. 223 ff.; Sallust (Phil.) *De Diis et Mundo* 4; Julian *Orationes* v. 165 ff.

[2] Cumont, *Oriental Religions in Roman Paganism*, p. 50.

Just when this religion had its inception it is impossible to state with any exactness. It is clear, however, that from the sixth century B.C. onward the worship of the Great Mother was dominant in Asia Minor. The earliest monuments of the cult, the so-called Niobe of Mount Sipylus and two reliefs from the vicinity of Prymnessus, date from the middle of the sixth century at least.[1] Herodotus was acquainted with certain external features of this worship, and he knew the Great Mother as belonging to Sardis and enthroned on Mount Dindymon.[2] By the beginning of the fifth century Pessinus had become a center of her cult, and a hundred years later Asia Minor generally was familiar with it. Considerably before the period of Alexander, therefore, the worship of Cybele and Attis was well established and widely spread in Asia Minor—mountains like Dindymon, Ida, and Tmolus, and cities like Cyzicus, Sardis, and Pessinus being the important centers of the cult.

The Great Mother early emigrated from her Asian home and traveled to Europe, first by way of the Hellespont and later by the Aegean Islands. Pindar knew her worship at Thebes[3] and Aristophanes ridiculed the goddess from Athens.[4] The chorus of Euripides' *Bacchae* came from Mount Tmolus and sang the praises of the Great Mother as well as of Dionysus. By the end of the fourth century, the worship of the Mother existed privately in the seaport town of the Peiraeus, while the Emperor Julian had a story to tell concerning the introduction of the Great Mother's religion at Athens.[5] Admittedly, however, the cult of the *Magna Mater* was not especially popular in Greece.[6] The demand for a highly emotional type of religious experience was already well satisfied among the

---

[1] Ramsay, in *Journal of Hellenic Studies*, III, 35–41; V, 244–46.

[2] Herodotus i. 80; iv. 76; v. 102.   [4] Aristophanes *Aves* 875–77.

[3] Pindar *Fragmenta* 57B.   [5] Julian *Orationes* v. 159.

[6] Pausanias vii. 17. 9; vii. 20. 3; ix. 25. 3; iii. 22. 4.

Hellenes. In the orgiastic rites of Dionysus, the Greeks had religious practices of strikingly similar character which gave them the desired emotional stimulation.

The coming of the *Magna Mater* to Rome and the west was under the most dramatic circumstances. It was in the year 204 B.C.; Hannibal was still in Italy and Rome was thoroughly exhausted. Moreover, the people had become frightened because of frequent showers of stones and other unusual phenomena. In desperation the Sibylline Books were consulted, and it was learned that the enemy could be conquered if the Idaean Mother should be brought from Pessinus to Rome. Accordingly, a delegation was sent to King Attalus of Pergamum, who conducted them to Pessinus and gave them the sacred stone which was the Mother of the Gods. On her arrival in Italy, the goddess was officially welcomed by the "best man" of the Republic and the leading matrons of Rome. Miracles attended the event, the citizens made holiday, and an annual festival was instituted in honor of the goddess. As a result—so it seemed—the crops of that year were successful and Hannibal was driven out of Italy and conquered. So the *Magna Mater* came in triumph to the west in 204 B.C.[1]

Although the worship of the Great Mother was officially welcomed to Italy, it seems to have been regarded with suspicion, treated as foreign, and subjected to state regulation during the last two centuries of the Republic. Under the Empire, however, the cult came into its own. By the first century A.D. the legal restrictions of republican days were removed and the worship of the *Magna Mater* easily became one of the most popular and favored religions of the time. The Archigallus, or high priest of the cult, became the *Attis populi Romani*.[2] During the reign of Claudi-

---

[1] For the historian's account of the event see Livy xxix. 10–14. For the poet's rendering of the story, see Ovid *Fasti* iv. 178 ff.

[2] *Corpus Inscriptionum Latinarum* Vol. VI, No. 2183.

us, the annual festival was elaborated with even more impressive rites than those of its native Phrygian home and it took on its final form as one of the great festivals of the Roman Empire.[1] The literature of the first century shows the high degree of prominence attained by the cult during this period. Livy gave an account of the coming of the Great Mother to Rome.[2] Ovid, in the *Fasti*, devoted much space to an explanation of the origin and significance of her rites.[3] Vergil told how the Great Mother had protected Aeneas, the ancestral hero of the Roman race.[4] Horace made several references to the Great Mother's rites,[5] and Propertius recounted the story of Claudia, who led the Roman matrons in welcoming the goddess to Italy.[6] Even Maecenas composed a poem in honor of Cybele.[7] The satirists, on the other hand, were unsparing in making the *Galli* the butt of crude jokes.[8] Thus, during the period when Pauline Christianity was barely beginning to make itself felt as a missionary movement in the Graeco-Roman world, the cult of the Great Mother of the Gods had already won a place of prominence for itself in the life of the Roman Empire. It is important, therefore, to consider the phenomena of this gentile religion in relation to the development of early Christianity itself.

III

Our clearest index to the personal religious experience of the devotees of the Great Mother is found in a study of the cult ritual. Because of their public character we possess the most extensive information concerning the annual

---

[1] Joannes Lydus *De Mensibus* iv 41.

[2] Livy xxix. 10–14.

[3] Ovid *Fasti* iv. 178 ff.   [5] Horace *Odes* i. 16. 5; iii. 19. 18.

[4] Vergil *Aeneid* ix. 77 ff.   [6] Propertius iv. 11. 51.

[7] Baehrens, *Fragmenta Poetarum Romanorum, Maecenas*, 4.

[8] Martial ii. 45; iii. 81. Juvenal ii. 111; iii. 60; vi. 511; viii. 176.

spring festival of Attis, and the *Taurobolium* of the *Magna Mater*—ceremonials that had the official sanction of the Roman state. In considering the spring festival which Claudius incorporated as a part of the established religion of the Empire, it is important to bear in mind that at most it was but an elaboration of rites that had long been practiced in Asia Minor. We are specifically informed that the Roman ritual was celebrated *Phrygio more*.[1] It may reasonably be assumed, therefore, that the Roman ceremonies were not essentially different from their Asian originals.

The prelude to the annual festival began on the Ides of March. On the second festival day, which was designated *Arbor intrat* in the calendar of Philocalus, the guild of *dendrophori*, or tree bearers, were in charge of the ceremonial. It was the duty of the *dendrophori* to cut down a pine tree in the woods and bear it with due pomp to the temple of Cybele. The perennial pine was a natural embodiment of Attis, the spirit of vegetation. According to legend, it was under a pine tree that he had mutilated himself and died. He had himself been transmuted into a pine tree and carried in this form into the cave of Cybele where the goddess mourned her dead lover;[2] hence the pine tree borne by the *dendrophori* into the temple of Cybele was regarded as the corpse of Attis dead and treated with divine honors. It was swathed with fillets of wool as the body of Attis had been. Its branches were hung with garlands of violets, the flowers that sprang from his blood. From the middle of the stem was suspended an image of a young man, who was doubtless Attis himself.[3] The ritual

[1] Arrian *Tactica* 22; also Servius on Vergil *Aeneid* xii. 838.

[2] Arnobius v. 7; Ovid *Metamorphoses* x. 103–5.

[3] Julian *Orationes* v. 168; Lydus *De Mensibus* iv. 41; Arnobius *Adversus Nationes* v. 7, 16, 39; Sallust (Phil.) *De diis* 4; Firmicus Maternus *De Errore* 27.

fact was that the dead god was brought with funeral pomp to the temple of the *Magna Mater*.

The following day was one of fasting when the devotees of Attis mourned their god. It was a peculiar fast, however; Jerome called it "a gluttonous abstinence, when men ate pheasants in order not to contaminate cereals."[1] Meats, in general, were allowed, but fruits and vegetables were forbidden. This prohibition extended to wine also. The vegetable abstinence was a natural one. As the cutting down of the pine tree symbolized that the god of vegetation was dead, so the vegetable world shared in the defunct condition of the god. To partake of vegetables and cereals at such a season would be to violate the bruised and broken body of a god. This fast probably began with the fifteenth of March, and it had its influence as a physical preparation for the excessive emotionalism of the rites which marked the climax of the festival.

These rites came on the twenty-fourth of March, a day that was called, significantly enough, the "Day of Blood." At this time the Great Mother of the Gods inspired her devotees with a frenzy surpassing that which the followers of Dionysus knew. It was a madness induced not by wine, but by the din of crashing music, the dizzy whirling of the dance, and the sight of blood. The music which accompanied these rites was wild and barbaric, made by clashing cymbals and blatant horns, shrilling flutes and rolling drums. It was maddening music, noisy and savage. Lucian vividly described the wild tumult made by the *Galli* on Mount Ida blowing their horns, pounding their drums, and clashing their cymbals.[2] Music of this kind—the Anatolian prototype of modern jazz—was popularly known as Phrygian music.[3]

---

[1] Jerome *Epistulae* cvii. 10 *Ad Laetam*.

[2] Lucian *Deorum Dialogi* xii.   [3] Martial xi. 84.

To the accompaniment of these barbaric strains a dance was staged. With wagging heads and streaming hair, the devotees of the Great Mother whirled their bodies round and round in a dizzy dance, shouting and singing as they gyrated. Apuleius pictured such a dance performed in a Thessalian village by the mendicant priests of the Syrian goddess.

They went forth with their arms naked to their shoulders, bearing with them great swords . . . . shouting and dancing like mad persons to the sound of the pipe. . . . . They began to howl all out of tune and hurl themselves hither and thither, as though they were mad. They made a thousand gests with their feet and their heads; they would bend down their necks and spin round so that their hair flew out in a circle; they would bite their own flesh; finally every one took his two-edged weapon and wounded his arms in different places.[1]

This cruel custom of lacerating one's own flesh during the frenzied ritual was a distinctive characteristic of the Great Mother's cult. Slashing their arms with knives, or gashing their bodies, the worshipers sprinkled with their own blood the sacred tree that was Attis. When Martial was casting about for a comparison to make vivid the dangerous habits of a certain barber he could think of nothing more to the point than these bloody rites of the Great Mother. "He who desires not yet to go down to Stygian shades, let him, if he be wise, avoid barber Antiochus. White arms are mangled with knives less cruel when the frenzied throng raves to Phrygian strains,"[2] he declared. To the modern mind this sanguine rite seems cruel in the extreme. It is probable, however, that the devotees, wrought up to a very high pitch of excitement by the din of the noisy music and the frenzy of the wild dance, were largely insensible to the pain. This ghastly ritual formed a part of the mourning for the dead Attis. When

---

[1] Apuleius *Metamorphoses* viii. 27.   [2] Martial xi. 84.

the Great Mother saw the freely flowing blood of her worshipers, she could not doubt that they shared with her
in her sorrow. The blood may well have been intended,
also, to appease the *manes* of the dead Attis or to strength-
en him for his resurrection. To imitate Cybele in her grief
and to call Attis back to life were the purposes of this
bloody rite.

But the devotees of the Great Mother did not stop with
the shedding of blood merely. Keyed up to the highest
pitch of religious excitement, they followed the example of
Attis and emasculated themselves. With this final act of
self-sacrifice and consecration, the *Dies sanguinis* was
crowned and the devotee became one of the *Galli*, a
eunuch-priest of the Asian goddess.[1] This was the regular
practice in Phrygia, and in Rome, even, it is probable that
the custom was followed. In his account of the Syrian goddess, whose cult was strikingly like that of Cybele, Lucian
gave a description of this sacerdotal initiation. It is not
only a vivid depiction of the bloody scene itself but also a
good piece of psychological analysis, for it shows the
strange fascination of these barbaric rites and reveals their
mesmeric effect upon the spectators witnessing the supreme act of consecration. In abbreviated form Lucian's
account is as follows:

During these days they are made *Galli*. As the *Galli* sing and celebrate their orgies, frenzy falls on many of them, and many who had come
as mere spectators afterwards are found to have committed the great
act. Any young man who has resolved on this action, strips off his clothes,
and with a loud shout bursts into the midst of the crowd and picks up
a sword. He takes it and emasculates himself and then runs wild
through the city.[2]

For one who had performed this irrevocable sacrifice in a
moment of hot excitement a strong revulsion of feeling was

[1] Julian *Orationes* v. 168. [2] Lucian *De Dea Syria* 51.

later inevitable. This emotional reaction was powerfully depicted by Catullus in his famous poem bearing the name "Attis."[1]

Undoubtedly for the devotee of Cybele the rite of self-mutilation had distinct religious values. By the very act the devotee himself became another Attis. He had done in the service of the goddess what Attis had already done. The Attis in the poem of Catullus was not the original lover of Cybele but rather one of her priests, who by the fact of priestly initiation had become identified with the god. "Methought in a dream that I had become Attis, and that the festival of the so-called *Hilaria* was fulfilled to me by the Great Mother," wrote Damaskios, the last of the Neoplatonists.[2] The name Attis was actually used as a traditional title for the priesthood of the Great Mother.[3] Just as Attis was believed to have attained the state of deity by the passion of emasculation so by the way of self-mutilation, the *Gallus* became a god instead of mortal.

The act that made an Attis of the votary placed him in peculiarly intimate relationship to the Mother Goddess herself. The broken instruments of his manhood were treated as an oblation to the goddess.[4] Perhaps they were thrown into the lap of her statue, as the "Passion of St. Symphorian" suggests.[5] In the case of a goddess of fertility, like the *Magna Mater*, this was a significant act. Thus the ministers of the Great Mother, who personated her divine lover, made it possible for her to exercise her beneficent function in renewing the life of nature. As a new Attis the votary assumed the rôle of a bridegroom to the goddess. There were "marriage chambers" in the sanctuary of the

---

[1] Catullus lxiii.   [2] Quoted by Bousset, *Kyrios Christos*, p. 150.

[3] Polybius xxi. 37; *Corpus Inscriptionum Latinarum* Vol. VI, No. 2183.

[4] Prudentius *Peristephanon* x. 1061–67.

[5] Cited by Hepding, *Attis*, p. 72.

Great Mother at Lobrinon near Cyzicus.[1] In such a chamber the newly consecrated priest kept vigil during the night after his dedication, a bridegroom in the bridal chamber of his goddess. Indeed, a specific cult designation of the *Gallus* was "bridegroom."[2] This indicates that the experiences of the *Dies Sanguinis* and the following night were interpreted as a process of mystical union with the Great Goddess herself, and by means of certain obscure ritual acts there was developed a sense of intimate divine communion on the part of the devotee. From another standpoint the newly consecrated priest was thought of as a male counterpart of the goddess. Hence, he was called *Kubebos*.[3] By the fact of emasculation he had assimilated himself to the nature of the goddess.[4] As an indication of this transformation he henceforth wore feminine dress and allowed his hair to grow long. At some point in the ceremony there was also a solemn enthronement and the consecrated mortal was crowned in token of his deification.[5] Nothing less than this, in the experience of the *Gallus*, was the result of his act of devotion. It made him realistically and mystically one with his goddess.

The day following the "Day of Blood" brought a delirium of joy to replace the delirium of sorrow. Dead Attis had been buried and around his grave his devotees had mourned his death long into the night. Toward morning, however, a great light appeared in the darkness and the resurrection of the god was announced. Firmicus Maternus thus described the scene: "When they are satisfied with their fictitious grief a light is brought in, and the priest, having anointed their lips, whispers, 'Be of good

[1] Scholion to Nicander *Alexipharmaca* 8.

[2] Anthologia Palatina vi. 220; ix. 340.

[3] Suidas *s.v.*   [4] Hippolytus *Philosophoumena* v. 1.7.

[5] Plato *Euthydemus* 277 D; Sallust (Phil.) *De diis* 4.

cheer, you of the mystery. Your god is saved; for us also there shall be salvation from ills.' "[1] Then joy took the place of sorrow, for the resurrection of the god brought with it the assurance of salvation for men, and this chiefly included the promise of a happy immortality. On the twenty-fifth of March, the first day when daylight exceeded darkness, the resurrection of the god was celebrated with universal license. The day's celebration was known as the *Hilaria* and was characterized by the general good cheer. Mourning was not permitted; but instead there were masquerades and banquets. Even the *Galli* were eased of their wounds in their joy because of the resurrection of Attis.

There followed a day of much needed rest, the *Requiratio*. Then the festival closed with the *Lavatio*, or washing of the goddess in the Almo, a rite that aroused the scorn and sarcasm of Arnobius.[2] The silver statue of the goddess was placed in a wagon drawn by oxen and conducted in solemn procession to the Almo where it was washed in the water of the river. Amid rejoicing the statue was drawn back to its temple, showered with the flowers of springtime on its way. This was probably a rite of purification considered necessary because of the experience through which the goddess had passed on the *Dies Sanguinis*. After marriage, purification was deemed essential even for a goddess.[3] Because the *Magna Mater* had been mystically united with her ministers, such postnuptial purification was necessary in her case.

In this, the annual spring festival of their god and goddess, the *Galli* found the beginning of a new life for themselves. It was a highly wrought emotional experience induced by fasting, wild music, frenzied dancing, and the

---

[1] Firmicus Maternus *De Errore* 22.

[2] Arnobius *Adversus Nationes* vii. 32.   [3] Hepding, *op. cit.*, p. 216.

sight of flowing blood. The sorrow thus aroused was interpreted as a sympathetic sharing with the Great Mother in her grief at the death of her lover. The orgiastic rite reached its climax in the irrevocable sacrifice of manhood, an act whereby the devotee physically assimilated himself to divinity. He himself became Attis, a god, mystically united as a divine lover to the Great Goddess. In the resurrection of his god he felt himself personally participant and he found therein the assurance of a happy future life. The experience was a crudely physical one and realistic in the extreme. Yet it had a strange fascination because of its very realism, and it held out to the devotees who were willing to make the supreme sacrifice the promise of a divinization of human nature and an immediate communion with deity.

To this experience the figure of a new birth was not inappropriately applied. The pagan writer, Sallust the Philosopher, used this very terminology in describing the effect of the Attis festival on those who participated in it.[1] He said that those who passed through this form of initiation were actually treated as new-born babes and dieted on milk for some time afterward. His exact expression was: *hōsper anagennōmenōn*, "as of those who are being born again." Thus, at the annual spring festival the ministers of the Great Mother passed through a religious experience so fundamental that it seemed to them the beginning of a new life, essentially different from the life they had known before. It was a regeneration that transformed their beings, gave them a present communion with their god and goddess, and assured them of personal immortality.

IV

Another bloody rite of great importance connected with the cult of the Great Mother was the *taurobolium*, or sacri-

[1] Sallust (Phil.) *De diis* 4.

fice of a bull, with its variant the *criobolium*, or ram sacrifice. The origin of the *taurobolium* and its early relationship to the cult of the *Magna Mater* is obscure. Almost
certainly, however, it was of oriental origin localized in
Anatolia, and it probably had its inception in the primitive
practice of washing in the blood of an animal in order to
secure its vital energy. In the cult of the Great Mother,
however, the primitive notions attached to the practice
became transformed and spiritualized. When the rite came
to prominence in Italy early in the second century A.D. two
distinct motives were apparent, one official, the other personal. The *taurobolium* was officially performed vicariously
for the safety of the emperor, the empire, or a particular
community—*pro salute imperatoris, pro salute imperii, pro
salute urbis*, etc.[1] This was a purely official and sacerdotal
celebration, with the *Archigallus* presiding, and during the
second and third centuries this usage was especially prominent in Roman practice.

But the *taurobolium* might be a private ceremony also,
performed by an ordinary person who bore the expense of
it himself—*de suo, suo sumptu*, or *sua pecunia*.[2] In this case
the purpose was a purely personal one and the motive
which actuated the celebration was the purification and
regeneration of the individual. This private rite was performed on laymen as well as priests and by persons of all
classes and both sexes. It was strictly an individualistic
ceremony. During the third and fourth centuries, probably
because of Christian competition, the private celebration
of the *taurobolium* came forward into particular prominence. Between these two types of ceremony, however,
the official and the private, there can be no doubt as to
which was prior to the other. The rite in itself was essen-

[1] *Corpus Inscriptionum Latinarum* Vol. XII, Nos. 1569, 1782, 4321.

[2] *Op. cit.* Vol. IX, No. 3014; Vol. XII, Nos. 1, 1744.

tially of a private and personal nature and its public, vicarious usage was clearly a later adaptation. The devotees of the Mother and Attis certainly experienced it for their own benefit before ever the rite was enacted for the good of the community. Centuries before the *taurobolium* was performed in Italy for the safety of the state, it was enacted in Asia Minor for the benefit of the individual devotee.

The ceremony itself was picturesque. In the *Peristephanon* by the Christian poet Prudentius there is a description of the rite which purports to be by an eyewitness. A priest is the subject of the ceremony. With a golden crown on his head and adorned with fillets, he descends into a deep trench which is covered with a platform of perforated planks. A large bull, gleaming with gold and garlanded with flowers, is led on to the platform. Here he is stabbed to death by the consecrated spear, and his blood flows out over the covering of the trench and rains down on the expectant devotee below.

Through the thousand crevices in the wood the bloody dews run down into the pit. The priest receives the falling drops on his head, clothes and body. He leans backward to have his cheeks, his ears, his lips, and his nostrils wetted. He pours the liquid over his eyes and does not even spare his palate, for he moistens his tongue with blood and drinks it eagerly.[1]

When the life of the bull is extinct, its body is removed and the neophyte emerges from the trench, drenched and dripping with blood. He presents himself to the expectant throng of worshipers who do obeisance to him as to a god, as to one who has been born again to a divine life.

For the one who experienced the blood bath of the *taurobolium* this was exactly the meaning of the rite. He came up out of the trench reborn to a new kind of ex-

---

[1] Prudentius *Peristephanon* x. 1011 ff.

istence. In effect the bath of blood was believed to purify him from the sins and evils of his old life and make him a new man, or rather a divinized human. In some cases the efficacy of the rite was supposed to last for a period of twenty years, and then the grace was renewed.[1] In other instances, the conviction was that the effect of the rite was everlasting and that the devotee was *in aeternum renatus*, to quote the formula of the inscriptions.[2] There is a strong temptation at this point to question if this startling phrase and the whole conception of the new birth experience in the cult of the *Magna Mater* may not be due to Christian influence. There is not, however, a shred of evidence to substantiate this contention. Against it is the purely pagan character of the rite itself, its undoubted antiquity, and the fact that it naturally lent itself to the new-birth interpretation. Held as it usually was, though not invariably, at the time of the vernal equinox on the *Dies Saguinis*, the resurrection of vegetation and of the god of vegetation naturally suggested the regeneration of the individual. Thus the whole ritual became a sort of passion drama in and of itself, involving three parties: the god, the neophyte, and nature in a single cycle of events. The neophyte descended into the pit; Attis died; vegetation withered. The neophyte came up out of the pit; Attis arose from the dead; vegetation revived. In this way, at the spring festival of Attis, the regeneration of the individual was made to coincide with the rebirth of nature.

V

The Cybele-Attis cult included certain strictly private rites that are quite as important for the student of personal religion as the public ceremonies we have just exam-

---

[1] *Corpus Inscriptionum Latinarum* Vol. VI, Nos. 504, 512.

[2] *Op. cit.* Vol. VI, Nos. 510–12, 736.

ined. Julian, the Emperor, in discussing the March festival, made careful distinction between two series of rites following the cutting down of the sacred pine, one secret and mysterious, the other open to the public.[1] It is probable, therefore, that the secret rites of the cult were more or less co-ordinated with the public ceremonials. Augustine demanded to know of these esoteric rites, "What good is to be thought of their sacred rites which are concealed in darkness, when those which are brought forth into light are so detestable?"[2] This interrogation conveniently emphasizes the differentiation between the public and private rites of the Attis cult.

In the nature of the case the public rites were open to a more or less limited number of participants. The sacerdotal consecration of the *Dies Sanguinis* was a restricted type of initiation available only for men and to those only who felt impelled to make the supreme sacrifice. It was a masculine and priestly initiation. But the cult of the Great Mother welcomed women as well as men and included laymen as well as priests. Even the grace of the *taurobolium* was obtainable only by those who could bear the expense of the ceremony. The private rites of the cult, however, were accessible to a far larger group. They represented the lay type of initiation as contrasted with the priestly. Hence they are of more than usual importance from the point of view of personal religious experience.

Unfortunately, we know even less of these private ceremonials than of the secret rites in other mystery cults, and for much the same reason. Their secret has been too well guarded. Only a single formula has come down to us, in slightly variant forms, from the esoteric liturgy of the Attis cult. According to the version given by Clement of Alexandria the confessional of the initiate was:

[1] Julian *Orationes* v. 169.   [2] Augustine *De Civitate Dei* vi. 7.

> I have eaten out of the drum:
> I have drunk out of the cymbal:
> I have carried the *Kernos:*
> I have entered the bridal chamber.[1]

Firmicus Maternus repeated the formula in a more brief form:

> I have eaten from the drum:
> I have drunk out of the cymbal:
> I have become a mystic votary of Attis.[2]

In this formula two experiential elements stand out clearly. One is union with divinity by the semblance of a mystic marriage. "I have entered the bridal chamber." The votary entering the shrine of the goddess went there as a bridegroom. In the secret chamber divinity and humanity were united in marriage, and thus the devotee attained communion with his goddess. This was the lay equivalent for the priestly experience when the *Gallus*, as a new Attis, became the bridegroom of Cybele.

The second important element of mystical experience emphasized in this formula was communion with the deity by the act of eating and drinking.

> I have eaten from the drum:
> I have drunk from the cymbal.

The similarity of this confessional to the Eleusinian password is incontestable. Just as the initiate at Eleusis drank of the mixed barley potion and ate sacred food from the chest, so the devotee of the Great Mother drank from the cymbal and ate from the drum. The instruments mentioned, the drum and the cymbal, were the favorite musical instruments of the Great Mother. It was natural, therefore, that they should be used as cup and plate in this ceremony. Just what was the sacred food which the devo-

---

[1] Clement of Alexandria *Protrepticus* ii. 14.

[2] Firmicus Maternus *De Errore* 18.

tees shared we have scarcely a hint. We know only that it consisted of a beverage and of solid food.

Much more important than to know these external details is to understand the psychological effect of this communion meal on the participants. Was it merely a common meal that gave the votaries fellowship with one another, binding them together in a brotherhood like that of a great family? It may have had this meaning incidentally, but certainly this was not the inclusive significance of the rite for the votary. It was a communion with divinity rather than a communion with one's fellow devotees. Firmicus Maternus, in denouncing this rite, contrasted it specifically with the Christian sacrament of the eucharist.[1] His words show clearly that there was a genuine parallelism between the Christian rite and the pagan. Both were believed to communicate divine life to the devotee and assure him of salvation. Maternus concluded his invective against the pagan rite with the appeal, "It is another food that gives salvation and life. Seek the bread of Christ and the cup of Christ!" Apparently, therefore, the sacred meal in the Cybele-Attis cult was a genuine sacrament that enabled the devotee to absorb the divine life in a realistic manner. In the liturgy of the cult, Attis himself was addressed as a "reaped ear of corn."[2] It is not unlikely that a corn product, or some other vegetable food in which Attis was believed especially to dwell, formed a part of the sacred repast. In partaking of this meal, the devotee was enabled to share in a materialistic manner the life of his god. The common meal of the Great Mother's cult therefore was a means of attaining to a realistic type of mystical communion with divinity.

All these various rites in the cult of the Great Mother were crude enough. They were characterized by realism

[1] *Loc. cit.*   [2] Hippolytus *Philosophoumena* v. 1. 8, 9.

and naturalism. There was eating and drinking. There was a bath in blood. There was an orgy of self-induced sorrow and joy that had its climax in self-multilation. Yet these very rites with all their primitive crudity and cruelty became transmuted into vehicles for really deep religious experience. The act of eating and drinking became a sacrament of communion wherein the devotee partook of a divine substance and thus attained actual union with his deity. The semblance of a mystic marriage whereby the initiate as a divine lover was united to the goddess was another means of attaining the same end. The blood bath of the *taurobolium* brought with it the washing away of the sins and evils of an old life. It was a regenerating experience by which the neophyte was reborn for eternity. The passion drama depicting the death of natural life and its renovation in the springtime was an allegory of personal resurrection to eternal life. Even the act of self-mutilation became the means whereby the devotee, like Attis himself, effected his own deification and assimilated himself to the nature of the Great Mother. In the cult of the *Mater Deum* the communion of eating and drinking, the semblance of mystic marriage, the purification in the bath of blood, and the mortification of the flesh, all functioned as sacraments of spiritual regeneration.

VI

For the student of Christian origins a knowledge of the regenerative rites of the Great Mother is doubly important because her worship was remarkably like that in a whole group of cults with which Paul, the Christian apostle, had early familiarity and contacts that were intimate. These were the religions indigenous to the lands of Syria and Cilicia, where Paul was brought up and where he had his early missionary experience. Unfortunately, our knowledge of these gentile cults is fragmentary and chaotic. They had nothing like the solidarity of the Greek and major Oriental systems, and it would be utterly impossible to reconstruct their history or to outline their ritual in any detail. Still it is possible to distinguish among them certain common elements that show a general resemblance to the Phrygian worship of the Great Mother. Usually, the central place in the cultus was held by a mother-goddess who embodied the power of life, and a somewhat subordinate position was assigned to a youthful male deity who like Attis died and rose again.

The prototype for this diversified, yet measurably unified complex of religious systems seems to have been the Babylonian cult of Ishtar, the deified personification of motherhood. She was known to biblical writers as Ashtoreth, and to the Greeks as Astarte or Aphrodite. With her was associated a young and active deity called Tammuz, who was slain but afterward revived. As in the case of Attis, lamentations formed an important part of his worship. In Ezekiel's day this practice was adopted by Jews, even, and among the "abominations" which the prophet saw perpetrated at the very gate of the Jerusalem temple was the weeping of women for Tammuz![1] In Phoenicia the mother-goddess was worshiped under the name of Ashtart, and as early as the third century B.C. her cult was so pre-eminent that the kings of Sidon served her as priests.[2] She, too, had her consort, Eshmun by name. Their houses were built together, and they were simultaneously glorified.

To the Greek world this immortal pair was familiar as Aphrodite and Adonis, the goddess of love and her impetuous young husband. "The Fourth Venus," said Cicero,

[1] Ezekiel 8 :14.

[2] See Cook, *A Text Book of North Semitic Inscriptions* (Oxford, 1903).

"was a Syrian . . . . who is called Astarte and is said to
have been married to Adonis."[1] Greek and Latin writers
delighted to retell the story of their love and of Aphrodite's
loss. The tale was that of an ardent young hunter who, all
too rash, was wounded to death by a boar. Thus young
Adonis died; but the grief of his goddess-lover brought
about his restoration to life. In the cult of these divinities,
also, traditional lamentations were a conspicuous element
of the ritual. Sappho more than once referred to this weeping for the god, while Bion wrote a lament for Adonis
which, though a conventional literary product and not an
actual cult hymn, yet gives a fairly accurate impression
of the mourning songs sung at Adonis' festivals.[2]

The annual celebrations in honor of the god were
elaborated as a drama of marriage and passion. Around a
ritual marriage bed the wedding of the divine pair was
celebrated. There followed a lament for the dead Adonis
ending in a forecast of the resurrection. Sometimes that
joyous event was actually represented. At all the important centers of Adonis worship, not only in Syria and
Cyprus but also in Athens and Alexandria, the festival of
Adonis was one of the great events in the religious calendar. Theocritus, in one of his *Idyls*, described such a festival as it was conducted at the court of Ptolemy II early in
the Hellenistic period. The marriage song sung at this celebration began with a description of the wedding tableau
and included an adequate account of the Adonis festival
as a whole.

The bridal bed for Adonis spread of my own making is;
Cypris hath this for her wrapping, Adonis that for his.
Of eighteen years or nineteen, is turned the rose-limbed groom;
His pretty lip is smooth to sip, for it bears but flaxen bloom,

---

[1] Cicero *De Deorum Natura* iii. 23.

[2] An excellent translation of Bion's *Lament* is given in J. M. Edmonds, *The Greek Bucolic Poets*, pp. 385 ff.

And now she's in her husband's arms, and so we'll say good-night;
But tomorrow we'll come with the dew, the dew, and take hands and
    bear him away
Where plashing wave the shore doth lave, and there with locks undight
And bosoms bare all shining fair will raise this shrilling lay:

"O sweet Adonis, none but thee of the children of gods and men
'Twixt overworld and underworld doth pass and pass again:

.   .   .   .

Adonis sweet, Adonis dear,
Be gracious for another year;
Thou'rt welcome to thine own alway,
And welcome we'll both cry today
And next Adonis-tide."[1]

Another Syrian goddess who gained considerable prominence in the Roman world was Atargatis. Her consort was Hadad, with whom the belief in immortality was connected at an early period. In his ritual, as in that of Adonis, an elaborate show of grief was a characteristic factor, and the prophet Zechariah knew of the lamentations for Hadad.[2] But it was the goddess who attracted the attention of the Roman world. In the eyes of the Greeks she was the "Syrian goddess," and among Latins this *Dea Syria* became popular as *Iasura*. During the latter days of the Republic her cult was notably propagated by the agency of slaves and under the Empire Syrian merchants became conspicuous as her missionaries. She was especially popular with the lower classes, though some in high stations affected her cult. Marius was one of her devotees and Nero "held in contempt all religious rites except those of the Syrian Goddess"—though his esteem for her was not a lasting one.[3] The great slave uprising in Sicily in 134 B.C. was led by a slave who claimed to be inspired by the goddess herself—a revealing illustration of the loyalty she commanded for this class in society.

---

[1] *Op. cit.*, pp. 193 ff.

[2] Zechariah 12 : 11.   [3] Suetonius *Nero 56.*

Her rites were such as would appeal to the proletariat and conserve religious values for them. They were realistic, picturesque, sensuous, and fascinating in their strangeness. Apuleius in an incidental account of the missionary operations of her traveling priests gave a memorable picture of their methods in actual practice among the rural population of Thessaly.[1] The account was not a very complimentary one, and it was doubtless exaggerated. Certainly the itinerant priests of the Syrian goddess were generally actuated by more worthy motives than this particular group was represented to be. Still the description of their religious exercises was detailed by Apuleius with all the vividness of life itself, and it may be considered a true representation of the cult rites on festal occasions. Lucian, who was himself a Syrian and wrote as one wholly familiar with this religion, also described the rites in a way that parallels and confirms the account of Apuleius.[2] The exercises were essentially the same as those that formed the climax of the Great Mother's festival and made eunuch priests of her male devotees. To the accompaniment of wild music men danced themselves into a frenzy and then lacerated and mutilated themselves unsparingly. Here again the central experience of the cult was ecstatic in character, with a cruel and crudely physical emotionalism. But it was not without its mystical content; for in this way the devotees sought to affiliate themselves with their pitiless goddess.

Altogether the cults of Cilicia and Syria may be grouped in the same class as the Anatolian worship of the Cybele. They were redemption religions, the deities of which were revered as the saviors of the individual man. In their propagandist efforts they aimed at universalism

---

[1] Apuleius *Metamorphoses* viii. 24 ff.

[2] Lucian *De Dea Syria* 50 ff.

through individualism. They were still tainted with much of the grossness of primitive naturalism; yet this very fact was not a disadvantage with the humbler folk in society whom they captivated by the barbaric appeal of their ritual. They were religions of enthusiasm which aroused fear, pain, hope, joy, all culminating in ecstasy. By mortification, by stimulating music, by self-mutilation, and like means, these Syrian zealots strove to rise to a higher state than mere mortality and unite themselves with divinity. This was their rebirth to a new life and immortality.

BIBLIOGRAPHY

I. THE CYBELE-ATTIS CULT

BENNETT, F. M., *Religious Cults associated with the Amazons*. New York, 1912.

CUMONT, FRANZ, *Oriental Religions in Roman Paganism* (Chicago, 1911), pp. 46–72.

DILL, SAMUEL, *Roman Society from Nero to Marcus Aurelius* (London, 1920²), pp. 547–59.

FARNELL, LEWIS RICHARD, *Cults of the Greek States* (Oxford, 1907), III, 289–306.

FRAZER, J. G., *Adonis, Attis, Osiris* (London, 1922), I, 261–317.

GRAILLOT, H., *Le Culte de Cybele, Mère des Dieux*. Paris, 1912.

HEPDING, HUGO, *Attis seine Mythen und sein Kult*. Giessen, 1903.

LOISY, ALFRED, *Les Mystères païens et le Mystère chrétien* (Paris, 1921²), pp. 85–122.

SHOWERMAN, GRANT, *The Great Mother of the Gods*. Madison, Wis., 1901.

SCHMIDT, ERNST, *Kultübertragungen* (Giessen, 1909), pp. 1–30.

TOUTAIN, JULES FRANÇOIS, *Les cultes païens dans l'Empire Romain* (Paris, 1907), Part I, Vol. II, 73–119.

WISSOWA, GEORG, *Religion und Kultus der Römer* (Munich, 1912²), pp. 317–27.

II. SYRIAN CULTS

CUMONT, FRANZ, *Oriental Religions in Roman Paganism* (Chicago, 1911), pp. 103–34.

VON BAUDISSIN, W. W. F., *Adonis und Esmun*. Leipzig, 1911.

FRAZER, J. G., *Adonis, Attis, Osiris* (London, 1922), I, 1–259.

LAGRANGE, MARIE-JOSEPH, *Études sur les religions Semitiques*. Paris, 1905.

SMITH, W. R., *Religion of the Semites*. London, 1894².

STRONG AND GARSTANG, *The Syrian Goddess*. London, 1913.

TOUTAIN, JULES FRANÇOIS, *Les cultes païens dans l'Empire Romain* (Paris, 1907), Part I, Vol. II, 35–72.

VELLAY, CHARLES, *Le Culte et les Fêtes de Adonis-Tammous dans l'Orient antique*. Paris, 1904.

WISSOWA, GEORG, *Religion und Kultus der Römer* (Munich, 1912²), pp. 359–68.

CHAPTER VI

DEATH AND NEW BIRTH IN MITHRAISM

AMONG the most ancient and most honored gods of Roman paganism was the Persian Mithra. He came to the empire out of a more remote oriental antiquity than did the Great Mother of the Gods. In the hymns of the Vedas, as in those of the Avesta, his name appeared; in the former as Mitra, in the latter as Mithra. To be sure his character was but dimly traced in the Vedas. Only a single fragment remains that was dedicated especially to him,[1] and other references to him were quite incidental. Still, enough traits are preserved to make clear the resemblance of the Vedic deity to the Iranian Mithra. Fundamentally, he was the god of light, invoked together with Heaven under the name of Varuna, even as in the Persian system Mithra was associated with Ahura. Certain ethical qualities of his character are also distinguishable; for he was regarded as the upholder of truth and the enemy of error, even as Mithra was revered by the Persians. These traits of resemblance are sufficiently clear to make the primitive identity of the two deities quite certain and to push the origins of Mithraism far back into the unknown period when the ancestors of the Persians and the ancestors of the Hindus were living together.

I

In the Avesta the character of Mithra was depicted with special clarity, one of the longest of the yashts, the tenth, or *Mihir Yasht*, being dedicated to him. The quali-

[1] *Rig-Veda* iii. 59.

ties there ascribed to Mithra remained fairly constant through the later centuries of paganism, and are important to know for an appreciation of the ethical quality of this Persian religious system. In the *Mihir Yasht*, as in the Vedas, Mithra was represented as the genius of heavenly light, "who first of the heavenly gods reaches over the Hara, before the undying, swift-horsed sun; who foremost in a golden array, takes hold of the beautiful summits, and from thence looks over the abode of the Aryans with a beneficent eye!"[1] He was not himself the sun, moon, or stars; he was more than they. He was the genius of celestial light who appeared before sunrise and at nightfall went over the earth after the setting of the sun and surveyed everything that is between the earth and the heavens.[2] As the beneficent god of light, Mithra was the dispenser of physical blessings. His light fostered life and happiness and his heat made the earth fruitful. The usual epithet applied to him was "the lord of wide pastures," and he was the one who gave to man an abundance of material possessions, good health, and a numerous progeny.[3]

But the Avestan thought of Mithra did not remain on the material level merely. It reached high ethical altitudes. Being the "ever waking, ever watchful" god, who with his "hundred ears and hundred eyes" constantly watched the world, Mithra naturally became the guardian of truth and the preserver of good faith. Throughout the *Mihir Yasht* he was referred to as the "truth-speaking, undeceived god, to whom nobody must lie." Ahura Mazda himself was represented as laying this solemn injunction on Zarathustra. "Break not the contract (mithrem), O Spitama! neither the one which you have entered into with one of the unfaithful nor the one you have entered into

[1] *Yasht* x. 13.

[2] *Yasht* x. 95.   [3] *Yasht* x. 65, 108, 112.

with one of the faithful who is one of your own faith. For Mithra stands for both the faithful and the unfaithful."[1] To those who obeyed this injunction, and otherwise honored Mithra, the god guaranteed his protection. He was the divinity "whom the poor man, who follows the good law, when wronged and deprived of his rights invokes for help with hands uplifted . . . . and to him with whom Mithra, the lord of wide pastures, has been satisfied, he comes with help."[2]

The wrath of Mithra was as terrible as his blessings were rich and full; for he was the implacable foe of all evil who, "never sleeping wakefully maintains the creation of Mazda."[3] He was even engaged in ceaseless combat with the spirits of evil, and to wicked men he brought endless troubles. "To whom shall I in my might impart sickness and death?" he asks. "To whom shall I impart poverty and sterility? Of whom shall I at one stroke cut off the offspring?"[4] The response is:

"Thou bringest down terror upon the bodies of men who lie to Mithra; thou takest away the strength from their arms, being angry and all powerful; thou takest the swiftness from their feet, the eyesight from their eyes, the hearing from their ears." "On whatever side there is one who has lied unto Mithra, on that side Mithra stands forth, angry and offended, and his wrath is slow to relent."[5]

This character of militant virtue was one of the prime attributes of Mithra.

The god's championship of righteousness and opposition to evil was not confined to this life merely. It extended to the future, and became the guaranty of safety and security to the faithful ones in the world to come. Their prayer for protection was a prayer that included the future

---

[1] *Yasht* x. 2.

[2] *Yasht* x. 84–87.   [4] *Yasht* x. 110.

[3] *Yasht* x. 103.   [5] *Yasht* x. 23, 19. Cf. 38.

as well as the present. "Mayest thou keep us in both worlds, O Mithra, lord of wide pastures! both in this material world and in the world of the spirit, from the fiend Death, from the fiend Aeshma, from the fiendish hordes that lift up the spear of havoc and from the onsets of Aeshma."[1] This clear conception of Mithra, the god of light and truth and the opponent of evil, was one of Persia's best gifts to the religious life of the Roman Empire.

II

From the time of his admission to the Zoroastrian pantheon until his last fatal battle with Christianity itself, Mithra was a conquering deity. His cult from the first became increasingly popular and powerful and his own position as the object of popular devotion, once established, remained a dominating one. It is true the price he paid for admission to the Avestan system was that of submission to Ahura Mazda. Like other ancient nature divinities, he was classified as one of the creatures of Mazda, one of the Yazatas. But he quickly became the most powerful of them all and was distinguished as the intermediary between Ahura, the god of light, and Ahriman, the god of darkness. It was here that Plutarch located him in his exposition of Persian dualism.[2] Later, however, Mithra completely overshadowed with his glorious and vivid personality the vague figure of Ahura himself. Proofs might be multiplied showing what a conspicuous rôle Mithra played in the religion of the Persian empire. He was peculiarly the god of the "great kings," their special guardian, whom they invoked on the eve of great undertakings and by whom they swore their mighty oaths.[3] He was the one

[1] *Yasht* x. 93.

[2] Plutarch *De Iside et Osiride* 46, 47.

[3] Plutarch *Alexander* 30; Xenophon *Cyropaedia* vii. 5. 53; *Oeconomicus* iv. 24.

Iranian god who made a real impression on the literature
of classical Greece—an eloquent testimony to the exalted
position he occupied in the religious system of Persia.

With the extension of Persian power by military conquest there followed a great accession of influence to
Mithraism. It was during the days of the Achaemenides
that Mithra finally acquired the character of lord of
armies, which remained a predominant trait throughout
the rest of his history. Where Persian arms met with success, there Mithra became known. The whole great Persian empire was missionary territory for his official clergy,
the Magi. In Babylon they became superior to the indigenous priests. Yet victorious Mithraism felt the effects of
its Chaldean conquest and ever thereafter bore the marks
of its victory. In Chaldaea Mithraism learned astrology
and after that it continued as an astronomical religion.
Under the early Achaemenides the Magi penetrated Asia
Minor also, and there the indigenous religions paled before
Mithraism. The Magi captured Pontus and Cappadocia,
where Strabo knew of their sanctuaries.[1] They penetrated
Galatia and Phrygia and remained there in considerable
numbers.[2] Lydia, apparently, received its contingent of
Magi, for Pausanias, writing in the period of the Antonines, told of a Mithraic sanctuary attributed to Cyrus
where the descendants of these early missionaries still
chanted their hymns in a barbarian tongue.[3] While the
provinces of Asia Minor were yet under the suzerainty of
the "great kings," Mithraism became firmly established
there.

It might be expected that a religion so closely identified
with the fortunes of the Persian empire would share in the
downfall of the kingdom of Darius. Exactly the opposite

---

[1] Strabo xv. 3, 15.

[2] Eusebius *Praeparatio Evangelica* vi. 10. 16, 37.   [3] Pausanias v. 27. 3.

occurred during the Hellenistic period. The Diadochi were quite as friendly to Mithraism as ever the satraps of the great king had been. In Pontus, Cappadocia, Armenia, and Commagene, dynasties were established which represented the Achaemenian tradition in opposition to the Hellenizing tendencies of the Greek kings of Pergamum and Antioch. These Anatolian rulers made Mithra the special object of their loyalty, and the very personal character of their devotion was attested by the frequency with which the name "Mithridates" occurred in their families.[1] For the prosperity of Mithraism in Asia Minor during the Hellenistic period, however, royal patronage was not chiefly responsible. Rather it was the ready adaptation that Mithraism itself made to the new religious demands of the times. It threw off its official and markedly Persian character and began to operate as a private cult brotherhood rather than as a racial or nationalistic religion.[2] Men were admitted to its membership, not by the fact of birth into a particular racial or national group, but by special initiation. Like the contemporary cults of Cybele and Demeter, it addressed its appeal to men as individuals. The downfall of the Persian empire could not check the growth of such a brotherhood, any more than the political misfortune of proud Athens could lessen the attractiveness of the Eleusinian mysteries. Apparently, too, under the stimulus of religious competition, the followers of Mithra began to engage in unusually vigorous propaganda on behalf of their cult.

It was during the Hellenistic period and in Asia Minor that Mithraism made its final modifications and took on

[1] For a list of theophorus names see Cumont, *Textes et Monuments figurés relatifs aux Mystères de Mithra*, II, 78.

[2] For the historical relationship of the Mithraic cult brotherhoods to the official Mithraic clergy, the Magi, see Loisy, *Les Mystères païens*, pp. 165 ff.; also Cumont, *op. cit.*, I, 239 f.

the definitive form it maintained through the imperial period.[1] In the uplands of central Asia Minor, the god entered into an alliance with Cybele that became famous in Roman times. Quite naturally, too, he was associated with Helius, the sun-god. An external but altogether notable result of the contact of Mithraism with Hellenism was the sudden tendency to represent the god in human form. Here in Asia Minor, toward the beginning of the second century B.C. Mithraism learned from a Pergamene sculptor to chisel that remarkably impressive group of "Mithra Tauroctonus," which thereafter stood like an altar-piece in the apse of the god's cave-sanctuaries.[2] Thus the vague personification of oriental imagination came to assume a precise and definite form altogether appealing to occidental taste. The very fact of standardized representation had its influence in a more precise definition of the character of Mithra. All of these accretions of art and legend tended to make the Iranian religion of Mithra a Hellenized product. To adopt M. Cumont's vivid figure, above the Mazdean substratum and the thick sediment of Chaldean astrology and the rich alluvial deposits of beliefs local in Asia Minor, there grew up a luxuriant vegetation of Hellenistic art that partly concealed the original nature of Mithraism.[3] This Hellenistic overgrowth is a picturesque, if indirect, testimony to the popularity of Mithraism in Asia Minor during the three centuries preceding the Christian era.

By the beginning of the Christian centuries the domain of Mithra extended from the Indus in the east to the Euxine on the north. In the plateau countries of Asia Minor, he was strongly intrenched. One of the great cham-

[1] For a detailed discussion of the syncretism of this period as it affected Mithraism see Cumont, *op. cit.*, I, 34 ff.

[2] Cumont, *op. cit.*, I, 179 ff.   [3] *Op. cit.*, I, 240.

pions of Mithraism at this time was Mithridates Eupator (120–63 B.C.), a foeman worthy of the best generals Rome could send against him. The Magi were his supporters, and M. Cumont conjectures that if he had realized his ambitious schemes Mithraism would have become the official religion of his great Asian empire. It is probable, however, that his defeat by Pompey was not an unrelieved disaster for Mithraism since it opened the way for a further dissemination of the cult through the agency of refugees, slaves, and prisoners.

About this time Mithraism came prominently to Roman notice in another section of Asia Minor—in the land of Paul's birth—as the religion of the Cilician pirates.[1] These bold freebooters dared dispute naval supremacy with the Romans and audaciously plundered the most venerable shrines around the eastern Mediterranean. In all this they may well have considered themselves the champions of the invincible god whose help, they were assured, would win them the victory. It was Pompey who forcibly suppressed the champions of Mithra (66 B.C.). In Paul's native land, however, the religion of Mithra still continued to be influential, and in Tarsus he was worshiped for centuries thereafter.[2]

For Mithra these military disasters in Asia Minor signalized the beginning of his conquest of Italy and the Empire. According to Plutarch it was when the Cilician pirates were defeated that the Romans first became acquainted with the rites of Mithra. In speaking of the pirates and their religion, Plutarch affirmed, "The secret rites of Mithra continue to the present time, having been first instituted by them."[3] It is altogether probable, then, that the defeat of the pirates resulted in bringing to Rome

[1] Plutarch *Pompey* 24, 29.

[2] Cumont, *op. cit.*, II, 189, Mon. 3.   [3] Plutarch *Pompey* 24.

from Asia Minor slaves and prisoners who were devotees
of Mithra. In this very humble manner the mysteries of
the Persian god were first brought to the capital city of
the Mediterranean world.[1] The successful conclusion of the
Mithridatic Wars undoubtedly brought about a similar
immigration of slaves, captives, and traders, as well.

Later, when Rome began to consolidate her eastern
conquests, the way was cleared for the establishment of
more intimate relations between Italy and Anatolia. Under Tiberius, Cappadocia was incorporated as part of the
empire. Western Pontus was added under Nero. Once
these official administrative relations were established with
the very provinces where Mithraism was popular, it was
inevitable that Mithraic influences should increasingly be
felt in Rome and Italy. By the middle of the first century
A.D. the mysteries were so highly esteemed by the Romans
that the emperor himself was initiated by the Magi who
came with Tiridates to Rome.[2] Plutarch, a little later, referred to the rites of Mithraism as a familiar religious
phenomenon and spoke with approval of the Mithraic view
of life.[3] Thus, Mithraism, which during the Hellenistic
period was little known outside the Orient, had, by the
middle of the first century A.D., become familiar to Rome
and Italy. A full century before Paul of Tarsus brought
the Christian gospel to the imperial city, his fellow-countrymen of Cilicia had introduced the gospel of Mithra
there; and by the time the Christian apostle came to Rome,
the religion of the Iranian god was already well known in
the city.

[1] Note that the captives whom Pompey brought back after the capture of
Jerusalem in 63 B.C. were settled in the *Regio Transtiberina* of Rome. The
Romans found these captives to be poor slaves but active propagandists for
their native religion.

[2] Pliny *Historia Naturalis* xxx. 6. Cf. *Dio Cassius* lxiii. 1, 2, 5.

[3] Plutarch *Pompey* 24; *De Iside et Osiride* 46, 47.

Just as Asia Minor in the last century B.C. sent out the emissaries who won Rome for Mithra, so in the next century Asia Minor sent out the missionaries who won many of the frontier provinces of the Empire as well. In this case the missionaries were soldiers recruited from the upland provinces of Asia Minor; from Pontus, Cappadocia, Commagene, and Lesser Armenia—again the districts in which the cult of Mithra was well established. Even before these sections were annexed to the empire, while they were still in the position of client kingdoms, Rome made use of them as recruiting grounds. During the Parthian Wars under Claudius and Nero, large oriental contingents were added to the Roman armies, for the most part as auxiliaries, but also as legionaries. It has been suggested that the soldiers of the Third Legion who paid homage to the rising sun at the battle of Betriacum (A.D. 69) were devotees of Mithra. Thus already in the first century A.D. was begun that unique movement of religious propaganda in the ranks of the Roman army which was so significant for the later dissemination of the Persian religion.

For Mithraism soldiers were the best kind of missionaries. Mithra himself had been for long centuries the god of battles, and his cult was an exclusively masculine one. Soldiers, on the other hand, were pious to the point of being superstitious. The dangers to which they were constantly exposed caused them to seek the assurances of a religion that would guarantee safety for the present and salvation for the future. The oriental devotees of the militant god Mithra, who had found these assurances in his religion, were not in the least exclusive. They gladly welcomed and initiated their companions in arms as members of their cult brotherhoods. True to the camaraderie of soldier life, these neophytes in turn became missionaries for

Mithra; and so the movement grew. Introduced into the Roman army early in the first century by semi-barbarian recruits from Asia Minor, Mithraism spread like an epidemic through the ranks of the legions. Henceforth it was the religion of the Roman army, and its chief centers of influence were the garrison towns of the frontier provinces. In notable instances the founding of Mithraic shrines and other military dedications in northern centers like Aquincum and Carnuntum can be traced back directly to soldiers who came from first-century Anatolia. During the next two centuries Mithraism spread to the farthest limits of the Empire. Mithraic monuments were scattered from the Euxine Sea to the mountains of Scotland, and from the banks of the Rhine to the Sahara Desert. Viewing a map showing this diffusion of the Mithraism,[1] one is ready to credit the famous dictum of Renan that "if Christianity had been arrested in its growth by some mortal malady, the world itself would have become Mithraistic."

To one section of the Empire only did Mithra remain a stranger. That was to Greece. Within the confines of Hellas, a single late inscription has been found at the Piraeus and a solitary bas-relief at Patros.[2] To the Greeks with their old memories of Persian wars Mithraism was too oriental to make an appeal. Notwithstanding this failure in Greece, however, and quite apart from later success, it is important to remember that in the first century Mithraism was not only well established in Asia Minor, but it had also already begun a lively missionary campaign in the heart of Italy and in the ranks of the Roman army. Hence, in summarizing the religious influences which were

[1] Such a map is found at the conclusion of Volume I of Cumont's *Textes et Monuments*.

[2] Cumont, *op. cit.*, II, 469, inscription No. 220a.

significant in the Graeco-Roman world when Christianity had its initial development, considerable account must be taken of Mithraism.

III

It is therefore important to examine the practices of this cult in order to determine whether or not they were expressive of a radical type of religious experience properly characterized as a new birth, such as many other contemporary cults fostered by their initiation ceremonies. In making this search, one is much handicapped by a lack of materials with which to work. The mysteries of Mithra, like the other private cults, were strictly secret and the liturgy, which for the faithful was such an important part of their religion, has all but completely disappeared. Scarcely a trace is left of either hymn or prayer, and only scattered hints may be gathered here and there as to the character of the ceremonies included in the Mithraic rites. Most of these hints, even, come to us from prejudiced Christian sources. Mithraic monuments, however, are comparatively abundant, and from these one may derive indirect suggestions concerning the cult ritual. At least it is possible to gather from the remains of *Mithraea* a general impression of the effectiveness of Mithraic rites.

The sanctuaries of Mithra were caves in the mountains or underground crypts,[1] recalling the primeval cave in which the god performed the life-giving act of slaying the cosmic bull. These chapels were always small, and when the brotherhood grew beyond a convenient size—a hundred members at the maximum—other *Mithraea* were established. In small shrines such as these, the impressions made on the mind of the neophyte were bound to be very intimate and personal. It was a place, too, for mystical

---

[1] Cumont, *op. cit.*, I, 57 ff.

religious experience, where the devotee could feel himself close to divinity. In the limited nave of the chapel stood venerated images: the torch-bearers, the mysterious lion-headed Cronus, and the "Petrogenes Mithra" rising from the generative rock. In the center of the apse stood the group of "Tauroctonus Mithra," a pathetic tableau, but the central scene of a great salvation drama. Around it were grouped in small panels other scenes from the life of Mithra, from which M. Cumont has ably reconstructed various episodes in the cosmic myth of the Iranian god.[1] The ceiling was decorated to represent the heavens, and astronomical symbols were frequent elsewhere in the decorations. The crypt as a whole was arranged like a microcosm wherein the individual neophyte had an opportunity to come close to things divine. Such were the physical surroundings amid which the candidates for initiation participated in the Mithraic sacraments. Though the sanctuaries were small, they were effectively arranged and lighted to make the initiatory rites highly impressive.

Although we know almost nothing of Mithraic initiation, one important fact is clear, it was no simple affair. There were various degrees of initiation which admitted the candidates to different grades of privilege. A text of Jerome, together with various inscriptions, preserves the number and names of the different degrees.[2] They were seven, each one called a *sacramentum*, ranging from the lowest, or Raven (*corax*), grade to the highest grade, that of the Father (*pater*). Between were the degrees known as Occult (*cryphius*), Soldier (*miles*), Lion (*leo*), Persian (*Perses*), and Courier of the Sun (*heliodromus*). Apparent-

---

[1] Cumont, *op. cit.*, I, 305 ff.

[2] Jerome *Epistolae* cvii. 2 (to Laeta). M. Cumont has assembled the literary and epigraphic *testimonia* relative to these grades in *Textes et Monuments*, II, 535.

ly, in the process of initiation, the celebrants donned sacred masks appropriate to the particular degree conferred; the Occult wore a veil, the Persian a cap, while the Soldier, Raven, and Lion each wore disguises that can easily be imagined. Such masked figures appear now and then on Mithraic bas-reliefs.[1] A Christian of the fourth century wrote in ridicule of these practices: "Some flap their wings like birds, imitating the cry of crows; others growl like lions; in such manner are they that are called wise basely travestied."[2] To be understood adequately, these Mithraic disguises must be interpreted as the late survivals of very primitive religious practices. Their genesis goes back to the time when deity was conceived and represented under the form of animals typically. Then the worshiper, in order to identify himself with his god, took on the animal name and semblance of the deity; he put on the skin of his lion-god and was himself called a "Lion." So the Raven and Lion masks of Roman Mithraism were but tardy survivals of the animal skins that were donned in primitive times that the devotee might realistically charge himself with the power of his god.

Other peculiar ceremonies also were performed at each grade of initiation. For example, Tertullian told of the rite of the crown, enacted during the sacrament of the Soldier.[3] At the sword's point a crown was offered the candidate "as though in mimicry of martyrdom," Tertullian said. But the initiate was taught to push it aside with his hand and affirm, "Mithra is my crown!" Thereafter he never wore a crown or garland, not even at banquets or at military triumphs, and whenever a crown was offered him he refused it saying, "It belongs to my god." This was taken

[1] Cumont, I, 175, Fig. 10.

[2] Pseudo Augustine, *Quaestiones veteris et novi Testamenti.*

[3] Tertullian *De Corona* 15.

as proof that he was a soldier of Mithra. Tertullian himself was the son of a centurion. He was quite familiar with this ceremony and spoke of it with rare appreciation. Was his father, then, a soldier of Mithra as well as of Rome?

The same author, in another passage, told of a rite of sealing which appropriately formed a part of the initiation of the Mithraic soldier. Just as the recruits to the army had a mark burned in their flesh before they were admitted to the oath, so the Mithraic initiate as a part of his *sacramentum* had a sign burned on his forehead. "Thus Mithra marks on the forehead his own soldiers," said Tertullian.[1] In this way the solemn vow of the initiate as a soldier of Mithra was as indelibly impressed upon his mind as the seal was on his forehead. Of the ceremonials connected with the other grades of initiation we know almost nothing.[2]

In addition to the rites that may be related to a particular *sacramentum* there were certain other ceremonials of real importance which cannot be definitely localized in the Mithraic ritual. One such group of requirements were in the nature of preliminary austerities intended to test the moral courage and physical endurance of the candidates. As early as the period of the Avesta, such preparations were prescribed for the worship of Mithra. In the *Mihir Yasht* it was recorded:

Zarathustra asked him: "O Ahura Mazda! How shall the faithful man drink the libations cleanly prepared, which if he does and he offers them to Mithra, the lord of wide pastures, Mithra will be pleased with him and without anger?" Ahura Mazda answered: "Let them wash their bodies three days and three nights: Let them undergo thirty strokes for the sacrifice and prayer to Mithra, the lord of wide pastures."[3]

[1] Tertullian *De Praescriptione Haereticorum* 40.

[2] For an extended commentary on the individual grades of initiation see Loisy, *Les Mystères païens*, pp. 172 ff.

[3] *Yasht* x. 121, 122.

These antique prescriptions were probably the origin of the trials imposed on candidates in Roman Mithraism. Neither the number nor the precise nature of the various ordeals through which the initiates were made to pass are known, though later writers, the Christian Fathers especially, delighted to elaborate them in detail and to give their number very explicitly. Gregory of Nazianzen, for example, spoke indefinitely of "tortures" which the initiates had to endure;[1] his commentator Nonnus, however, enlarged on the theme by telling of "eighty punishments" by water, fire, frost, hunger, thirst, and prolonged journeyings, all arranged in a series of increasing severity. According to another statement, the initiate was blindfolded, his hands were tied with the entrails of chickens, he was made to leap over a ditch filled with water and, finally, the act was brought to an end when a "liberator" appeared who cut the disgusting bonds with a sword.[2] So far as specific detail is concerned, all this gratuitous information need not be taken seriously. Certainly the Mithraic shrines were so small and so limited in equipment that such ordeals could scarcely be more than a matter of pretence. At one point in his commentary, however, Nonnus was doubtless correct—the tests in general were intended to develop a Stoic apathy and to cultivate a steady control of the emotions.

Distinctive among the preliminary Mithraic tests was a simulated murder. Apparently, there was performed by the initiate, more likely on the initiate, the feint of a murder. The historian Lampridius in telling of the mad freaks of the emperor Commodus said that during the Mithraic ceremonies "he polluted the rites by a *real murder* where a certain thing was to be done for the sake of inspiring terror."[3] Probably at the time the emperor was officiat-

[1] Gregory of Nazianzen *Orationes* iv. 70.

[2] Pseudo Augustine *Quaestiones veteris et novi Testamenti.*

[3] Lampridius *Commodus* 9.

ing as a *Pater* at one of the lower degrees of initiation, perhaps that of the Soldier, when he committed the cruel deed.
Doubtless in its origin the simulated murder of Mithraism
was real—if not a human sacrifice, at least a mortal combat. Later it became a less dangerous test and finally a
mere liturgical fiction. The wholesale charges of murder
which were made against the devotees of Mithra by late
and hostile writers are as little deserving of credence
as similar charges that were made against the Christians.[1]

A simulation of death in the Mithraic mysteries, however, is perfectly intelligible. Death was the logical preliminary to a renewal of life; hence the pretence of death
by the neophyte was a perfectly natural antecedent to the
regenerative experiences of baptism and sacramental communion that followed in the Mithraic ritual. That this
was precisely the interpretation put upon this bit of liturgical fiction is clearly suggested by a passage in Tertullian.
In discussing the Mithraic rites of baptism and communion, the Christian lawyer affirmed: "Mithra there brings
in the symbol of a resurrection."[2] This striking use of the
phrase *imago ressurrectionis* is doubly significant. It proves
that a simulation of death was an integral part of Mithraic
ritual, and also that it was but antecedent to an experience
of regeneration.

Various ceremonies figured in the Mithraic liturgy
which were calculated to induce this process of spiritual
renewal. Among the most important were the ablutions
which from the earliest times were prominent in the cult
of Mithra. The ceremony consisted either of sprinkling as
with holy water, or of complete immersion as in Isiac practice. In the grottoes of the Persian god, water was always

---

[1] For a convincing discussion of this point see Cumont, *Textes et Monuments*,
I, 69 f.

[2] Tertullian *De Praescriptione Haereticorum* 40.

at hand,[1] and in certain instances, at Ostia, for example, vaults have been found which may have served the purpose of immersion.[2] Mithraic baptism, like the later Christian rite, promised purification from guilt and the washing away of sins. Christian Fathers noted the similarity and were quick to charge the Devil with plagiarism at this point. Tertullian declared:

> The Devil, whose business is to pervert the truth, mimics the exact circumstances of the divine sacraments in the mysteries of idols. He himself baptizes some, that is to say, his believers and followers; he promises forgiveness of sins in the sacred fount, and thus initiates them into the religion of Mithra.[3]

Again, and this time for the sake of rebuttal, the Christian lawyer stated the case for pagan baptism in the following words: "Well, but the nations, who are strangers to all understanding of spiritual powers ascribe to their idols the imbuing of waters with the self-same efficacy (as Christian baptism)." Then he countered with the argument, "But they cheat themselves with waters that are widowed. For washing is the channel through which they are initiated into the sacred rites of some notorious Isis or Mithra."[4] From Tertullian's *ex parte* statement of the case, even, it is clear that the neophyte came out of the baptism of Mithra with his conscience lightened from the weight of previous guilt. The waters of baptism were believed to wash away the defilements of the old life, and to induce a spiritual renewal.

Provision was also made in the Mithraic ritual for nourishing the new spiritual life in a realistic manner. At initiation, honey was applied to the hands and tongue of the candidate. According to Porphyry, this was done in

[1] Porphyry *De Antro Nympharum* 18.

[2] Cumont, *Textes et Monuments*, II, 523 f.

[3] Tertullian *De Praescriptione Haereticorum* 40.

[4] Tertullian *De Baptismo* 5.

both the Lion and the Persian grades of initiation.[1] As Porphyry said explicitly, honey was supposed to be a powerful preservative; hence it would serve to keep the initiate from the blemish of sin. In the Mithraic liturgy, however, it was believed to have a positive efficacy also, as its application to the tongue of the candidate suggests. Placed in the mouth of the neophyte, it was supposed to communicate to him some marvelous virtue. It was customary to put honey into the mouths of new-born children. So in Mithraism the spiritually new-born were fed with honey. So later, in primitive Christianity and among the Marcionites, the baptized were given a drink of milk mingled with honey.[2] Furthermore, in Mithraic thought honey was a celestial substance produced under the influence of the moon where, according to their cosmic myth, the seed of the divine bull that Mithra slew at the beginning of time had been gathered.[3] By its origin, then, honey was a powerful agent for nourishing the new spiritual life of the initiate. It was charged with mystical properties. It was the food of the gods themselves, and its absorption by the initiate endowed him with divine powers.[4]

Another means whereby the new divine life was nourished in the neophyte was by participation in a sacrament of eating and drinking. Mithraic theology traced this nourishment also back to the bull of their cosmic myth; for from the blood of the moribund victim of Mithra sprang the vine which supplied the votaries of the god with the life-giving wine of their sacrament.[5] Their

[1] Porphyry *De Antro Nympharum* 15.

[2] Tertullian *Contra Marcion* i. 14.

[3] *Corpus Inscriptionum Latinarum* Vol. III, No. 1002.

[4] For a discussion of the liturgic use of honey see Usener, *Milch und Honig* (*Hermes* [1902], LVII, 177 ff.).

[5] Cumont, *op. cit.*, I, 186 f.

communion included bread as well as wine. In the famous bas-relief from Konjica, Bosnia, there is a most interesting representation of a Mithraic communion.[1] Before two re-clinging communicants stands a tripod supporting tiny loaves of bread, each distinctly marked with a cross. One of the standing figures in the group, easily identified as a Persian, presents the communicants with a drinking cup. Other participants in this ceremony are clearly Mithraic initiates of different orders. This bas-relief shows in an unusually circumstantial manner that the Persian mystery religion, like the Christian, had its sacramental communion with its bread and wine.

The likenesses between the two rites did not fail to impress the Christian apologists who once more accused the demons of thievery. Justin Martyr, in speaking of the Christian Eucharist, asserted, "The wicked demons have imitated this in the mysteries of Mithra, commanding the same thing to be done. For that bread and a cup of water are placed before the initiate with certain incantations in these mysteries, you either know or can learn."[2] The similarities between the two communions, Mithraic and Christian, are indeed striking. Both were memorial services, celebrated in remembrance of the divine hero of the cult; for Mithra at the close of his redemptive career and just before his ascension to heaven, partook of a last supper with Helius and other companions of his labors. On the back of the great pivoted bas-relief at Hedderheim this original last supper was depicted.[3] Whenever the initiates participated in the Mithraic communion, they recalled this mythical love-feast.

---

[1] Cumont, *op. cit.*, I, 175, Fig. 10.

[2] Justin Martyr *Apologia* i. 66. Cf. Tertullian *De Praescriptione Haeretico-rum* 40.

[3] Cumont, *op. cit.*, II, Plate 8. Compare also Fig. 149, p. 294; Fig. 154, p. 298; Fig. 156, p. 300; Fig. 161, p. 304, and Fig. 421, p. 488.

But it meant more to them than this. From their communion they gained assurance for the future. Supernatural effects were expected from the assimilation of the consecrated elements. From the bread and wine they gained not only vigor of body and wisdom of mind but also the power to combat evil spirits and a divine substance that assured them of the boon of immortality. Thus the sacramental collation served to nourish the new life of the neophyte in a realistic way.

The sequence of these few ritual remains—the preliminary trials and the simulated death of the candidate, the regenerative bath of baptism, and finally the nourishing of the new life by means of honey and the consecrated elements of the Mithraic communion—serves to show that the idea of death and rebirth to a new life figured prominently in the ritual of the Persian god. If additional evidence is needed, it is found in the fragments of what was probably in its original state a Mithraic liturgy now preserved in an Egyptian magical papyrus dating from about A.D. 300[1] Professor Albrecht Dieterich, who published this as *Eine Mithrasliturgie*, is of the opinion that the liturgical parts, which consist of invocations, go back to a Mithraic ritual of the final grade of initiation in use perhaps as early as the first century. The rest of the Paris papyrus is composed of magical formulas and other occult matter. Notwithstanding all this extraneous material, it is not unlikely that the author of this religio-magical cento had access to a genuine Mithraic ritual of which he made considerable use for his own purposes. The figure of the death and rebirth of the initiate comes prominently to view at several points in this liturgical text, and it becomes quite apparent that initiation into the mysteries of Mithra was comprehensively thought of in this figurative way.

[1] Bibliothèque Nationale, *Suppl. Gr.* 574. See Dieterich, *Eine Mithrasliturgie* (Leipzig, 1910).

The opening prayer of the liturgy begins:

O! first genesis of my genesis! First beginning of my beginning! First spirit of the spirit that is within me! . . . . May it please thee to translate me, who am trammelled by the nature which underlies me, to an immortal genesis . . . . that I may be born again in spirit; that I may be initiated, and the sacred Spirit may breathe on me!

At different points in the liturgy, this spiritual genesis is specifically contrasted with natural birth. "Though I was born a mortal from a mortal mother . . . . having been sanctified by sacred ceremonies I am about to gaze with immortal eyes on the immortal aeon." Again the contrast between the natural birth and the spiritual rebirth is even more clearly brought out in the words addressed to the supreme god, "I, a man . . . . begotten in mortal womb by human seed, and today begotten again by thee, a man who has been called from so many thousands to immortality according to the plan of a god wonderful in his goodness, strives and longs to adore thee according to his human ability." The concluding words of the liturgy mark a high point of ecstatic expression and form a fitting conclusion for a Mithraic ritual. "O Lord! Having been born again, I pass away, being exalted the while. Having been exalted, I die! Coming into being by life-begetting birth and freed unto death, I go the way as thou hast ordered, as thou hast established the law and ordained the sacrament."

Few if any ancient texts contain a clearer appreciation of the radical religious experience of rebirth to immortal life than does this magical papyrus with its fragments of a Mithraic liturgy. By itself alone it is startling testimony to the prominence of the idea in gentile religious circles. Taken in conjunction with the few well attested ritual acts of Mithraism which were obviously intended to symbolize and induce an experience of spiritual rebirth, this evidence becomes quite convincing. It is certain that the devotees of Mithra viewed initiation as a rebirth to immortality.

IV

Finally, it is relevant to note the quality of the new life induced by the Mithraic ritual, particularly in its ethical aspects. From its very inception the cult of Mithra was characterized by soundly moral elements. If etymology counts for anything, it would seem that from early times the conception of Mithra himself was an ethical one, for his name was related to a common noun which in the Sanskrit meant "friend" or "friendship" and in Avestan "compact." As a result of Mithra's alliance with Zoroastrianism, his ethical character became strongly accentuated and he was clearly defined as the special guardian of truth. Zoroastrianism, with its apotheosis of moral dualism, gave Mithra his permanent function as the champion of right and the leader of the forces of good against the powers of evil and darkness. Obviously, it would be an unhistorical procedure to identify the ethics of first-century Mithraism with Avestan morality. On the other hand, except in the case of Armenian Mithraism,[1] there is no evidence that the cult's remarkable career of conquest resulted in a deterioration of its ethical quality. Mithraism was heir to the high ethics of ancient Persia and it guarded this heritage well.

Still when it comes to a discussion of the moral elements of the Mithraic life, the treatment has to be general, for sheer lack of specific evidence. There were certain "commandments" that had to be carefully observed by the initiate in order to be sure of the salvation that Mithra offered, and these were obligatory on all, the high and the lowly, the senator and the slave alike.[2] What the specific precepts were is unknown.

Nevertheless, certain characteristic features of the Mithraic ideal stand out with clarity. Primarily, it was

---

[1] Strabo, xi. 532.   [2] Julian *Convivium* 336.

an ideal of perfect purity. The ritual prescribed repeated ablutions and purifications and these were intended to wash away the stains of sin.[1] The very conformity to ritual practice at this point showed a sensitiveness to moral turpitude. The Mithraic life was also one of steady self-control and of asceticism even. Rigorous fasts and abstinences were enjoined,[2] and continence was encouraged as a special virtue.[3] More broadly, the resistance of all sensuality was a mark of the Mithraist. Chiefly, however, the Mithraic life was characterized by militant virtue. The good of this religion dwelt in action, and a premium was placed on the energetic virtues rather than on gentler qualities. Even its mysticism was a matter of active co-operation between Mithra and his soldiers, and this kind of mysticism discouraged dependence and stimulated individual effort. So virile and aggressive was this religion that sometimes it seemed cruel and heartless in the rigor of its discipline. In the largest terms, life for the Mithraist was a prolonged struggle, a part of the great cosmic warfare of good against evil, right against wrong.

In this war the initiate was assured of victory, for he had the help of an invincible god who was hailed in Persian as *nabarze*, in Greek as *anikētos*, and in Latin as *invictus* and *insuperabilis*.[4] Mithra was an unfailing help to mortals in their struggles, the protector of holiness, the defender of truth, and the intrepid antagonist of all wickedness.[5] The very presence of the god who was eternally vigilant and forever young was the assurance of success. Just as in the physical realm he gave victory in human warfare, so in the moral realm he gave his victory over evil instincts, the

[1] Tertullian *De Praescriptione Haereticorum* 40.

[2] Porphyry *De Abstinentia* iv. 16.   [3] Tertullian *loc. cit.*

[4] Cumont, *op. cit.*, I, 208, note 6; also II, 532–33.

[5] *Op. cit.*, Vol. II, inscriptions Nos. 3, 45, 60, 71, 144, 156, 188, 223a, 472, 486, 548, *et al.*

spirit of falsehood, and the temptations of the flesh. So far as the present was concerned, therefore, the Mithraic life was one of assured victory in the contest with evil.

As to the future, the initiate into Mithraism was guaranteed a righteous judgment and a happy immortality. He felt secure about the judgment, for Mithra, the guardian of truth, would preside at the great assize which determined his eternal destiny. According to the picture suggested by the Emperor Julian, Mithra was also the guide who assisted the soul on its heavenly journey and, finally, like a fond father, welcomed the soul to its heavenly home.[1] The seven grades of Mithraic initiation had a very direct relation to the future fate of the soul; for the heavens themselves were divided into seven spheres, each presided over by a different planet. Through these spheres lay the journey of the soul up to the heaven of the fixed stars. According to Celsus, this was represented in the Mithraic shrines by a sort of ladder containing eight gates, one above the other, the gates being of different metals.[2] From the different Mithraic sacraments the initiate learned the appropriate formulas which would admit him to the various spheres. As the soul passed from one sphere to another, it cast aside various earthly impurities and desires like different garments and finally, purified of all vice, it entered the empyrean, there to enjoy eternal bliss.[3] In addition to this general hope of immortality, more or less vague in character, certain Mithraic circles cherished a vivid eschatology involving a return of Mithra to the earth, a bodily resurrection of the dead, the destruction of the wicked, and the rejuvenation of the universe.[4] Whatever

[1] Julian *Convivium* 336.

[2] Origen *Contra Celsum* vi. 21, 22; see also Cumont, I, 117 f., 309 f.

[3] Bousset, "*Die Himmelreise der Seele*," in *Archiv für Religionswissenschaft*, IV (1901), 160 ff.

[4] Plutarch *De Iside et Osiride* 46, 47.

the particular form of the hope, the Mithraic initiate felt a calm assurance regarding the future.

This study of Mithraism has shown that the cult of the Iranian god held out to its devotees the hope of a blessed immortality and the assurance of victory in the struggle of life, on the basis of certain initiatory rites which were viewed as marking the beginning of a new kind of existence. The preliminary tests, the simulated death, the purification of baptism, the feeding of the initiate with honey, and the participation in a sacramental communion all served to stress the idea that initiation was a rebirth to a new life. Mithraic sacraments were both the symbols and the effective causes of this spiritual regeneration.

BIBLIOGRAPHY

CUMONT, FRANZ, *The Mysteries of Mithra*. Chicago, 1910.

CUMONT, FRANZ, *Oriental Religions in Roman Paganism* (Chicago, 1911), pp. 135–61.

CUMONT, FRANZ, *Textes et Monument figurés relatifs aux Mystères de Mithra*. Brussels, 1896–99.

DIETERICH, ALBRECHT, *Eine Mithrasliturgie*. Leipzig, 1910.

DILL, SAMUEL, *Roman Society from Nero to Marcus Aurelius* (London, 1920²), pp. 585–626.

GASQUET, A. L., *Le culte et les mystères de Mithra*. Paris, 1899.

GEDEN, A. S., *Select Passages Illustrating Mithraism*. London, 1925.

GRILL, J., *Die persische Mysterienreligion im römischen Reich*. Tübingen, 1903.

HALLIDAY, W. R., *The Pagan Background of Early Christianity* (London, 1925), pp. 281–311.

LAJARD, FELIX, *Recherches sur le culte public et les mystères de Mithra en Orient et en Occident*. Paris, 1867.

LEGGE, F., *Forerunners and Rivals of Christianity* (Cambridge, 1915), II, 224–76.

LOISY, ALFRED, *Les Mystères païens et le Mystère chrétien* (Paris, 1919), pp. 161–203.

PHYTHIAN-ADAMS, W. J., *Mithraism*. London, 1915.

TOUTAIN, J., *Les cultes païens dans l'Empire romain* (Paris, 1911), Part I, Vol. II, 121–77.

CHAPTER VII

ISIAC INITIATION

THE chief contribution of Egypt to the religion of the Roman Empire was the cult of Isis in the form of a Hellenized development of that ancient Egyptian religion. From very early times Isis and Osiris held a unique position in the religious thought of the Egyptian people. Herodotus noted in his day that "no other gods were worshiped in the same way by the whole of Egypt save only Isis and Osiris."[1] The worship of other deities varied from place to place in different sections of the country. By comparison with these the related cults of Isis and Osiris were undiversified, and their hold on the religious loyalties of the Egyptian people remained more or less constant not only in different localities but in various ages as well. It is surely an impressive fact that in Graeco-Roman times the reformed and Hellenized cult of Isis functioned as vigorously as the antique Osirian religion had functioned in the times of the Pharaohs.

I

The various traditions gathering around the divine names of Osiris and Isis were summarized in connected form by Plutarch.[2] In addition to Plutarch's convenient narrative, there are a number of Egyptian monuments that preserve fragments of the tragic tale. The oldest of these are a series of liturgical texts, hymns, prayers, and incantations from the walls of the pyramids of Sakhara. Quite apart from Plutarch's rendition of the story, it would

[1] Herodotus ii. 42.   [2] Plutarch *De Iside et Osiride* 12-20.

be possible, from these pyramid texts, to reconstruct completely the Osirian legend.[1] In its developed form, this tradition included many different strands. The essential elements of the tradition, however, were as follows: Osiris on earth had reigned as king over the Egyptians, "making them reform their destitute and bestial mode of living, showing them the art of cultivation, giving them laws, and teaching them how to worship the gods. Afterward he traveled over the whole earth, civilizing it."[2] His wicked brother Set, or Typhon, plotted against him and succeeded in accomplishing his violent death. When Isis, his wife, heard of the terrible deed, she put on mourning and wandered distractedly far and wide searching for the lost body of her husband. After a long search she recovered the body and carefully embalmed it. Over the corpse she and her sister Nephtys joined in a lament that became classical —a type of the Egyptian lamentations for the deceased.[3] With the aid of the faithful god Anubis, her son Horus, and Thoth, Isis performed certain magical rites over the body of Osiris which had the effect of revivifying the corpse and restoring her husband to life. Thereafter he was translated to the nether regions where he reigned as "Lord of the Underworld and Ruler of the Dead."[4] Here he presided at the bar of judgment and assigned to the souls of the departed their proper reward for virtue or punishment for sin.

This brief summary of the Osirian tradition itself suggests that, in the religious thought of Egypt, Osiris was a

[1] This has, indeed, been successfully accomplished by Professor J. H. Breasted in his *Development of Religion and Thought in Ancient Egypt*, pp. 18 ff.

[2] Plutarch *De Iside et Osiride* 13. Cf. Tibullus i. 7. 29 ff., and Diodorus Siculus i. 14, 17, 20.

[3] Dennis, *The Burden of Isis, Being the Laments of Isis and Nephtys Translated from the Egyptian*.

[4] Plutarch *De Iside et Osiride* 79.

dying and reviving god like Adonis and Attis and Dionysus, and as such a personification of the yearly vicissitudes
of vegetable life in the ever recurrent struggle of life and
death in nature. He was also an embodiment of the ideal
Pharaoh and a personification of the righteous man who,
facing the mystery of death, sought the assurances of religion regarding the future. So also Isis, like Demeter and
the *Magna Mater*, was a mother-goddess personifying the
power of life in nature and the unquenchable human hope
for a final triumph in the conflict of life with death. She
also embodied the beneficent influences of culture and religion; for she had taught men the arts and government
and the mysteries.[1]

Traditionally, the rites of the Osirian religion, like those
of Eleusis, were established by the goddess-mother herself.
Plutarch, again, was a recorder of this tradition. His account of the establishment of the Osiris cult was as follows:

> But the avenger of Osiris, his sister and wife Isis, who extinguished
> and put a stop to the madness and fury of Typhon, did not forget the
> contests and struggles she had gone through, nor yet her own wander-
> ings, nor did she suffer oblivion and silence to envelop her many deeds of
> wisdom, many feats of courage, but by intermingling with the most
> sacred ceremonies images, hints, and representations of her sufferings
> of yore she consecrated at one and the same time both lessons of piety
> and consolation in suffering for men and women when overtaken by
> misfortune.[2]

In the ancient Egyptian calendar of religious feasts,
with its many celebrations in honor of a variety of gods,
the rites of Osiris held a place of singular honor. When
Herodotus visited Egypt, he found that next to the most
important native religious festival was the one in honor
of Isis held in her great temple at Busiris in the Nile delta.[3]

[1] Diodorus Siculus i. 27. Cf. an inscription from Ios translated by Deissmann, *Light from the Ancient East*, pp. 136 ff.

[2] Plutarch *De Iside et Osiride* 27.   [3] Herodotus ii. 59–61.

The Greek historian showed great reverence for these rites and was very reticent about giving any precise information concerning them. He did, however, say this much: "There, after the sacrifice, all the men and women lament in countless numbers; but it were profane for me to say who it is for whom they lament." Also in speaking of similar ceremonies at Sais, Herodotus gave but slight additional information and gave that very guardedly.

> There is also at Sais the burial of him whose name I deem it forbidden to utter in speaking of such a matter . . . . and there is a lake hard by, adorned with a stone margin and wrought to a complete circle. . . . . On this lake they enact by night the story of the god's sufferings, a rite which the Egyptians call the mysteries. I could speak more exactly of these matters, for I know the truth, but I will hold my peace.[1]

The information that Herodotus records, scanty as it is, yet is sufficient to betray the general character of these religious celebrations. They were in the nature of a passion drama and they featured lamentations in which the spectators participated. The suggestion is an obvious one that the death and resurrection of Osiris constituted the subject matter of this drama and that the lamentations were the traditional lamentations of Isis for her husband.

Herodotus' reserve about giving any detailed information concerning the Osiris festivals calls attention to a fact of some importance. Even in ancient Egypt the Osirian cult included both public rites and secret ceremonies as well.[2] Certain things were done and certain explanations were made which were regarded as matters of great sanctity. Only privileged people were permitted to share them. Herodotus was so impressed by the sacred character of these revelations that he kept the secret conscientiously. One would hardly be justified, on this basis, in speaking

---

[1] *Op. cit.* ii. 170–71. Cf. ii. 132.

[2] Herodotus is confirmed at this point by Iamblicus vi. 5. 7.

of an Osirian initiation into a secret fraternity, perhaps. Nevertheless, there was a differentiation between the public and the private Osirian rites even in ancient Egypt, and this is an important distinction to keep in mind for the understanding of a significant development of Isiac ritual in Hellenistic times.

Osirian rites such as Herodotus mentioned were repeated at annual festivals at the great temples of the god in different parts of Egypt. These sacred dramas were performed for the benefit of Osiris himself, and a statue of the god formed the center of interest in the celebration. On a stela of the Twelfth Dynasty dated about 1875 B.C. a state official, Igernefert by name, recounted with some minuteness how he conducted "the ceremony of the golden chamber for the Lord of Abydos (Osiris)."[1] Igernefert told of the preparation of various properties for the drama and of the part that he himself played in the performance. The scenes included first of all a procession of the followers of Osiris, with an attack by his enemies. The death of the god formed the second scene, to which Igernefert made allusion quite as guardedly as Herodotus. "I performed the great going-forth. I followed the god in his footsteps." Then came the resurrection and final triumph of the god. "I avenged Osiris on the day of the great battle, I overthrew his enemies upon the river of Nedit," declared Igernefert, referring to such a bloody struggle as that to which Herodotus also made allusion.[2] Then the drama was brought to a joyful close by the return of the Lord of Abydos to his palace, i.e., the return of the image of the god to its temple.

Not only were there occasional celebrations of the

[1] The text has been published in H. Schäfer's *Die Mysterien des Osiris in Abydos* (Leipzig, 1904).

[2] Herodotus ii. 63.

Osirian drama such as this but in later times, especially, there were also daily commemorations of the passion and resurrection of the god. These were enacted in the chapels of the god and doubtless formed the secret part of the Osirian ritual. Bas-reliefs from temples and various ritual remains enable us to reconstruct the liturgical acts and recitations of these miniature passion plays. There was the search for the body of Osiris and the prolonged lament of Isis and Nephtys over the corpse. In response to their cries Horus, Anubis, and Thoth came and purified the body and prepared it for restoration to life. Next certain magical rites were performed. By means of the adze of Anubis the mouth, eyes, and ears of the corpse were opened, other members of the body were put into motion, and each organ was recalled to life separately. Then, to insure resurrection, vegetable rebirth was represented by the germination of grain, and even an animal rebirth was simulated. The priest playing the part of Anubis assumed a recumbent position under the skin of a sacrificed animal. Here he symbolized the foetus in the womb, or, more specifically, Osiris being conceived anew. Coming out from under the skin, he typified Osiris being reborn.[1] These rites completed, Osiris was alive once more. His image was crowned and adored and offerings were made to him. In these daily rites Osiris, represented by his image, passed through a ritual rebirth.

The question at once arises, Were the benefits of these rites extended to men, as well as to the god? In the Egyptian funeral ceremonies is found the answer to this question, for the burial rites of ancient Egypt were but Osirian ceremonies repeated according to the principles of sympathetic magic. The deceased man was the dead Osiris and at his funeral the sacred drama was re-enacted. His wife

[1] Moret, *Mystères Égyptiens*, pp. 31–34.

and sister played the parts of Isis and Nephtys. His son was Horus and his friends were the helping gods. Professional priests assumed rôles not otherwise provided for. Upon the corpse of the dead man were performed the same rites that traditionally had been enacted over the dead Osiris. His mouth, eyes, and ears were opened and the ceremonies of vegetal and animal rebirth were repeated. Just as Anubis "passed under the hide" in order to effect the rebirth of Osiris,[1] so the presiding priest "laid himself down under the hide of a cow in the land of transformation." By the mimicking of birth when he issued from the skin it was believed that he accomplished the spiritual renaissance of the defunct.[2] "He who renews life (after death)" was an epithet applied to the man thus favored. Such a man went to join his god on the plains of Aalu, where, if he so chose, he might himself become a god. Many a man so privileged was specifically called "Osiris" after his death.[3] A familiar Egyptian text testifies most clearly to this future hope for one who had shared in Osirian rites; "As truly as Osiris lives," so ran the text, "he also shall live; as truly as Osiris is not dead, shall he not die; as truly as Osiris is not annihilated, shall he not be annihilated."[4]

These Osirian funeral rites, however, were entirely in the interests of the dead, to insure them a rebirth to immortality. Was this grace ever granted to a living person, so that even before death he might be certain of the future benefits these powerful rites could assure? In the case of the Pharaoh this was done. During the *Sed* festival a ritual death and rebirth was enacted for the benefit of the royal

[1] *Book of the Dead* xvii.

[2] Moret, *Mystères Égyptiens*, pp. 66–71, 82 ff.

[3] See Wiedemann, *Realms of the Egyptian Dead*.

[4] Erman, *Die Aegyptische Religion*, pp. 96 and 97.

personage himself.[1] Only in later times and as a special favor were others granted this grace.[2] Generally speaking, the advantages of ritual rebirth in Egyptian religion were conferred upon the dead and were confined to the future life.

II

Notwithstanding the clear suggestions of postmortem regeneration to be found in the Egyptian cult of Osiris, it is to a modification and further development of this ancient religion that one must turn to find clear examples of the spiritual rebirth of the individual during his lifetime. In the Hellenistic cult of Serapis and Isis, such experiences may be isolated. This new cult was but an adaptation of the venerable Egyptian religion to the spirit and needs of Hellenistic times. Hence it assumed that individualistic, universalistic character so typical of other contemporary religious movements. It welcomed to its membership non-Egyptians as well as Egyptians. Osirian religion had been a pure product of the Nile Valley. The new religion, itself a syncretism, did not know any geographical or racial distinctions. Other contrasts, more or less superficial, might be drawn which recorded in an external way the degree to which the old Egyptian religion was modified to meet the social needs of the Alexandrian age. The ancient system had centered in the god, Osiris; but in the reformed cult of Hellenistic times he was replaced to a considerable extent by a new divinity, Serapis, and popular interest was transferred to the more appealing personality of Isis. She dominated the Hellenistic cult quite as Demeter held supreme place in the Eleusinian mysteries, or the *Magna Mater* in those that emanated from Phrygia. In the ancient Osirian religion, the public ritual with its strong appeal to the masses was important. In the Hellenized

[1] Moret, *Mystères Égyptiens*, pp. 73–84.   [2] *Op. cit.*, pp. 90–96.

worship of Isis, the significant ceremonials were those secret rites that had such deep meaning for the individual.
These were only some of the ways in which the new cult
showed adaptation to the very personal needs of individual
religionists in the Hellenized world.

The inception of this significant reform has been concealed under an overgrowth of tradition and legend. These
traditions, varying in detail, were summarized by two
prominent writers of Roman times, Plutarch and Tacitus.[1]
The general purport of their accounts was to the effect that
Ptolemy Soter, the first of the Macedonian rulers of Egypt,
had a dream in which he saw a huge statue of Pluto, located at Sinope in Pontus. The king was commanded to bring
this colossus to the growing city of Alexandria and instal
it there as the center of a new religion. It was a magnificent
piece of craftsmanship, composed of gems and precious
metals, the work of Bryaxis, the companion of Scopas. By
stealth and diplomacy Ptolemy accomplished his purpose,
and the colossus was installed with due pomp as the god
Serapis in a magnificent temple, or Serapeum, especially
built to receive it. According to both renditions of the
story, Ptolemy had recourse to the assistance of Manetho,
an Egyptian priest, and Timotheus, "one of the race of the
Eumolpidae, who was invited from Eleusis to preside over
the mysteries." By the collaboration of an Egyptian priest
and an Eleusinian priest—so legend affirmed—Ptolemy
was enabled to institute his new religion.

Whatever of historical truth or of fable may have been
repeated by Plutarch and Tacitus, two points stand out
clearly from the traditional background. In the first place
the projection of the new cult of Serapis was but a part of
Ptolemy's plan to bring about a fusion of races in his Egyptian kingdom; and in the second place the cult itself was

[1] Plutarch *De Iside et Osiride* 28; Tacitus *Histories* iv. 83, 84.

adapted to this purpose, for it was a combination of Egyptian and Hellenistic elements.

The political purpose of this new cult was ill-disguised. It was intended to serve as one more cultural bond uniting the inhabitants of Ptolemy's Egypt. We cannot be sure that Alexander cherished the scheme of uniting his great world empire by the bonds of religion as well as by commerce and culture. It is perfectly patent, however, that Ptolemy purposed this very thing and gave his official patronage to the cult of Serapis for this very reason. From the first the new cult was intended to furnish a common religious meeting ground for the Greek inhabitants of Egypt and the natives also.[1]

For this purpose nothing was better adapted than a modification of Osirian rites. Through centuries of history the masses of Egyptian people had shown a decided preference for the worship of the god Osiris, so that other Egyptian divinities were forced to include him in their cults. Recognizing their own Osiris in the new god Serapis, the natives of Egypt, as a rule, were ready to give him their adherence. The Greeks, on the other hand, had long since identified Osiris with their own Dionysus and Isis with Demeter.[2] In the rites of the Egyptian divinities and the myths that clustered about them, they found strange correspondences with their own myths and rituals. Osiris had been torn to pieces even as their own Dionysus had been. Isis had mourned for him as Aphrodite had bewailed Adonis or the Great Mother had lamented her Attis, and she had sought for his body even as the sorrowing Mother of Eleusis had sought for her lost daughter. In the finding and restoration of Osiris, the Egyptians rejoiced even as the Eleusinian devotees shared the joy of their goddess in

[1] Cumont, *Oriental Religions in Roman Paganism*, p. 75. Cf. Legge, *Forerunners and Rivals of Christianity*, I, 30 ff.

[2] Herodotus 2. 42, 48, 145.

the restoration of Persephone. The resemblances between the Graeco-Oriental mysteries and the Egyptian cult of Osiris were many and salient, and the Egyptian religion easily lent itself to the process of Hellenization.

Consequently, the new religion of Ptolemy became, roughly, a compound of the old religion of the Pharaohs and the mysteries of Greece and Asia Minor. Whether or not Manetho the Egyptian priest and Timotheus the Eumolpid collaborated in the institution of this Hellenized Egyptian religion, the cult of Serapis and Isis was such a composite as would have been produced by such men. On a foundation Osirian and Egyptian was erected the shrine of Serapis which in externals, at least, was decidedly Hellenistic in character.

III

In order to estimate the extent to which the reformed Osirian religion was influential in the Graeco-Roman world, it is necessary to trace the missionary successes of this cult during the Hellenistic and early imperial periods. It was disseminated from the Serapeum at Alexandria in somewhat the manner that the Jewish religion spread from the temple at Jerusalem. In Egypt itself the new religion of the Ptolemies was readily adopted. The Egyptians had long been familiar with the process of changing the divine government of heaven in a manner paralleling the political changes on earth. So they acceded to the Serapis of Alexandria as they had previously accepted the Amon of Thebes. Moreover, they recognized the essential identity of their beloved Osiris with the new god Serapis. In the second century A.D. there were no less than forty-two Serapeums in the Nile Valley. Egypt, then, was an effective missionary base for the Isiacists.[1]

---

[1] Aelius Aristides viii. 56. Legge contends that the native Egyptians refused to adopt the new cult and that it thrived only in the Greek centers of Egypt. See Legge, *Forerunners and Rivals*, I, 51.

Because of the political prestige of the Lagides and the extensive commerce of Alexandria, the Hellenized religion of Isis quickly spread over the eastern Mediterranean world. King Nicocreon, of Cyprus, consulted the oracle of the Serapeum and, receiving a satisfactory response, he introduced the cult into his island.[1] Ptolemy I (323–285 B.C.) was responsible for the establishment of the cult in Athens where a Serapeum was built beneath the Acropolis.[2] About the same time a Serapiast brotherhood was instituted at the Piraeus.[3] Ptolemy Euergetes (246–221 B.C.) sent a statue of Isis to Seleucus Callinicus who built a sanctuary for it in Syrian Antioch.[4] The next two hundred years saw Isiac brotherhoods established in Asian centers, such as Smyrna, Cyzicus, and Ephesus, and on the islands of Rhodes, Delos, and Tenedos, as well as in Thessaly and Thrace.[5] A full century before Jesus of Nazareth was born, Egyptian sailors and merchants had propagated the cult of Isis all along the coasts of Syria, Asia Minor, Greece, and among the Aegean Islands. When Paul began his missionary work in these regions, he everywhere met with Isiac establishments that were already centuries old. Here the worship of the Alexandrian deities became so firmly rooted that even the political vicissitudes that befell the Ptolemies did not seriously affect it. Even to the last days of paganism, Isis remained a power in the eastern Mediterranean world.

In the Latin west even more than in the Greek east the Alexandrian cult proved itself genuinely popular. It

[1] Marcrobius *Saturnalia Convivia* i. 20.

[2] Pausanias i. 18. 4.

[3] *Corpus Inscriptionum Graecarum* Vol. I, No. 120. Foucart, *Les Associations religieuses*, p. 207, inscription 24.

[4] Libanius, *Orationes* xi. 114.

[5] Lafaye, *Histoire de culte des divinities d'Alexandrie*, pp. 35–38.

was probably through the Campanian ports, Puteoli in
particular, that the cult of Isis made its initial appearance
in Italy. A city ordinance of Puteoli dated 105 B.C. made
mention of a Serapeum in that city.[1] It was not a new
foundation, and the Isiac brotherhood itself must have
been in existence there at least a half century earlier. The
religion of Isis, then, antedated the arrival of Paul in
Puteoli by at least two centuries. Perhaps at about the
same time the first Isium of Pompeii was built.[2] It is a
safe conjecture that Isis worship came to Italy early in the
second century B.C., during those stirring years of religious
excitement following the arrival of the *Magna Mater* from
Pessinus, and at the time when the dignified Roman Senate
was trying to hold in check the excesses of the Dionysus
cult.

About the middle of the first century B.C. the immigrant religion was subjected to fierce persecution in Italy.
Five times during the years between 59 and 48 the Senate
ordered the destruction of Isiac shrines. Yet so popular
was the worship of the Egyptian goddess that in at least
one instance the consul himself had to undertake the work
of destruction which he was unable to find a workman to
do.[3] Even the Christian advocate Tertullian had to admit
that "the altars which the Senate had thrown down were
restored by popular violence."[4] Again, after the defeat of
Antony and Cleopatra at Actium, there was a natural reaction against things Egyptian, and as a consequence Isis
was banished beyond the *pomerium*.[5] In A.D. 19, because
of a real or pretended scandal involving a priest of Isis, the
devotees of the goddess experienced a bloody persecution

---

[1] *Corpus Inscriptionum Latinarum* Vol. X, No. 1781; Vol. I, No. 577.

[2] Mau, *Pompeii*, p. 163.   [3] Valerius Maximus i. 3. 3.

[4] Tertullian *Apologeticus* 6; *Ad Nationes* i. 10.

[5] Dio Cassius *Historia Romana* liii. 2.

and were banished wholesale to Sardinia along with the Jews.[1] Yet Isiaism, like Christianity later, seemed to thrive on persecution, and at no time during this period did the devotion of the masses to the Egyptian goddess perceptibly weaken. On the contrary, there is every indication that the history of the Isiac cult in Italy was the story of a really popular religion that triumphed even in the face of official opposition.[2]

Contemporary Latin literature is rich in allusions that show the great influence of the Alexandrian religion in Italy at the beginning of the Christian era. Conspicuous among the devotees of Isis were the mistresses of men of letters in the Augustan age. Tibullus, sick in Corcyra and despairing of his life, wrote to his fiancée Delia to seek the aid of the Egyptian goddess to whom she was so devoted.[3] Propertius, on the other hand, complained bitterly of his Cynthia's loyalty to Isis rather than to himself and did not hesitate to heap up words of reproach against the goddess. "Once more those dismal rites have returned to plague us," he grumbled. "Now for ten nights Cynthia has sacrificed. A curse upon the rites which the daughters of Inachus sent from the warm Nile to the matrons of Italy!"[4] Ovid, despairing of his lady's life, addressed his prayer directly to the goddess whom Corinna particularly adored: "O Isis . . . . by thy sistrums I pray thee . . . . turn hither thy countenance, and in one spare us both! For thou wilt give life to my lady and she to me."[5] Seneca's nephew, Lucan, paid his respects to the worship of the Alexandrian divinities in his *Pharsalia*.[6] So did Martial and Juvenal in their

---

[1] Josephus *Antiquities* xviii. 3, 4, 5; Tacitus *Annals* ii. 85; Suetonius *Tiberius* 36.

[2] Dill, *Roman Society from Nero to Marcus Aurelius*, p. 565.

[3] Tibullus i. 3.   [5] Ovid *Amores* ii. 13. 7 ff.

[4] Propertius ii. 33.   [6] Lucan *Pharsalia* viii. 831.

Satires, and though they had scant respect for the Egyptian religion, at least they witnessed to its immense popularity and the great loyalty of its adherents.[1] Juvenal in particular described a touching scene that illustrates the devotion of a typical worshiper to the goddess Isis.

In winter she will go down to the river of a morning, break the ice, and plunge three times into the Tiber, dipping her trembling head in its whirling waters, and crawling out thence naked and shivering, she will creep with bleeding knees right across the field of Tarquin the Proud. If the white Io[2] shall so order, she will journey to the confines of Egypt, and fetch water from hot Meroe with which to sprinkle the Temple of Isis which stands hard by the ancient sheepfold. For she believes that the command was given by the voice of the goddess herself.[3]

Citations such as these from first-century Latin literature bespeak a really great popularity for the Isis cult in the Roman world of that day.

With its place at Rome secure, the cult was in a strategic position to carry on its propaganda on an imperial scale. Lucan, who in his *Pharsalia* spoke of Isis and Osiris as enthroned in Roman temples, referred to them also as the deities of all the world.[4] Plutarch, with his elaborate attempt to reinterpret the Isis-Osiris religion in philosophical terminology, is perhaps the most weighty witness to this wider influence of the Alexandrian cult; for Plutarch tried to do for the Egyptian gospel what Philo earlier attempted for Judaism, and what only a little later the author of the Fourth Gospel essayed to do for Christianity.[5] He aimed to reinterpret the Egyptian religion in universal terms that should appeal to the philosophically minded.

Of the actual influence of the cult in Roman provincial

[1] Martial xii. 29.

[2] Io is here identified with Isis.

[3] Juvenal vi. 522 ff.

[4] Lucan *Pharsalia* viii. 831 and ix. 158.

[5] Plutarch *De Iside et Osiride*.

areas even in the first century, there is plenty of evidence. Toutain is familiar with over a hundred different documents of various dates that attest the existence of Isiac communities scattered all over the Roman provinces.[1] The extent of this Egyptian *Diaspora* in the mid-first century measures the advantage enjoyed by Isiaism over early Christianity in the matter of missionary propaganda. When Paul first conceived his stupendous scheme of world wide evangelization, he was chronologically far behind his Isiac competitors, and wherever he went in that gentile world he found that they had preceded him. In both the western and the eastern halves of the Mediterranean world, the Isis cult was widely known and genuinely popular before the Apostle to the Gentiles began his work.

IV

Among other factors that accounted for the great popularity of the Isis religion in the Graeco-Roman world was the impressiveness of its rites. In the Hellenistic development of Isiaism, as in the ancient religion of the Pharaohs, both public and private ceremonials were included in the cult. Notwithstanding their public character, the former rites were of a kind to foster a feeling of intimacy on the part of the devotee with his goddess. The public ritual included a regular daily liturgy with matins at the beginning of the day[2] and a benediction in the afternoon. During the latter part of the forenoon and the early part of the afternoon, Isiac shrines were left open, and the images of the goddess were exposed to the silent adoration of the worshipers. Prayer, meditation, and contemplative devotion were thus encouraged.[3] The daily liturgy was

[1] Toutain, *Les cultes païens dans l'Empire romain*, Part I, p. 17, col. 2.

[2] Apuleius *Metamorphoses* xi. 20; also Arnobius vii. 32.

[3] Apuleius *op. cit.* xi. 17; Ovid *Amores.* ii 13. 7; Tibullus i. 3.

brought to a solemn but joyful close with the chanting of hymns, the dismissal of the people, and the closing of the shrine.[1] By services such as these, regular and somewhat elaborate, the faith of the people in the Alexandrian divinities was renewed from day to day.

In addition to the daily liturgy, there were public festivals at different seasons that were conducted with an elaboration of pageantry dear alike to the south European and to the Oriental. Most solemn, most stirring, and quite the most popular of these was the November festival celebrating the passion and resurrection of Osiris. It was a festival of great antiquity, directly elaborated from the dramatic performances at Abydos and elsewhere, in which, from the Twelfth Dynasty onward, the sufferings of Osiris had been reproduced.[2] As in the passion play at Eleusis, the worshipers themselves participated actively in the sacred drama. When Isis mourned and sought for her husband, her devotees beat their breasts and shared her sorrow with an effusive display of grief. Again when the god was found, the worshipers joined in an equally extravagant demonstration of gladness.[3] By this alternation of extreme sorrow and joy the devotees of Isis realized a sympathetic and highly emotional communion with their deity. In this respect the psychological influence of the November passion play of Osiris was strikingly like that of the spring festival of Adonis, or of the September drama at Eleusis.

In addition to these public ceremonies, there were rites which were private in character and fostered a very individualistic type of religious experience. Membership in the

[1] Apuleius op. cit. xi. 17.

[2] See Schäfer, Die Mysterien des Osiris in Abydos unter Sesostris III (Leipzig 1904).

[3] Juvenal viii. 29; Ovid Metamorphoses ix. 693; Lucan viii. 831; Minucius Felix Octavius 21; Lactantius Divinae Institutiones i. 21.

Isiac community, as in the other mystery cults, was contingent upon participation in certain prescribed initiatory rites, the details of which were kept strictly secret. These private ceremonies were a direct development from the esoteric rites of ancient Egypt, where the priests of Osiris reserved certain interpretations and ceremonies, and imparted them only on promise of secrecy. This condition obtained in the worship of Isis at Abydos and elsewhere.[1] In the Hellenization of the cult, such private rites were readily adapted to purposes of initiation and were developed along lines similar to the rites of Eleusis. Tradition implied that Timotheus the Eumolpid was in part responsible for this development.

The most valuable, and almost the only source of information concerning these important rites is Lucius Apuleius' account of his own initiation at Cenchraea. By following his narrative through it is possible to trace, step by step, the procedure in Isiac initiations. One is impressed at the outset by the genuine eagerness of Lucius for the grace of admission to the order of Isis, an eagerness tempered by a distrust of his own ability to attain it. For—to quote Lucius's own words—"I had learned by diligent inquiry that her obeisance was hard, the chastity of the priests difficult to keep, and the whole life of them . . . . to be watched and guarded very carefully."[2] While awaiting the desired privilege, Lucius lived the life of a recluse in the cloisters of the temple, attending reverently on the regular services of worship. Such a novitiate as this was apparently expected of those who desired initiation, and rooms were provided for them in connection with the temple where they lived with the priests in a sort of monas-

---

[1] Iamblicus *De Mysteriis* vi. 5–7; Chaeremon in Porphyry *Epistola ad Anebon* 31.

[2] Apuleius *Metamorphoses* xi. 19.

tic community. The chief priest, in a kindly manner, restrained the urgency of Lucius "as parents commonly
bridle the desires of their children." He assured him that
initiation was no light matter but that "the taking of such
orders was like a voluntary death and a difficult recovery
to health." The pontiff urged him to await a sign from the
goddess herself, and at the same time gave specific directions as to the preparatory abstinences to be observed.[1]
Lucius had not long to wait. In a vision of the night time
the expected sign was vouchsafed to him and Mithra, the
principal priest of Isis, was assigned to him as a mystagogue.[2]

On the following morning the formal initiation rites
began. The great priest produced "out of the secret place
of the temple certain books written with unknown characters . . . . whereby they were wholly strange and impossible
to be read by profane people," and thence he interpreted
to Lucius "such things as were necessary to the use and
preparation of his order." At the propitious time after the
impartation of this instruction, Lucius, attended by a company of initiates, was brought to the place of baptism, and
there, "demanding pardon of the gods," the priest baptized
him and "purified his body according to custom."[3] Christian writers knew of this Isiac baptism and made plain that
a powerful efficacy was credited to it—indeed the selfsame
effect of purification from sin and spiritual regeneration
that Christians attributed to their baptismal rite.[4] In the

[1] *Op. cit.* xi. 21.

[2] *Op. cit.* xi. 22. The reason given for this assignment was that the destinies
of Lucius and Mithra were joined "by the ordering of the planets." This
astrological reference and the juxtaposition of the name Mithra constitute an
interesting illustration of religious syncretism in the cult of Isis.

[3] *Op. cit.* xi. 22, 23.

[4] Tertullian *De Baptismo* 5. Cf. Firmicus Maternus *De Errore Profanarum
Religionum* 2.

thought of the Isiac community, the waters of baptism were identified with the life-giving waters of the sacred Nile and these in turn with the waters of the primordial ocean whence all things, even the gods, had been created. Osiris himself had been reborn, after his passion, from the waters of the Nile. So for the initiate these sacred waters had a life-giving power, and Isiac baptism was in effect regarded as a regenerative rite that meant new life to the one who experienced it.

At the afternoon benediction on the day of baptism, the chief priest imparted to Lucius certain secret instructions and commanded him to observe various abstinences for a period of ten days. The ascetic prescriptions included an abstinence from meat, wine-drinking, and other pleasures of the flesh. Strict chastity was a particular point of insistence. It was this moral requirement particularly that made Lucius hesitate to apply for admission into the Isiac order.[1] It was this requirement of purity also that made the erotic Latin poets rail so loudly against the Egyptian goddess.[2] Plutarch, too, stressed in particular this feature of Isiac discipline. "By means of a perpetually sober life," he affirmed, "by abstinence from many kinds of food and from sexual indulgence, Isis checks intemperance and love of pleasure, accustoming people to endure her service not enervated by luxury, but hardy and vigorous."[3] After a ten-day period of ascetic isolation of this kind, Lucius was in an impressionable state, sensitive to the full suggestiveness of the further initiatory rites.

On the tenth day at sunset the initiation was held. After the priest had presented gifts to Lucius according to

[1] Loisy, *Les Mystères païens*, pp. 134 and 149, n. 2; Apuleius *Metamorphoses* xi. 19.

[2] Propertius ii. 33. Cf. Tibullus i. 3.

[3] Plutarch *De Iside et Osiride* 2.

ancient custom, the laity and the uninitiated were commanded to depart. Then the great priest took the candidate by the hand and led him to "the most secret and most sacred place of the temple" where the initiation ceremony itself took place. Here the curtain falls and Lucius refrains from telling us exactly what happened. He conscientiously kept his vow of secrecy. "You would perhaps demand, studious reader, what was said and done there: truly I would tell you if it were lawful for me to tell; you would know if it were convenient for you to hear; but both your ears and my tongue should incur the like pain of rash curiosity."[1] The curtain of secrecy, however, is but a thinly drawn veil intended to protect Apuleius and his readers from the charge of sacrilege; for he immediately proceeds to give a general impression of the ceremonies without describing a single rite or repeating a single formula. From this general characterization it is possible to get a fairly definite conception of what took place in the holy of holies of the Isiac sanctuary.

Understand that I approached the bounds of death, I trod the threshold of Proserpine, and after that I was ravished through all the elements, I returned to my proper place; about midnight I saw the sun brightly shine; I saw likewise the gods celestial and the gods infernal, before whom I presented myself and worshiped them.

These figurative words of Lucius, taken in conjunction with the plainer words of the priest who characterized Isiac initiations as "a voluntary death and a difficult recovery of health,"[2] make it practically certain that a ritual death and resurrection were the central features of the initiation ceremony. Since this was an Isiac initiation, the ritual could have been none other than an adaptation of the ancient Osirian rites that in Egypt from antiquity had been practiced on the living Pharaoh, on the mummies of the

[1] Apuleius *Metamorphoses* xi. 23.   [2] *Op. cit.* xi. 21.

dead, and on the statues of the god. In remotest antiquity these rites, so the devotees believed, had been efficacious in causing the regeneration of Osiris after his passion; and now they were practiced on the initiate himself that he might realize communion with Osiris in this life and share in his immortality. In the secret of the sanctuary the initiate participated in a repetition of the ancient drama, himself the central figure, the new Osiris whom Isis, by her power, exalted to an immortal regeneration.[1]

Back of Lucius' figurative language, it is possible to distinguish the main events in the Osirian drama. At the beginning of the ceremony, the initiate approached the bounds of death. In other words, he assumed the rôle of the dead Osiris over whom the vivifying funeral rites were performed. Osiris, restored to life, had not returned to his earthly kingdom, but had gone to preside over the realm of the dead. So the initiate, having been treated as the dead Osiris and restored to life, "trod the threshold of Proserpine." As Osiris he made an infernal journey and visited the realms of the departed. The admixture of solar imagery in Lucius' description should not confuse us. According to contemporary cosmology, the sun each night visited the subterranean regions. In the rite of initiation, therefore, the votary as a new Osiris made both the infernal and the celestial journey like the sun. At midnight he saw the sun brightly shine in the realm of the dead, and likewise he mounted up into the heavens and saw the gods celestial as well as the gods infernal. In doing all this he was but playing the part of the dying and rising god Osiris in the salvation drama of the Isis cult.

It is superfluous to inquire just what tableaus were presented to the eyes of the initiate at this point or how the scenic effects were managed. A first-century imagina-

---

[1] Loisy, *Les Mystères païens*, pp. 151 ff.

tion, habituated to simple stage effects, and stimulated by fasting, meditation, and special suggestion, was capable of conjuring up very vivid pictures on a comparatively simple basis. This was particularly true in the case of a pious believer like Lucius, with an abundance of faith and a strong predilection for mystical experience. For him the rite of initiation, however managed, had as its central significance a real death to the old mortal life, and a resurrection to a new eternal life, dramatically represented as an Osirian journey to the regions infernal and celestial.

How complete the regeneration effected by initiation was believed to be is suggested by the rites that took place on the following morning.[1] At the conclusion of the usual morning office, Lucius was brought in "sanctified with twelve stoles." His vestments were of fine linen embroidered with flowers, and from his shoulders there hung down to the ground a precious cope, the "Olympian stole," covered with symbolical figures. In his hand a lighted torch was placed and on his head a garland of flowers "with white palm branches sprouting out on every side like rays." Thus clothed, Lucius took his stand on a pedestal in the middle of the temple before the statue of the goddess herself, and when the curtains were drawn aside and he was exposed to public view, the faithful contemplated him with the admiration and devotion due a god. This was essentially a rite of deification, and Lucius with his Olympian stole, his lighted torch, and his rayed crown was viewed as a personification of the sun-god. Even without his self-identification[2] one could easily have guessed it from the

---

[1] Apuleius *Metamorphoses* xi. 24.

[2] "Thus I was adorned like the sun and made in the fashion of an image" (*op. cit.* xi. 24.)

garments and emblems he wore, the rayed crown especially. He was now treated as Osiris-Ra, and his apotheosis
was a fitting climax to his experiences of the night before
when "at midnight he saw the sun brightly shine and saw
likewise the gods celestial and the gods infernal." Lucius
was now more than man. Hitherto he had been treated as
a human being. Now he was regarded as divine.

His initiation was brought to a close with a sumptuous
banquet "celebrating the nativity of his holy order." The
feast was a joyous one like a birthday banquet and, coming
at the conclusion of the initiation ceremonies, it served to
accentuate the fact that Isiac initiation was believed to
effect the complete regeneration of the candidate. If we
may take the initiation of Lucius as a representative Isiac
initiation of the early empire—and we are certainly justified in so doing—it is clear that from start to finish the
initiate was made to feel he was passing through an experience that would transform his very being and make a new
man of him. At the outset the priest characterized the
rites as a voluntary death and a recovery of health. He
assured Lucius specifically that Isis had the power to make
men new-born individuals (*quodam modo renatos*), and thus
to set their feet in the way of salvation. The rites themselves were cast in the form of a ritual death and a resurrection culminating in a celestial journey.[1] And finally a
birthday banquet marked the conclusion of the ceremonial.
Figuratively, the Isiac initiation was represented as a
process of regeneration and initiates were referred to as
men who had been reborn (*renati*). This was the regular
cult formula. Actually, the rites were believed to accom-
plish the transformation and divinization of human nature.

[1] *Op. cit.* xi. 21.

V

What were the main characteristics of the new life induced by this ritual regeneration? In the first place, it was a life of present security lived under the protection of a kindly mother goddess. To her devotees Isis assured long life and happiness here on earth. The goddess said to Lucius in a vision:

> You shall live blessed in this world, you shall live glorious by my guide and protection. And if I perceive that you are obedient to my commandment and addicted to my religion, meriting by your constant chastity my divine grace, know that I alone may prolong your days above the time that the fates have appointed and ordained.[1]

In order to know what assurance this sense of divine protection gave to the devotees of Isis, one needs only to read the pages of Apuleius or turn to Aristides' fervid encomium of Serapis. Lucius addressed his goddess as the "holy and perpetual preserver of the human race, always munificent in cherishing mortals."[2] Similarly, Aelius Aristides, writing after the experience of a shipwreck from which he was saved, as he believed, through the intervention of Serapis, spoke of his god as the one who "purifies the soul with wisdom, and preserves the body by giving it health," the one who "is adored by kings and private persons, by the wise as by the foolish, by the great as by the small, and by those on whom he has bestowed happiness as well as those who possess him alone as a refuge from their trouble."[3] The strong fervor of such devout religionists as these leaves no doubt that the experience of Isiac initiation gave real assurance to the devotees of the goddess as they faced the inevitable uncertainties of life.

For the future, initiation meant the certain hope of a happy immortality. Of Serapis the grateful Aristides declared that he was "the savior and leader of souls, leading

---

[1] *Op. cit.* xi. 6.　　[2] *Op. cit.* xi. 25.　　[3] Aristides *In Serapide* 89.

them to the light and receiving them again. . . . . We can never escape his sway, but he will save us and even after death we shall be the objects of his providence."[1] Apuleius, secure under the present protection of Isis, regarded the future also with equanimity. In his account of the vision which gave to Lucius promise of a happy life here on earth, the author represented Isis as saying to her devotee concerning the future, "When after your allotted space of life you descend to Hades, there you shall see me in that subterranean firmament shining (as you see me now) in the darkness of Ackeron, and reigning in the deep profundity of Styx, and you shall worship me as one who has been favorable to you."[2]

Again and again on tombs of Isiac initiates this hope of a blessed immortality was recorded. The expression *eupsuchei*, "be of good courage," was so often iterated as to become almost a motto of the Isiac religion. In figurative language, the craving for immortality was represented as a thirst for the refreshment of a drink of cold water—a natural metaphor for people living in a hot climate like that of Egypt. "May Osiris give you fresh water," was a typical prayer which members of the Isis cult inscribed on the tombs of their loved ones.[3] It is hardly necessary to multiply illustrations; for the most indubitable item of Isiac faith was this assurance of immortality. Reborn through the rite of initiation, the mystic believed himself born again to a superhuman life, the immortal life of the gods. Among the various assurances which the Alexandrian religion gave to seekers for salvation in the Roman world, this promise of immortality was most welcome.

[1] *Op. cit.* 93.

[2] Apuleius *Metamorphoses* xi. 6.

[3] Kaibel, *Inscriptiones Graecae* Vol. XIV, Nos. 1488, 1705, 1782, 1842; also *Corpus Inscriptionum Latinarum* Vol. VI, No. 20616.

BIBLIOGRAPHY

APULEIUS, *Metamorphoses*, or *The Golden Ass*. Translation by W. Adlington, "Loeb Classical Library." New York, 1915.

BOULAGE, T. P., *Les Mystères d'Isis et d'Osiris*. Paris, 1912.

BUDGE, E. A. T. W., *The Book of the Dead*. London, 1913.

BUDGE, E. A. T. W., *Osiris and the Egyptian Resurrection*. London, 1911.

BUREL, JOSEPH, *Isis et Isiaques sous l'Empire romain*. Paris, 1911.

CUMONT, FRANZ, *Oriental Religions in Roman Paganism* (Chicago, 1911), pp. 73-102.

DENNIS, JAMES TEACKLE. *The Burden of Isis*. London, 1910.

DILL, SAMUEL, *Roman Society from Nero to Marcus Aurelius* (London, 1920²), pp. 560-584.

FRAZER, J. G., *Adonis, Attis, Osiris* (London, 1922³), II, 1-218.

GRUPPE, OTTO, *Griechische Mythologie* (Munich, 1897-1906), pp. 1562-82.

DE JONG, K. H. E., *De Apuleio Isiacorum Mysteriorum teste*. Leiden, 1900.

LEGGE, F., *Forerunners and Rivals of Christianity* (Cambridge, 1915), I, 28-89.

LOISY, ALFRED, *Les Mystères païens et le Mystère chrétien*. Paris, 1921².

MORET, ALEXANDRE, *Rois et dieux d'Égypt*. Paris, 1911.

MORET, ALEXANDRE, *Mystères égyptiens*. Paris, 1913.

REISNER, GEORGE ANDREW, *The Egyptian Conception of Immortality*. London, 1912.

SCHÄFER, HEINRICH, *Die Mysterien des Osiris in Abydos unter König Sesostris III*. Leipzig, 1904.

TOUTAIN, JULES FRANCOIS, *Les cultes païens dans l'Empire romain* (Paris, 1907), Part I, II, 5-34.

WEBER, WILHELM, *Drei Untersuchungen zur ägyptischgriechischen Religion*, Heidelberg, 1911.

WISSOWA, GEORG, *Religion und Kultus der Römer* (Munich, 1912²), pp. 351-59.

CHAPTER VIII

THE NEW BIRTH EXPERIENCE
IN HERMETICISM

IN HELLENISTIC and Roman times Egypt was peculiarly productive of a distinctive variety of religious temperament, notably fervid in its emotionalism, markedly ascetic in its tendencies, and supremely desirous of the culminating experience of absorption into deity. During the Alexandrian period Egyptian mystics, acting under the charm of ancient religious tradition, asked for the privilege of initiation into the cult of Isis and sought in her ascetic discipline and in the impressiveness of her liturgies the satisfaction of their aspirations. Much later, when Christian emperors were ruling in the Mediterranean world, Egyptian mystics were more than likely to turn anchorite and to seek in the solitude of the desert the experience of oneness with the divine; or perhaps they would lose themselves as members of a Christian monastic community.. During the interim centuries, while pagan emperors ruled from Rome, Alexandria in Egypt was much under the spell of able and sincere religio-philosophical teachers, such as Ammonius Saccas and Plotinus and their predecessors. There flourished in the Egyptian metropolis at this period an eclectic Platonism that earlier was related to Neo-Pythagoreanism and later was developed as Neo-Platonism. During these centuries Egyptian mystics, particularly those who had intellectual interests, were likely to be found frequenting the lecture hall of some popular teacher or seeking the realization of their desires in the fellowship of a religio-philosophical brotherhood.

Of the earlier phases of this important religio-philo-sophical development there are few literary remains. The considerable Neo-Pythagorean literature has perished and the teachings of Ammonius Saccas, the founder of Neo-Platonism, were oral and esoteric. But there yet remains from these centuries the so-called Hermetic literature, writings in Greek and Latin attributed to Hermes Trismegistus and composed of ethical, religious, and philosophic instruction. Obviously, these writings are the remnants of what must have been a far more extensive body of religious literature. Even in the decimated state in which we know them, they give unmistakable evidence of having been produced at different times and in different communities during the early imperial period. As the scattered and scanty memoranda of a distinctive and more or less widespread religious quest in the Graeco-Roman world, these enigmatic writings are extremely interesting and valuable.

I

The *Corpus Hermeticum* proper, which is the important section of this literature, includes a collection of fourteen tractates popularly but mistakenly named "Poimandres" from the dominant first number of the series, together with three others grouped under the name of "Asclepius." These tractates comprehend a variety of literary types: dialogues, discourses, hymns, prayers, epistles, an apology, and a theophany. But with all this diversity of literary *schema* there is a certain unity about the *Corpus*. The writings generally profess to be revelations. On the one hand, they describe what one of the main characters, Hermes or Asclepius or Tat, has seen or learned from his divine father and teacher; on the other hand, a prophet of religion proclaims to men the revelations he has received through his experience with the deity. Viewed as a revelation literature, the Hermetic writings show more of unity than their diversity of literary form would lead one to expect.

As to the dates of this literature, the student is faced with an apparent contradiction; the Hermetic literary tradition was a very ancient one, yet the *Corpus* that we know is not definitely attested until comparatively late in Christian times. To Hermes, or Thoth,[1] as the "Lord of Divine words," native priests in Egypt ascribed the inspiration and authorship of their sacred books, which Greek writers denominated "Hermetic" in accordance with this native literary tradition. Plato, Strabo, and Iamblicus vouch for this literary fiction, while Clement of Alexandria and Tertullian, among early Christian writers, are witnesses to the same tradition.[2] It is not until the time of Lactantius (*ca.* A.D. 325), however, that we find references and quotations which can be verified by comparison with extant Hermetic works.[3] His appreciative references to "Hermes" prove the existence in the early years of the fourth century of certain surviving numbers of the *Corpus*, together with other tractates that are now lost. The tone of contemporary references proves that in Lactantius' day the Trismegistic writings had considerable vogue.[4] Thus, while the Hermetic literary fiction was pre-Christian and ancient, it was not until the end of the third Christian century that the tractates of our *Corpus* emerged into the clear light of literary history. Most of them were much older than this. Just how much older they were is the problem.

[1] On the equivalence of Hermes and Thoth see Cicero *De Deorum Natura* iii. 56.

[2] Plato *Phaedrus* 274C. Cf. *Philebus* 18B. Strabo xvii. 25. Iamblicus *De Mysteriis* i. 1; viii. 1. Clement of Alexandria *Stromateis* vi. 4. 35. Tertullian *Adversus Valentinianos* 15; *De Anima* ii. 33.

[3] Lactantius *Divinae Institutiones* i. 6; ii. 15; iv. 6–9, 13, 27; vii. 4, 9, 13, 18; also *De Ira Dei* 11.

[4] See especially Arnobius *Adversus Nationes* ii. 13.

In a comparative study of religious phenomena during the earliest Christian centuries, the question of the dating of these documents is one of considerable importance. If, for example, the Hermetic *Corpus* was a third-century product and recorded only post-Christian developments, one would hardly be justified to give it consideration in connection with the genesis of early Christianity. Unfortunately, critical opinion concerning the dating of these documents is still in a very chaotic state.[1] By far the most definite scheme of chronology is that outlined by Richard Reitzenstein in his *Poimandres* studies, where he definitely dates not only the collection as a whole but also the *Poimandres* as the earliest of the series.

For the dating of this tractate, Dr. Reitzenstein lays special stress on a striking literary parallelism between it and the *Shepherd* of Hermas.[2] At the beginning of *Poimandres* the situation and sequence of events are remarkably like those of the fifth vision of Hermas. In both instances a supernatural being appears as a shepherd to the future prophet and pledges to remain with him. On being challenged as to his identity, the "shepherd" transforms himself before the prophet's eyes and shows him a vision.[3] The parallel is an unusual one surely; and Dr. Reitzenstein argues that the transformation of the shepherd narrated by the Christian writer is meaningless unless

---

[1] To cite the widest divergence of judgment on the point: Sir Flinders Petrie considers many of the Hermetic documents as pre-Alexandrian and dates the *Corpus* as a whole between 500 and 200 B.C. St. George Stock, on the other hand, would confine the composition of the *Corpus* to the narrow limits between the Edict of Milan, A.D. 313, and the death of Lactantius in A.D. 330. Neither of these extreme views, however, can be assigned much weight. See Flinders Petrie, *Personal Religion in Egypt*, chapters iii and v; St. George Stock, art., "Hermes Trismegistus," in the *Encyclopaedia of Religion and Ethics*, VI, 628.

[2] Reitzenstein, *Poimandres*, pp. 11 ff.

[3] Compare Hermas *Visions* v with *Corpus Hermeticum* i. 1 ff.

a knowledge of the pagan *Poimandres* is presupposed on his part. He further notes the remarkable titular similarity between the two documents, the *Poimandres* (*Shepherd of Men*) of Hermes and the *Shepherd* of Hermas. On the basis of literary analogy, therefore, Dr. Reitzenstein argues for dating the first number of the Hermetic *Corpus* earlier than the *Shepherd* and at least as early as the end of the first century A.D.[1]

Granted the parallelisms emphasized, they fall just short of proving the direct literary dependence of the Christian apocalypse on the pagan writing. Contact with oral tradition, which was even more characteristic of Hermetism than of Christianity itself, would be sufficient to explain the peculiar literary phenomena in question. Under the circumstances, literary analogy furnishes an insecure basis for the chronological placement of *Poimandres*.

This uncertainty as to the precise time when Hermetic literature had its beginning raises the further question as to what date may be assigned to the final assembling of these documents. In answer to this question there is something like an agreement of opinion among scholars that the collection was brought together about the end of the third century A.D. It is hardly necessary to detail the reasons for this conviction, but two main points stand out. The representation of the sun as the demiurgic orderer of all things and as a charioteer wearing a rayed crown suggests a time when the Mithraic cult was at the peak of its influence.[2] Also, the elaborate "Encomium of Kings" presupposes a plurality of kings exercising joint authority un-

---

[1] An item of internal evidence in favor of the first century dating of *Poiman-dres* is the appearance in it of the myth of the divine man, the doctrine that the human race was descended from an original father fashioned like a heavenly man. This myth was current in first-century Egypt.

[2] *C. H.* xvi. 7.

der one supreme ruler.[1] This corresponds with the arrangement under Diocletian and his colleagues (*imp.* 285–305 A.D.). On the basis of these suggestions, Dr. Reitzenstein concludes that about the time of Diocletian's triumph in A.D. 302 an Egyptian priest made a compilation of eighteen sacred documents, our *Corpus Hermeticum*, intended to prove to the rulers of the Empire that there was nothing in his religion deserving of official suspicion, but that its teachings were calculated to foster loyalty to the Empire and its rulers.[2]

Whether or not the Reitzenstein chronology for the Hermetic *Corpus* is accepted in detail, the general period that he suggests covering the first three Christian centuries is a very reasonable one for the writing and assembling of this literature.[3] As yet a more probable period for the composition of these documents and their collection into a specific *Corpus* has not been suggested. For our purpose, which concerns the religious needs and experiences of people in the Graeco-Roman world, this very general dating is sufficient. Were our problem one of documentary relationships between the Christian and Hermetic literatures, it would be necessary to be much more specific in chronology and to date the various documents quite exactly—as scholarship is not prepared to do at present. Since, however, we are concerned with the altogether more vital problem of religious needs and their satisfaction, it suffices to know that in the first century A.D. there were people who thought and felt and desired as they are represented in the Hermetic writings.

Of this we may be assured. Whatever the date of the

[1] *C. H.* xviii.

[2] Reitzenstein, *Poimandres*, p. 207; also pp. 371–74.

[3] On the question of dates, note the sane and convenient summary in Scott, *Hermetica*, I. 8 ff.

writings, Hermetic religion itself was older. A religion is always experienced and lived before ever it is recorded. Back of every religious literature, antedating it by a longer or shorter period, is the religious living of men and women who seek for the satisfaction of vital needs and desires. This general principle aside, however, the Trismegistic literature as it stands bears on its face the marks of its composite and pre-Christian origins. Many of the component elements can be isolated and labeled and dated in a general way, and a majority of these are definitely known to have been pre-Christian. The whole synthesis gives the impression of being a development that had its beginnings in Hellenistic Egypt, some time before Christianity had its beginnings in Palestine to the north. Its mythology, its literary structure, its magic, and its naïve reverence for things Egyptian point in this direction, and the combination of these with Greek and Oriental elements is such a product as would come from that religious clearing house of the Hellenistic world, the Egypt of the Ptolemies. More precisely, the combination of Stoic physics and Platonic mysticism represented by the Hermetic literature existed in Alexandria at least as early as the philosopher Antiochus, or about 100 B.C. The literature itself must undoubtedly be dated considerably later; but even in its present form it falls securely within the first three centuries A.D.

II

It would be both interesting and useful in this connection to know exactly the component elements and their proportions as they were represented in the conglomerate product of Hermeticism, and by such an analysis to trace the beginnings of this movement back to ultimate sources. What were the various strands of influence that went into the weaving of this many-colored web? To answer this question accurately, the student must make himself at home in some dozen different thought-worlds. One would need to be thoroughly acquainted with the traditional religions of ancient Egypt, and the syncretistic religions of the Hellenistic world; with the confused astrology of the Orient and the clear philosophies of classical Greece; and above all with the religio-philosophical aggregates that were so highly important in the Hellenistic and Graeco-Roman periods, and are all but completely ignored by the purists of today. In an age of high specialization such as ours there are few scholars who have the versatility requisite for unraveling such a tangled skein as that of Hermeticism.

It is not surprising, therefore, to find a characteristic variety of opinion concerning the blend of elements found in this religion. While there is more or less agreement as to what constituent elements were involved, the scholars violently disagree concerning the proportion of the various elements and their assignment to primary or secondary place in the combination. Dr. Reitzenstein, for example, regards the fundamental strain to be Egyptian.[1] Zielinski, on the other hand, furnishes an antidote to this Egyptian prepossession by emphasizing the Hellenic and philosophical components of Hermeticism.[2] M. Cumont brings to the fore as well-nigh coimportant with these ingredients, a stress on the Semitic and Oriental contributions to the complex.[3]

The significant point emphasized by all this discussion

---

[1] Reitzenstein, *Poimandres*, pp. 59–116.

[2] Zielinski, art., "Hermes und die Hermetik" in *Archiv für Religionswissenschaft*, VIII (1905), 321–72, and IX (1906), 25–60.

[3] Cumont, *Oriental Religions in Roman Paganism*, pp. 88, 233 f. At the present time the question of possible Christian influence on Hermeticism has come to the fore. For variant views on this question see: Heinrici, *Die Hermes-Mystik und das neue Testament*, pp. 163 ff.; Windisch, art., "Urchristentum und Hermesmystik," in *Theologisch Tijdshrift*, LII (1918), 186–240. See especially pp. 191 f.

is that the religion of Hermes was a syncretism, and as such was characteristic of the period when Christianity came into being. The early imperial era, like the Hellenistic period that preceded it, was one of syncretism in religion as in most other departments of life. The Greek cults had become orientalized and the eastern cults had been Hellenized. In philosophy eclecticism was the order of the day, and even those who were nominal adherents of a particular school freely made use of ideas borrowed from other systems. Hermeticism itself was a syncretism quite typical of this general period, and doubly so because it represented an amalgamation of various philosophies with different religions. There was a substratum of religious experience, essentially mystical in character, that sought in these writings to give itself intellectual justification. A blend of ideas, Greek, Oriental, and Egyptian, philosophical, mythical, and magical, was elaborated and erected on this basis of mystical experience, to give the effect of a system of theology. To others it may be left to differentiate and classify and evaluate the various theoretic elements that compose the superstructure; our interest is in the basic item of personal religious experience.

What the student would like to know quite exactly about this religious experience is how to classify it as to type, and how significant an item it was in the religious life of the early imperial period. Was it primarily individual experience that is mirrored in these writings—or do they record the experiences of groups of individuals? To what extent was there a definite social movement back of the *Corpus?* How widespread and influential was that movement? Could it be classified as a cult? What, for example, was the relation of Hermetic religion to the mystery religions so popular during this period? These are some of the interrogations that arise as one studies the literature.

Again it is Dr. Reitzenstein who has assumed the most unequivocal position on this complex of problems. He maintains that this literature presupposes a definite religious movement with clergy and cult practice and various communities, that had its. beginnings in Hellenistic Egypt and lasted through the third Christian century. The first tractate of the series, according to his view, was the product of a peculiar "Pimandres" community, founded probably about the time of Jesus' birth. In the early part of the next century, its influence spread to Rome.[1] During the third century it lost its identity among the Hermetic communities generally, and finally in the fourth century the whole movement disappeared from view.[2]

Other scholars are inclined to take issue with Dr. Reitzenstein in his historical reconstruction. W. Kroll declares, "Least of all can I believe in communities of Poimandres, Nus, Anthropos, etc. at the time of the birth of Christ; and our writings are not to be considered liturgies of such communities; on the contrary their character is purely literary."[3] Indeed, it must be granted that external evidence is lacking to prove the existence of a Hermetic religion with clergy or cultus. Must we then grant the further possibility that Hermeticism had a purely literary existence and was at best but a sporadic and individualistic expression of religious aspiration?[4]

Internal evidence makes it clear that this was not the case. The character of the Hermetic documents themselves proves that Hermeticism was a real religion that had its social as well as its individual aspect. Public preachments

[1] This would explain the singular parallelism between *Poimandres* and *The Shepherd of Hermas*.

[2] Reitzenstein, *Poimandres*, p. 248.

[3] W. Kroll, art., "Hermes Trismegistos" in Pauly-Wissowa, *Real Encyclopädie*, VIII, 820.

[4] Cumont, *Les Religions Orientales*, p. 340, n. 41.

as well as private instruction went into the making of the *Corpus Hermeticum*, and even the most intimate of the dialogues were framed to include cult remains in the form of hymns and prayers. So the "Secret Discourse on the Mountain" includes the "Hymn of Rebirth" and the *Poimandres* revelation ends with a triple *ter-sanctus* to the Father God.[1] The prophet of *Poimandres*, when he had made a successful beginning of his evangelization, taught his followers how to give thanks to God at the time of the sun's setting.[2] Hermetism, too, had its baptism and the Trismegistic prophet, like John the Baptist, summoned men to "Repent and be baptized!"[3] These cult remains are so indigenous to this literature and are handled with such naïve sincerity that the student cannot regard them as literary fictions. It is a living religion that one is dealing with here. On the basis of these practices and the general representation of the *Corpus*, the student is justified in thinking of Hermetism as a definite religious movement proceeding from Hellenistic Egypt with communities gathered about prophetic leaders. How extensive its influence became in the Graeco-Roman period, who can tell?[4]

There is one addendum that should be made concerning cult practices in the religion of Hermes. While they were treated with reverence, they were allegorized and "spiritualized" and the emphasis was very little on rite and very much on personal religious experience. Trismegistic religion had its baptism, to be sure; but the important thing was not the physical rite, but the hyperphysical immersion in spirit that it entailed.[5] In the Asclepius there is a dra-

---

[1] *C. H.* xiii. 16; i. 31. Cf. v. 10 ff.

[2] *C. H.* i. 29. Cf. xiii. 16; also *Asclepius* xli. 1.   [3] *C. H.* iv. 4.

[4] On this point see Reitzenstein, *Poimandres*, pp. 160–90.

[5] *C. H.* iv. 4. *Nous* (lit. "mind") is the Hermetic equivalent of spirit and is thus rendered throughout this chapter.

matic illustration of this attitude toward ritual. Tat and Asclepius have just been receiving instruction from the Thrice-Greatest One himself.

Having come forth from the sanctuary, they began their prayers to God, looking towards the south; for when a man wishes to pray to God at sunset, he ought to face southward, as at sunrise he ought to face eastward. But when they had begun to pray, Asclepius whispered, "Tell me, Tat, shall we propose to your father that we should add to our prayer, as men are wont to do, an offering of incense and perfumes?" Trismegistus heard; and much disturbed, he said, "Hush, hush, Asclepius; it is the height of impiety to think of such a thing with regard to him who alone is good. Such gifts as these are unfit for him; for he is filled with all things that exist, and lacks nothing. Let us rather adore him with thanksgiving; for words of praise are the only offering that he accepts."[1]

Such was the typically inconsistent attitude of Hermetic religion toward liturgical performance. Prayers must be made in a certain way; but it were profanation to offer incense! Thus, while the external ceremonial features of Hermeticism should not be neglected, the chief concern of Trismegistic religionists was the cultivation of inward experience.

III

Did Hermeticism with its unusual emphasis on personal religion foster an experience of individual regeneration such as was prominent in the mystery cults in connection with their initiation ceremonies? Of this there can be no doubt. One of the most important tractates of the *Corpus*, the "Secret Discourse on the Mountain," is specifically and exclusively devoted to *palingenesia*, and the entire process of Hermetic rebirth is there described and enacted before the reader's imagination.[2] The characters of the dialogue are Hermes and his son Tat. The latter begins the colloquy by reminding his father that in his general discourses he

---

[1] *Asclepius* xli. 1 f.   [2] *C. H.* xiii.

has affirmed that no one could ever be saved without regeneration.[1] Tat had longed to learn the secret of rebirth
and his father had promised to share it with him when he
had become a stranger to the world. This, Tat protests,
he has already done and so he does not hesitate to ask his
father to fulfil the promise and communicate to him the
complete tradition of rebirth. Like the Nicodemus of the
Johannine dialogue, Tat puzzles in literalistic fashion as
to how a man can be born again—of what seed and from
what womb he comes to rebirth. Hermes replies that spiritual wisdom conceiving in silence is the womb, true good
the seed, and God himself the author of the act.[2] Thus
the reborn individual becomes a son of God endowed with
divine powers. Tat does not understand this and asks further explanation concerning the manner of rebirth. To this
demand Hermes rejoins:

What can I say, my son? . . . . I can tell you nothing but this; I see
that by God's mercy there has come to be in me a form which is not
fashioned out of matter, and I have passed out of myself, and entered
into an immortal body. I am not now the man I was; I have been born
again in spirit, and the bodily shape which was mine before has been
put away from me. I am no longer an object colored and tangible, a
thing of special dimensions; I am now alien to all this, and to all that
you perceive when you gaze with bodily eyesight. To such eyes as
yours, my son, I am not now visible.

As Tat listens to his father's discourse, he is seized with
ecstasy and seems to lose his reason. He finds himself confused and speechless and incapable of thought even. At
last he asks, with genuine anxiety, if it is impossible for
him to realize this spiritual good. Without hesitation
Hermes reassures him on this point. "Heaven forbid, my
son. Draw it into you and it will come; will it, and it comes
to be. Stop the working of your bodily senses, and then
will deity be born in you. But if you would be born again,

---

[1] Cf. John 3: 3, 5.   [2] Cf. I Peter 1:22 f.; I John 4:7 and 5:1.

you must cleanse yourself from the irrational torments of matter."

The reference to material torments prompts Tat to question as to what they are. In reply Hermes enumerates twelve evil propensities which are bound up with man's physical nature. They are ignorance, grief, intemperance, sensuality, injustice, avarice, folly, envy, deceit, anger, rashness, and malice. In the picturesque language of Hermes, these evil propensities and many more of the same tribe creep through the prison house of man's body and, like torturers, torment the prisoner who is there confined. Hermes concludes:

But when God has had mercy on a man, they depart from him together, one and all; and then is reason built up in him. Such is the manner of the rebirth.

And now, my son, speak not but keep solemn silence; so will the mercy come down on us from God.

In the pause that follows, the silence is broken only by the voice of Hermes calling upon the ten "Powers of God," virtues all, to come and possess Tat, driving out the evil inclinations of the flesh: knowledge of God to replace ignorance, joy instead of sorrow, self-control in place of intemperance, continence where sensuality was, righteousness in lieu of injustice, generosity to drive avarice away, truth instead of error, and the more abstract qualities of goodness, life, and light to take the place of all the other brutish torments. The invocation of Hermes is an efficacious rite whereby his disciple is enabled to realize the desired change in immediate experience.

No longer has there come upon us any of the torments of darkness; they have flown away with rushing wings. Thus, my son, has the spiritual being been made up in us; and by its coming to be we have been made gods. Whoever, then, has by God's mercy attained to this divine birth, abandons bodily sense; he knows himself to be composed of powers of God, and knowing this is glad.

True to the word, Tat's first reaction to all this is ecstatic: "Father, God has made me a new being, and I perceive things now not with bodily eyesight, but by the working of the spirit." Thus freed from the limitations of sense, Tat feels himself completely at one with the universe. "I am in heaven," he exclaims, "in earth, in water and in air. I am in beasts and plants. . . . . I am present everywhere!" Then, as his ardor cools somewhat, Tat pauses to ask about his transformed being. "Tell me, Father, will this body which is composed of divine Powers ever suffer dissolution?"

To this interrogation Hermes quickly answers:

Hush! Speak not of a thing that cannot be; it would be impious to say that. Has the eye of your spirit been blinded? The physical body which is an object of sense differs widely from that other body which is of the nature of true being. The one is dissoluble, the other is indissoluble. The one is mortal, the other is immortal. Do you not know you have become a god, and son of the One, even as I have?

As yet Tat's eagerness is not fully satisfied and he asks to be taught the "Hymn of Rebirth" which is known only to those who have experienced regeneration. With specific directions as to how the hymn is to be uttered at the time of sunset Hermes imparts to him the secret ode. Even with this esoteric information the eager neophyte is not completely satisfied. He must sing his own song of praise, and like Epictetus he will not be restrained from doing so. This, then, is Tat's own song of regeneration:

O thou first author of the work by which the rebirth has been wrought in me. To thee, O God, do I, Tat, bring offerings of speech. O God, thou art the father; O Lord, thou art the spirit. From me accept such praises as thou willest. For by thy will it is that all is accomplished for me.[1]

At this point the dialogue closes with an expression of gratification on the part of Hermes that his instruction has

[1] *C. H.* xiii. 21.

come to deathless fruition in the regeneration of Tat. He further charges his disciples to keep the tradition of the rebirth a secret, that it may not be defiled by calumniators.

IV

From this ordered account of the regeneration of Tat, together with casual references in other tractates of the *Corpus*, it is possible to reconstruct the various steps in the process of rebirth as the disciple of the Thrice-Greatest Hermes realized them in sequence. They may be enumerated thus:

1. THE CALL TO REPENTANCE

This was the prophet's part in the process. It consisted of a preliminary proclamation of the Hermetic gospel and it might be either public or private. Trismegistic religion had its prophetic tradition of public preaching as well as its esoteric tradition of private instruction. It may fairly be questioned as to whether the two are consonant or represent entirely different streams of development. Nevertheless, in the Hermetic *Corpus* as we know it both phases are found, and some memorable examples of prophetic preaching are quoted directly.

The visionist of *Poimandres* after he had been shown man's destiny by the Shepherd began to preach to others the beauty of piety and gnosis.[1] The content of his message was as follows:

O people, men born of earth, who have given yourselves up to drunkenness and sleep in your ignorance of God; awake to soberness, cease to be sodden with strong drink and lulled in sleep devoid of reason. . . . . O men, why have you given yourselves up to death, when you have been granted power to partake of immortality? Repent, you who have journeyed with error, and joined company with ignorance; rid yourselves of darkness, and lay hold on light; partake of immortality, forsaking corruption.

[1] *C. H.* i. 27 f.

Entirely similar in content, though even more vigorous and picturesque in language, is the sermon which comprises a whole tractate, the seventh in our *Corpus*. Here, in order to enforce his sermon the preacher makes free use of figures suggested by life in wineshops and seaports and also the contrasted pictures of the tombs of the dead and the dwellings of the living.[1] It was in response to such a general proclamation of the Hermetic gospel as this one wherein the assertion had been made that no one could be saved without rebirth, that Tat sought to learn from his Father the secret of the process.[2]

2. INTIMATE INSTRUCTION

The second step in the process, private instruction under the tutelage of a "Father," was far more characteristic of Trismegistic religion than the work of evangelization just noted. This step is represented by the greater number of Hermetic documents that remain today, most of them being dialogues between Hermes and Tat or Asclepius. In all of these there are two characters only; and even in the *Asclepius*, where, according to the account, Tat and Ammon were admitted to the conversation, they did not assume speaking rôles, but merely listened to the dialogue.[3] At this stage of the process the seeker became the disciple and was allowed to ask questions, but further than this he did not participate. If one judges from the recorded dialogues, the "Father's" answers were sometimes confusing rather than specifically informing, and on the whole were intended to stimulate the disciple's emotions rather than satisfy his intellect. Thus the dialogue took the place, in a general way, of the initiatory rites of the mysteries, which were designed, as Aristotle said, not to instruct but to put one in a proper frame of mind. And yet, throughout the

[1] *C. H.* vii.   [2] *C. H.* xiii. 1.   [3] *Asclepius* i.

dialogues of the Hermetic *Corpus* a show is made of rationalization—or one should rather say, an attempt at
intellectualization especially along philosophical lines more
or less familiar to the Graeco-Roman world.

3. THE DISCIPLE'S SELF-PREPARATION

The disciple, however, was not expected to be wholly
passive and receptive in the process. There were important matters of mental and moral preparation and purification for which he alone was held responsible. On the
one hand he was expected to train himself to regard the
things of sense as illusory. Hermes informed Tat that he
could not communicate to him the secret of rebirth until
he had become an alien to the phenomenal world. So Tat
made it a primary item in his personal preparation to teach
his thought to be a stranger to the illusion of the world.[1]

On the other hand an ascetic as well as a mental discipline was prescribed and the seeker was expected to purify
himself from fleshly appetites and sensual passions. "Hate
your body," was the Hermetic demand; and when Tat expressed to his "Father" the desire to be baptized, Hermes
replied, "If you do not first hate your body, my son, you
cannot love yourself. But if you love yourself you will have
spirit."[2] This was the chief burden of the Hermetic prophet's message—to persuade men to cease from intoxication
of sensation that ends in sensuality.[3] This was, once more,
the point of Hermes' urgency when he told his son Tat to
"cleanse himself from the irrational torments of matter."[4]

In all this, great stress was placed on the exercise of the
individual's own will-power. When Tat was fearful lest he
should not be able to attain the desired good, Hermes said
to him, "Will it, and it comes to be. Stop the working of

[1] *C. H.* xiii. 1.   [3] *C. H.* i. 27; also vii. 1 ff.
[2] *C. H.* iv. 6.   [4] *C. H.* xiii. 7 ff.

your bodily senses, and then will deity be born in you."[1] An absolute choice was presented to the disciple, between the temporal and the eternal, and the choosing was left to him. Hermes said:

> It is not possible, my son, to attach yourself both to things mortal and to things divine. There are two sorts of things, the corporeal and the incorporeal; that which is mortal is of one sort, and that which is divine is the other sort; and he who wills to make his choice is left free to choose the one or the other.[2]

From reading certain sections in Trismegistic treatises, one might get the impression that this religion regarded the human will as all powerful and that all a man had to do was to will to be reborn and he would become so.[3] But the Hermeticist did not conceive the process thus simply. Rebirth in this religion, like that in the New Testament, was a birth from above dependent finally on God's will, not man's. He who was reborn was first begotten of God.[4]

4. SILENT MEDITATION

It was a distinctive feature of Hermetic rebirth that it was usually realized in religious meditation either in solitude or at most in the company of one's "Father." The prophet of *Poimandres* thus described his own state when there came to him the vision that made him a prophet: "Once on a time, when I had begun to think about the things that are, and my thoughts had soared high aloft, while my bodily senses had been put under restraint by sleep,—yet not such sleep as that of men weighed down by fulness of food or by bodily weariness."[5] While he was in this condition, the theophany occurred, followed by the vision of creation. Reviewing the experience, he wrote of

---

[1] *Loc. cit.*   [2] *C. H.* iv. 6 f.   [3] See especially *C. H.* xi. 20.
[4] *C. H.* xiii. 2. Compare John 3:3; I John 4:7; 5:1, and Peter 1:3, 23.
[5] *C. H.* i. 1.

it afterward, "My bodily sleep had come to be sober wakefulness of soul; and the closing of my eyes true vision; and my silence pregnant with good; and my barrenness of speech, a brood of holy thoughts."[1] In his case, apparently, meditation ended in downright sleep and the vision was a dream!

Silence on the part of the subject was considered essential for the realization of rebirth. "Then only will you see the vision, when you cannot speak of it," said Hermes to Tat, "for the knowledge of it is deep silence, and suppression of all the senses."[2] There is something almost magical about the way silence figured in the Hermetic process of regeneration. It will be recalled that this was the final caution of Hermes to his son before the latter realized the experience of rebirth. "Speak not, but keep solemn silence; so will the mercy come down on us from God."[3] Silence was a *sine qua non* in the Hermetic process.

5. ECSTASY

What was the outcome in experience of all this hushed stage setting? In a word it was ecstasy, partly self-induced, partly the reaction from the "Father's" discourse. There was real agony of spirit in Tat's incoherent speech, uttered under the stress of emotion aroused by Hermes' words:

Father, you have driven me to raving madness. . . . . You have reduced me to speechless amazement. . . . . I must indeed have gone mad, father; I have lost the wits I had. I thought your teaching had made me wise, but when you put this thought before me, my senses are stopped up."[4]

But in the recorded experience these disquieting emotions, due to a perfectly natural mental confusion, ended finally in an ecstasy of very different order, an exalted sense of

[1] *C. H.* i. 30.
[2] *C. H.* x. 5.
[3] *C. H.* xiii. 8.
[4] *C. H.* xiii. 4 ff.

harmony with the universe, so that Tat could exclaim that
he felt himself in heaven, on earth, in water, and everywhere![1] This was a carefully cultivated emotionalism, to
be sure; yet it was emotionalism of a refined sort. There
was nothing crudely physical about it, nor did it tend to
harmful excess. It was a highly attenuated mental emotionalism induced by meditation and quiet conversation.

It was typical of Hermeticism that this ecstasy, like
Paul's Damascus experience, was spoken of in terms of
vision and described as a glowing light. Thus Hermes,
when pressed by Tat's eager questioning, characterized his
own experience. He had seen a simple vision, mercifully
sent to him by God himself. It was a thing that could not
be taught and could not be seen with the natural eye—yet
it had accomplished his spiritual birth.[2] It was a vision,
he declared in another passage, which flooded a man's
mental horizon up to the limit of his ability to apprehend
it, but not beyond. It did not, like the sun, blind the eyes
with firelike blaze, but it did hold the mind enthralled, so
that he who perceived it was conscious of nothing else.[3]
Such was the limitless vision that surprised the *Poimandres*
prophet—a vision of light, "sweet and joyous." When he
expressed a desire to know the meaning of it all, he was
told by the Shepherd of Men, "That light am I, even
Spirit, the first God. . . . . Now fix your thought upon the
light and learn to know it."[4] One may conclude, therefore,
that a photism, conceived as a theophany, was a usual
feature of Hermetic ecstasy.

6. THE INTERPRETATION OF THIS EXPERIENCE

It is exceedingly important to know how the followers
of Trismegistic tradition interpreted this overflow of emo-

[1] *C. H.* xiii. 11.　　　[3] *C. H.* x. 4 ff.

[2] *C. H.* xiii. 3.　　　[4] *C. H.* i. 4–6.

tion. What central significance did it have for them? Nothing was more central than this. It meant a special spiritual endowment that added a new element to man's very being. In Hermetic terminology this new element was *nous*, the spirit of Trismegistic religion. The natural man had no share in spirit, which was a special divine gift that God had willed to set up among men as a prize.[1] The spirit, as Hermes said plainly to Tat, was the very essence of God himself, inseparable from his being and inherent in it as light is in the sun.[2] The figure was an inevitable one, for in certain Hermetic circles, at least, the sun itself was viewed as the reservoir of this spiritual essence, the container of its substance, whence it flowed to men in a mysterious manner. And so, in the ecstasy of a vision experience, when the human soul seemed bathed and flooded with light, it was but this ethereal light-substance flowing into man's being from its heavenly source and transforming him into divine essence.[3] It was said of this light-substance as of the spiritual air-substance in the Fourth Gospel, "No one knows whence it comes or whither it goes."[4]

This spiritual endowment Hermetic thought connected also with the rite of baptism. In a unique dialogue, the fourth, Hermes narrated to Tat how God had taken a huge bowl, filled it with spirit and sent it down to men, entrusting it to a messenger, who was commanded to preach thus to mankind: "Hearken, each human heart; dip yourself in this basin if you can, recognizing for what purpose you have been made, and believing that you shall ascend to him who sent the basin down." Some, according to the narration, did not heed the message and chose rather to remain in their ignorance. Others gave heed, baptized

[1] *C. H.* iv. 3.
[2] *C. H.* xii. 1.
[3] *C. H.* x. 6.
[4] *C. H.* xvi. 6. Compare John 3:8.

themselves in spirit, and so became initiates to Hermeticism.[1] In this realistic fashion the disciple of Hermes, like the early Christian, came to a realization of his spiritual birth, through the rite of baptism.

The endowment with spirit brought with it, also, a special mental equipment called "gnosis" which, according to the Hermetic scheme, was prerequisite to salvation. "And this alone, even the knowledge (*gnosis*) of God, is man's salvation," declared Hermes, "this is the ascent to Olympus; and by this alone can a soul become good."[2] The very first event mentioned in Tat's regeneration was the driving out of ignorance by the *gnosis* of God.[3] Such knowledge was not the result of sense-perception and reason. It stood in contrast to them.[4] Rather it was a special mental enlightenment, the gift of God, which freed men from the illusions of sense and gave them insight into reality and the purpose of existence. In this way the Hermeticist interpreted the mental emotionalism of his religious experience: as endowment with spirit and equipment with *gnosis*.

7. THE RESULTS OF HERMETIC REGENERATION

There were two important consequences that were believed to proceed from this spiritual rebirth. One related to the present and the other chiefly to the future. One was a matter of morals and the other was a metaphysical affair.

In the first place Hermetic rebirth meant the moral purification of the individual. He was reborn ethically as well as essentially. In the account of Tat's regeneration, this was represented as the conquest of a horde of vices by an all but equal number of virtues.[5] Elsewhere the same

[1] *C. H.* iv. 4.
[2] *C. H.* x. 15.
[3] *C. H.* xiii. 8.
[4] *C. H.* x. 9.
[5] *C. H.* xiii. 7 ff.

process was figured more positively as seeds of good, sown by God, coming to great and fair fruitage in "virtue, self-control, and piety."[1] In the moral life of the regenerate, the spirit was given a notable rôle to play, as the physician of the soul. Hermes said to Tat:

> As a good physician inflicts pain on the body, burning or cutting it, when disease has taken possession of it, even so the spirit inflicts pain on the soul, ridding it of pleasure from which spring all the soul's diseases, and godlessness is a great disease of the soul; for the beliefs of the godless bring in their train all kinds of evils and nothing that is good. Clearly then, spirit, inasmuch as it counteracts this disease, confers good on the soul, just as the physician confers health on the body."[2]

According to the Hermetic view, those who had no share in this divine endowment centered all their thoughts on the pleasures of the body and its appetites, in the belief that for its sake men came into being.[3] They became wicked and depraved, envious and covetous, murderous and impious. To them an avenging demon was always present, ever adding torment to insatiable desire.[4] But to the holy and good, the pure and merciful who lived piously, the spirit was ever present to help them win the Father's love by their upright lives.[5] The disciple of Hermes said of his *nous* as the disciple of Paul would have said of his *pneuma*, "a man can escape from wickedness if he has the spirit in him."[6]

On its metaphysical side Hermetic rebirth involved nothing less than deification. "This is the good; this is the consummation for those who have got *gnosis*—they enter into God,"[7] was the last word of the Shepherd of Men to his prophet before giving him his commission. Hermeticism emphatically maintained that it was perfectly possi-

---

[1] *C. H.* ix. 4. Compare Paul's "Fruits of the Spirit," Gal. 5:22.

[2] *C. H.* xii. 3.   [5] *C. H.* i. 22.

[3] *C. H.* iv. 5.   [6] *C. H.* xii. 7.

[4] *C. H.* i. 23.   [7] *C. H.* i. 26.

ble for man, even while residing in the human body, to become deified.[1] With this exalted thought of possibilities within human reach, the Hermetic thinker was almost inclined to respect man more highly than the gods. While none of the gods left their heavenly spheres to come down to earth, man, without leaving earth, could ascend to heaven and make himself divine—such was the power of his ecstasy. "We must not shrink from saying," Hermes concluded, "that a man on earth is a mortal god, and that a god in heaven is an immortal man."[2]

So far as the future was concerned, divinization meant immortality also. When the transformation of man's essence was complete by the process of regeneration, then he had a body that death could not touch or harm. "The natural body can be dissolved, the spiritual body cannot be" was as much a conviction of Hermes as of Paul, and the disciple of the former confidently expected that when he should depart from his earthly body, he would "be brought into the troop of the gods and the souls that have attained bliss."[3]

Altogether the rebirth experience of Trismegistic religion was a well-ordered process with clearly defined steps. There were certain preliminary items for which the leaders of the Hermetic movement were responsible—the Prophet's call to repentance and the Father's personal words of instruction. There were other items of psychological self-preparation for which the seeker and he alone was responsible—a profound distrust of sense-perception, a rigorous control of physical appetites, and a willingness to wait in quiet, silent meditation for the inflow of divine grace. The rebirth experience itself was in inward ecstasy characterized by all but complete disregard of external sensations, with heed given only to the weighty words of

[1] *C. H.* x. 6, 9. [2] *C. H.* x. 25. [3] *C. H.* xii. 12.

the Father. There was mental confusion followed by a sense of exaltation, chaos ending in clarification, and not infrequently a vision experience described as a wonderful light. The interpretation of it all was that man, in this supreme moment of ecstasy, was endowed with spirit, a deific light-substance, and equipped with *gnosis*, a divinely given mental illumination absolutely essential to salvation. As a result of this rebirth, the individual felt himself possessed of such divine power that he could live an upright moral life, and could face the future assured of immortality —a deified mortal while yet on earth.

V

One further question should be raised, whether the *palingenesia* of Hermeticism has significance per se only, or whether it may not have special importance in relation to general religious trends among Gentiles in the first-century world. When the Hermetic movement is viewed in relation to contemporary tendencies, it is found to have been exactly in line with certain other important movements of the period. The general *Weltanschauung* of the Graeco-Roman world was a religio-philosophical one, and there was a distinct tendency both on the part of religions and philosophies to approach each other.

On the one hand, the religions of the time, those that survived with any vigor the successive Macedonian and Roman conquests, were seeking intellectual justification for their cult practices and were endeavoring to rationalize their emotionalism. To recall a single and notable instance already cited, Plutarch, in his treatise on Isis and Osiris, tried to harmonize his religious and his philosophical heritages and to interpret the Egyptian cult in a manner that would appeal to a Greek-thinking world. A little earlier Philo, in his Alexandrian environment, made a voluminous effort to reinterpret the intractable religion of his fathers in a way to satisfy the contemporary demand for intellectual criticism and for mystical experience—both at the same time. Long before the period represented by the Hermetic *Corpus*, the crude physical emotionalism of the Dionysian brotherhoods had been restrained and reformed into the asceticism of the Orphic movement with its very elaborate theology. In Hellenistic times Oriental mysticism began to coalesce into pre-Christian Gnosticism with its elaborate speculations built on a *fundamentum* of mystical religious experience. Indeed, from one point of view Hermeticism itself took its place as a particular type of Gnosticism, originating in Egypt. Like the popular cults of the period it encouraged the emotional type of religious experience; but it refined its emotionalism and made it mental rather than physical. Like the popular cults also it had its rites; but they were reduced to a minimum and "spiritualized" as much as possible. As a religion Hermeticism went far in the direction of a philosophy.

On the other hand the contemporary philosophical movements were making distinct approaches toward religion and were giving scope, as never before, to the exercise of emotion in the quest for truth. The religious revival of the time of Augustus had its effect in the field of philosophy,[1] and those systems which yielded least to the popular demand for supernatural guaranties and emotional satisfactions were swept aside as unsatisfying. Epicureanism, the religion of the scientific-minded, yielded little and gained few adherents of note after Lucretius. Stoicism made greater compromise. Seneca and Epictetus clothed their moral and philosophical teachings in religious terms and gave them religious sanctions. Taught by the Syrian

[1] Benn, *The Greek Philosophers* (1914), chap. xiii, "The Religious Revival," pp. 474–522.

Posidonius, the Stoa had already become eclectic and had made place for astrology and mysticism and other characteristic features of oriental religion. In the first century A.D., probably at Alexandria, Pythagoreanism reappeared as a religious philosophy and made its way to Rome, where it enjoyed a temporary alliance with converted Stoicism.[1] A little later Platonism, rejuvenated but transformed almost beyond recognition, was to appear under the name of Neo-Platonism and dominate the Roman world as the great mystical philosophy of the third century.

In such a thought-world as this, the religion of Hermes held its place somewhere between cult and philosophy, at the point where these two strong tides flowing in opposite directions met and became one. Its thought content was an eclectic conglomerate, but completely infused with the religious spirit, and its feeling content was of an intellectualized variety. Thus the rebirth of Hermeticism, important per se, is even more significant as an example of the type of mystical experience encouraged by the religio-philosophical movements of the Roman world.

BIBLIOGRAPHY

CREED, J. M., art., "The Hermetic Writings" in *Journal of Theological Studies* (Oxford, 1914), XV, 513–38.

GRANGER, FRANK, art., "The Poemandres of Hermes Trismegistus," in *Journal of Theological Studies* (Oxford, 1904), V, 395–412.

HEINRICI, C. F. G., *Die Hermes-mystik und das Neue Testament.* Leipzig, 1918.

KENNEDY, H. A. A., *St. Paul and the Mystery Religions* (New York, 1913), pp. 104–14.

KREBS, ENGELBERT, *Der Logos als Heiland im Ersten Jahrhundert* (Freiburg, 1910), pp. 119 ff.

KROLL, J., *Die Lehren des Hermes Trismegistos.* Munster, 1928².

KROLL, W., art., "Hermes Trismegistos" in Pauly-Wissowa's *Real Encyclopadie* (Stuttgart, 1913), VIII, 791–823.

---

[1] Zeller, *Die Philosophie der Griechen*, Part III, Div. II, pp. 79–158.

MEAD, G. R. S., *Thrice Greatest Hermes*. London, 1906.

MÉNARD, LOUIS, *Hermes Trismegiste*. Paris, 1866.

PARTHEY, GUSTAVUS, *Hermetis Trismegisti Poemander*. Berlin, 1854.

PETRIE, W. M. FLINDERS, *Personal Religion in Egypt Before Christianity* (New York, 1909), chaps. iii and v.

REITZENSTEIN, R., *Poimandres*. Leipzig, 1904.

SCOTT, WALTER, *Hermetica*. Oxford, 1924–26.

STOCK, ST. GEORGE, art., "Hermes Trismegistus" in Hasting's *Encyclopedia of Religion and Ethics* (New York, 1914), VI, 626 ff.

WINDISCH, D. HANS, art., "Hermes und Hermes-mystik" in *Theologisch Tijdschrift* (Leiden, 1918), LII, 186–240.

ZELLER, E., *Philosophie der Griechen* (1903⁴), Part III, Div. II, pp. 242–54.

ZIELINSKI, art., "Hermes und die Hermetik" in *Archiv für Religionswissenschaft* (Leipzig, 1905–6), VIII, 321–72; IX, 25–60.

CHAPTER IX

THE MYSTICISM OF PHILO

TWO religions of Egyptian origin have already been investigated: the cult of Isis and the garbled philosophy of "Hermes Trismegistus." Both were typical gentile systems, characteristic products of Hellenistic syncretism. Each cultivated its own peculiar type of individual regeneration: the Isiac a realistic, emotional experience conditioned by the proper performance of cult rites, and the Hermetic a subjective, intellectualized experience all but completely divorced from ceremonialism. At the beginning of the Christian era, there was a third Egyptian syncretism which was characterized by a mysticism peculiarly its own, yet resembling in important ways the other types of mystical experience current in Alexandria. This, strange to say, was a Jewish syncretism—the religion of Philo the philosopher, the great Jewish contemporary of Jesus and Paul.

I

There is no man of Paul's period more important for an understanding of the Christian Apostle or of Hellenistic Christianity than is Philo of Alexandria. Even the casual student of the times cannot but be impressed by certain outstanding similarities between the environments and experiences of Philo and Paul. Both were Jews of the Diaspora, and each was reared in one of the great centers of Graeco-Oriental civilization; for Alexandria, even more markedly than Tarsus, was a focal point for Hellenistic culture with its characteristic blend of elements oriental and occidental. Reared in similar environments each at-

tained a certain prominence in his own racial group. For
Paul it was an early attainment when, as a young rabbinical student of favored family, he "outstripped many of his
own age and race in his special ardor for the traditions of
his fathers,"[1] and became the zealous defender of Jewish
orthodoxy against Hellenizing Messianists. As for Philo,
being related to the Alabarch Alexander,[2] he was a member
of one of the "best families" in the Alexandrian Jewish community. This fact is fixed whether or not the assertion of
Jerome that he was of priestly race is credited.[3] That Philo
himself, at least in his later years, rose to a position of influence on his own account is shown by the fact that when he
was of advanced age he headed the Jewish embassy to the
Emperor Caligula in A.D. 40.[4] Thus Philo, like Paul,
crowned his career with a journey to the imperial city, the
Alexandrian as head of a delegation of protesting provincials, and the Tarsian as a propagandist on trial for his
life.

Not only were Philo and Paul both Jews of the Diaspora prominent among their fellow-countrymen but they
were also both thoroughly *en rapport* with the gentile life
of the times. This their own writings certify even in matters of vocabulary and style. Paul wrote good Hellenistic
Greek in a manner suggestive alike of the informal letter-
writing of the period and of the fervent exhortations of
popular street preachers. Philo, on the other hand, formed
his diction according to that of Greek classical authors, the
influence of Plato being particularly notable.[5] He was familiar with the writings of the great Greek poets also,
Homer and Euripides and the others, and on occasion he

[1] Gal. 1:14.

[2] Josephus *Antiquities* xviii. 8. 1.　　[4] Philo *Legatio ad Caium*.

[3] Jerome *De viris illustribus* 11.　　[5] Siegfried, *Philo von Alexandria*, p. 32.

quoted from them.[1] He was acquainted with the works of
Phidias and mentioned them in no uncomplimentary manner[2]—a remarkable thing for a Jew to do. To the varied
play of contemporary gentile life he was also responsive.
Like Paul he was well acquainted with the athletic festivals
of the Graeco-Roman world, and had a detailed familiarity
with the rules of the games and the habits of competitors.[3]
Also he possessed extensive knowledge of the ordinary cur-
riculum of gentile education and discussed it with real insight.[4] The art of music and the practice of medicine commanded his attention.[5] Furthermore, he made extensive
observations and pronouncements on political and social
problems, thus displaying a keen interest in these important phases of the secular life.[6] Because he, a prominent
Jew of the Diaspora, was thus open to gentile influences,
the study of his religious experience is especially significant
in relation to the experiences of Hellenists generally.

Another reason why Philo is particularly important for
a study of religious developments in first-century life is
because his writings, like the Hermetic literature, represent
a blend of philosophy and religion such as was characteristic of the age. Here there is contrast between Philo and
Paul. The latter was consciously scornful of gentile philosophies. For the classical systems of Hellas he had little
use, and it was to Stoicism chiefly that he was responsive.

[1] Grossmann, *Quaestiones Philoneae*, p. 5, lists the Greek classics quoted by
Philo. Cf. Siegfried, *Philo*, pp. 137 ff.

[2] *De Ebrietate* 89 ff. The references to Philo's works in this chapter follow
the enumeration of the Cohn and Wendland edition.

[3] *De Agricultura* 111 ff.; *De Cherubim* 81 ff.

[4] *De Ebrietate* 49 ff. *De Congressu Eruditionis* 15 ff.; *De Somniis* i. 205.

[5] On music see *De Posteritate Caini* 105 ff.; *De Cherubim* 110. On medicine
see *Quod Deus sit immutabilis* 65 f.

[6] *De Josepho* 32 ff.; *De Fuga* 28 ff.; *De Somniis* i. 48 ff.

Philo, on the other hand, had a hearty admiration for the philosophy of the Greeks. Among gentile authors the philosophers were the ones whom he most highly esteemed. Parmenides, Empedocles, Zeno, and Cleanthes seemed to him divine men and members of a sacred company. But he showed the greatest fondness of all for Plato "the great" and "the most sacred,"[1] and probably he would have declared himself to be more indebted to Plato than to any other thinker of Greece. Certainly his own system, if we may thus characterize it, bore many of the characteristic marks of Platonism. His prejudice in favor of this classical philosophy was generally recognized in early times and gave rise to the proverb, "Either Plato philonizes or Philo platonizes."[2]

Notwithstanding this predilection, however, Philo borrowed freely from other systems as well wherever he found elements that were useful to himself. Pythagorean tradition was particularly attractive to him. He spoke of this school with veneration[3] and was himself characterized as a Pythagorean by Clement, of his own city.[4] But he was at least equally indebted to Stoicism, and recent writers have tended to emphasize his affinities in this direction. On the philosophical side, Philo presents a notable example of the eclectic tendencies of the time, and one reason why it is so difficult to reduce his thinking to a definite system is because of its syncretistic character.

In spite of his appreciation of Greek philosophy, Philo yet remained at heart a religionist consciously loyal to the

[1] *Quod omnis probus liber* 13.

[2] Jerome *De Viris illustribus* 11; Photius *Bibliotheca* 105.

[3] *Quod omnis probus liber* 2.

[4] Clement of Alexandria *Stromateis* i. 15. 72; ii. 19. 100. Cf. Eusebius, *Historia Ecclesiastica* ii. 4. 3, who emphasized both the Platonism and Pythagoreanism of Philo.

practices of his fathers. It was not one of the thinkers of
Greece but Moses himself who was the greatest of law-
givers and philosophers, he believed. The fundamental assumption on which his whole elaborate and disparate system was based was the absolute authority of the Mosaic
Law. In the Torah he found the perfect and supreme revelation of the divine wisdom. Each word in it was written
by Moses at specific, divine dictation, or at least under the
direct inspiration of God.[1] While the Pentateuch stood on a
solitary level above all the other sacred writings, Philo regarded the prophets also as interpreters of God, who made
use of them in revealing his will to men. This Jew of the
Diaspora, living at a considerable distance from the Jerusalem center of his religion, still found himself in sympathy
with the teachings of the prophets and maintained an in-
tense loyalty to the Law.

With his admiration for Greek philosophy and his loyalty to his own religion, Philo found himself in a dilemma.
He was unwilling to yield either the philosophy or the religion; so he sought to reconcile them. In this attempt he
was but trying to do what other thoughtful men of his own
race in the same environment had endeavored to do before
him. Over a century and a half earlier, Aristobulus had
worked out certain analogies between his ancestral faith
and the speculations of Plato, which he explained by the
assumption that the Greek philosopher borrowed his ideas
from Moses.[2] Taking this as his cue, Philo proceeded to
read into the Pentateuch whatever he considered worth
while in the different systems of gentile philosophy. This
was, of course, a difficult and violent procedure; but Philo
readily accomplished it by means of the allegorical method
of interpretation, an instrument borrowed from the Stoics.

[1] *Vita Mosis* ii. 187.

[2] Zeller, *Philosophie der Grichen*, Part III, Div. II, pp. 257 ff.

Thus, partly to satisfy his own mind, doubtless, and partly to make the treasures of gentile philosophy available for his fellow countrymen, but most of all to commend the Jewish religion to fair-minded Gentiles, Philo wrote his voluminous works. To philosophical speculation he sought to lend the authority of religion and to religion, on the other hand, he endeavored to give intellectual respectability by the addition of philosophical accretions. In working out this blend of philosophy and religion, he was operating in harmony with the tendencies of the times as the development of Neo-Pythagoreanism, Hermetism, Gnosticism, and the inception of Neo-Platonism indicate. For the very reason that Philo interpreted religious experience in religio-philosophical terminology, his interpretation has peculiar interest and value.

In view of Philo's earnest endeavor to combine disparate elements, Jewish and Hellenistic, religious and philosophical, it is not strange that his formulations should contain many contradictory features. From the study of his writings it is impossible to reconstruct any clear-cut, consistent system of thought. In the reading of Philo one is continually encountering contradictions and discrepancies, and it is a constant problem to know just which of two incongruous statements represents the real thought of the writer or whether either does. If, however, it is impossible to derive from the study of his writings a consistent impression of his way of thinking, it is at least possible to get a comprehensive view of his thoughts. His writings are so voluminous that they are to be reckoned among the most extensive source materials for the period. The student of Philo has at least the advantage of being able to follow the author's thought through the most varied ramifications, even though he is in danger of losing his way in the mass of conflicting opinions.

In studying the religious experiences of Philo and his contemporaries, we are concerned primarily with a single phase of religious mysticism, the experience of regeneration. Since this experience, as then conceived, involved the immediate relationship of man with the divine, the study of the Philonian formulation of this experience may properly begin with an examination of Philo's thought of God.

II

According to Philo's own statement, there were for him two basic problems in theology. "One is whether there is any deity at all? . . . . The other question is, supposing there be a God, what is he as to his essence?" With the first of these problems Philo as a good Jew had no real trouble, but the second he pronounced "not only difficult but perhaps impossible."[1] He struggled a great deal with this problem and generally succeeded in attaining a disheartening negative conclusion—that God is essentially unknown and unknowable. This, he argued, was not due to any obscurity on the divine side, but rather to human limitations. According to his theory, man must first become God—an impossibility—before he could hope to comprehend God. Philo's ultimate position concerning the essential nature of God was simply this: We know that God is, but we cannot know what he is. This bare conviction, he said, ought to satisfy the seeker after God. "It is sufficient for human reason to attain the knowledge that there is and exists something as the cause of the universe; but to press beyond this and inquire into essence or quality is superlative folly."[2] In theory, at least, that was the conclusion of the whole matter for this Jewish thinker.

It is well known that Philo on occasion emphatically

[1] *De Specialibus Legibus* i. 32 f.
[2] *De Posteritate Caini* 168. Cf. *Quod Deus sit immutabilis* 55.

asserted that God is completely bare of all qualities.[1] Then having emptied the term "God" of all qualitative content, he proceeded to fill it full again. He was not, after all, satisfied with the purely negative position that God is without quality. Instead he went on to make the assertion that God is at once the summation and source of all the good qualities known to men.[2] In his account of the embassy to the emperor, he spoke of the Uncreated and the Divine as "the first good and beautiful and blessed and happy, or if one is to speak the truth, that which is better than the good and more blessed than blessedness itself and whatever is more perfect than these."[3] Somewhat like a refrain in the writings of Philo there echoes the thought that "the active cause is . . . . better than virtue and better than knowledge and better than the good itself and the beautiful itself."[4] This Philonian God, though the summation of all excellent and admirable qualities, was by that fact superlatively exalted above his creatures instead of united with them.

Certain other characteristics of Philo's deity completely differentiated him from men. Philo ascribed to him eternal causality[5] and this, of course, put God into a class entirely by himself. Similarly, God was immutable while every created thing, by the very circumstance of creation, was subject to change.[6] Philo's infinite God was further removed from his creatures by being superior to the conditions of time and place.[7] In fine, the Philonian God was a personification of absolute perfection, the only perfect being in all the universe, a being full and complete in and of himself

---

[1] *Quod Deus sit immutabilis* 55; *Legum Allegoriarum* i. 36, 51.

[2] *De Specialibus Legibus* ii. 53.   [3] *Legatio ad Caium* 5.

[4] *Mundi Opificio* 8 f. Cf. *Praemiis et Poenis* 40.

[5] *De Virtutibus (Nobilitate)* 214. Cf. *De Gigantibus* 10.

[6] *Legum Allegoriarum* ii. 33.   [7] *De Posteritate Caini* 14.

and entirely self-sufficient. "His nature is entirely perfect, or rather God is himself the perfection and completion and boundary of happiness, sharing in nothing else by which he can be rendered better."[1] All of these characteristics peculiar to Philo's God: his creative power, his steadfastness, his superiority to time and place, his perfection, and self-sufficiency served to differentiate him completely from his creatures. The list of distinctive characteristics might be increased by reference to many other peculiar attributes. These, however, are sufficient to show on what a transcendent plane of solitary exaltation reposed the figure of Philo's God.

It is patent that the Alexandrian's conception of deity was an unusually exalted one. In view of the transcendence of the Philonian God, one might well question whether any relations were possible between the human and the divine. Admittedly, if Philo's abstract conception of the deity were carried to its logical conclusion, all mystical experience would be impossible for men.

III

Although Philo's God was far removed from humanity, man himself was not so far removed from the divine. The statement, paradoxical as it sounds, is no more contradictory than Philo's own thought as he expressed it. His idea of man was dualistic and very like the conceptions of human nature entertained by Orphics and Pythagoreans. In his opinion, man was a creature of higher and lower origin with a twofold nature to correspond with his beginnings. Following the Genesis account of creation, Philo affirmed that "the body was made by the Creator, taking a lump of clay and fashioning the human form out of it; but

---

[1] *Cherubim* 86. On the self-sufficiency of God see also *Legum Allegoriarum* i. 44.

the soul proceeds from no created thing but from the Father and Ruler of all things."[1] In another important passage in his writings, Philo emphasized the dual origin of man in mythological terminology obviously borrowed from a gentile source.[2] Commenting on the Genesis story of the angels of God who became enamored of the daughters of men, Philo said that these angels were souls hovering about in the air. Some of the souls, attracted by the pleasures of sense life, left their pure abode in airy space and descended into material bodies to live. Engulfed in bodies as in a river and sometimes swept away by the life of the senses, these souls yet remained on the Godward side of man with a strong tendency to strive upward and return to the place whence they came.[3] Whether Philo cast his thought in the gentile forms suggested by Plato or the Jewish forms suggested by Genesis, his emphasis was the same in both instances, on the dual origin of man, a being of heavenly origin on the one hand, of earthly origin on the other.

Corresponding with this view of the genesis of man was Philo's opinion of the constitution of human nature. Fundamentally, he believed man was a duad, consisting of a soul and a body.[4] So far as his body was concerned, man was but a part of the material universe. His physical being consisted of the same four elements of which the remainder of the cosmos was constituted. "For he is composed of the same materials as the world," wrote Philo, "that is of earth, and water, and air, and fire, each of the elements having contributed its appropriate part."[5] It is curious to

[1] *De Opificio Mundi* 134 f.

[2] Plato *Timaeus* 41–43, 69–70.

[3] *De Gigantibus* 6–15.

[4] *Legum Allegoriarum* iii. 161 may be taken as a typical passage.

[5] *De Opificio Mundi* 146; also *Quis Rerum Divinarum Heres* 153.

find in the writings of an Alexandrian Jew this echo of the physical speculations of Empedocles and the Ionians.

Since man was thus a part of the physical universe, he shared in all the imperfections of matter. Philo was conscious of the religious problem involved by the earthy constitution of the human body, and his attitude on the problem was a mingled one. Although in one passage he spoke of the body in a Pauline figure as a "sacred temple of the rational soul,"[1] his usual language was very different in tenor. Like the Neo-Pythagoreans of his own day and the Orphics of an earlier age, Philo spoke of the body as the prison-house of the soul, a clog and a hindrance to religious experience. "Away my friend, from that earthy vesture of yours," he exhorted, "escape from that accursed prison, the body, and from its pleasures and lusts, which are your jailors."[2] It was a matter of experience that the body, which was the seat of the sense life, actually weighed down the aspirations of the spirit. For the Alexandrian Jew, as for the Tarsian Christian, the body was a fertile seed bed for evil[3] in which natural impulses, left unrestrained, would come to full fruition in specific sins. On occasion Philo took the extreme position that man's physical nature was inherently evil in and of itself. Thus, because of his physical constitution, man was far removed from the perfect God.

This, however, was only half of the story. Man was not only body but body plus soul, and by this circumstance he was raised above the level of mere earthly existence. As a compound being of dual origin, one part heavenly and the other part earthly, man stood on the borderland between two different realms, his citizenship in both.[4] The

[1] *De Opificio Mundi* 137.

[2] *De Migratione Abrahami* 9.

[3] *Quis Rerum Divinarum Heres* 268. *Legum Allegoriarum* iii. 71.

[4] *De Opificio Mundi* 135.

higher element in the human constitution Philo emphasized equally with, if not even more strongly than, the
lower part of his nature. "The body has been fashioned
of earth," he granted, "but the soul belongs to the ether,
a fragment of the divine."[1] By reason of this higher element in his make-up, man had inherent within himself the
possibility of some sort of relationship with the deity.

Parenthetically, it should be noted that Philo's was not
an unmodified dualism pure and simple. At one important
point he complicated his theory by allowing for a twofold
division of the higher element in man, the soul. On the
one hand, Jew that he was, he viewed the soul as vital
energy, the principle of life in matter, essentially irrational
and possessed in common by both men and animals. On
the other hand, like a Stoic, he viewed the soul as man's
rational capacity, the impress of divine reason, an element
linking the human with the divine. Of these two parts of
the soul the latter was, or should be, the dominant and
superior element.

Philo's conception of the irrational part of the soul with
its troublesome sense-life need not concern us. Like the
body it was a negative and deterrent factor in religious experience. Not so the rational part of the soul, the intellect.
This element belonged peculiarly to man among created
beings and served to differentiate him completely from
other animals. Philo reiterated this point with emphasis:
"Man is the noblest of animals by reason of the higher
element among his component parts."[2] This reasoning
power not only differentiated man from the creatures of
earth but gave him kinship in heaven and related him, in
a way, to deity.[3] God himself was the creator and arche-
type of the rational nature,[4] and to this sovereign element

---

[1] *Legum Allegoriarum* iii. 161. Cf. *De Decalogo* 134.   [2] *De Decalogo* 134.

[3] *Quod Deterius Potiori insidiari soleat* 85; *De Decalogo* 134.

[4] *Quod Deterius Potiori insidiari soleat* 84; *De Opificio Mundi* 139; *De Fuga et Inventione* 69.

in the human constitution he had assigned the governance of the lower elements in human nature.[1]

Like contemporary Stoic teachers, Philo isolated in man's rational nature the all-important human factor in religious experience. In contrast to the material body and the animating principle, he viewed the intellect as a help rather than a hindrance in lifting man up to God. Instead of being an alien element, it was itself related to the divine, and was inherently capable of further fellowship with deity. Thus, while Philo's conception of God was so exalted as scarcely to admit of any interrelations between humanity and divinity, his conception of man was at once a lowly and an elevated one, humble in respect to man's body and sense life but exalted in respect to man's rational power. The latter element, Philo believed, itself closely akin to the divine, threw open to man the possibility for mystical religious experience.

IV

Being a creature of dual nature man was, in Philo's thought, the scene of an incessant conflict between the higher and lower elements in his constitution. The body constantly hindered the soul in its aspirations, and the soul was ever seeking deliverance from the imprisoning body. The rational element constantly strove to maintain its supremacy and the irrational desires were ever struggling to free themselves from restraint.[2] In man's lower nature there was a continual pull away from God.[3]

But Philo also recognized man's yearning for God, by virtue of the rational soul which was the dominant part of

[1] *De Agricultura* 26 ff.; *De Opificio Mundi* 66; *De Specialibus Legibus* (*De Victimis*) i. 201; *Legum Allegoriarum* ii. 6.

[2] *Quaestiones in Genesim* iv. 203.

[3] *Legum Allegoriarum* iii. 71; *Quis Rerum Divinarum Heres* 268; *Quod Deus sit immutabilis* 72; *Quis Rerum Divinarum Heres* 106 ff.; *De Decalogo* 5 ff.; *De Abrahamo* 41.

his constitution. Granting that the endeavor for fellowship with the divine might prove a futile one, Philo was yet convinced of the worth-whileness of the effort. "There is nothing better," he said, "than to search after the true God, even if the finding of him should escape human capacity, seeing that even eagerness of desire to understand him in itself produces unspeakable pleasures and delights."[1] Logically, then, the next task is to chart, following the lead of Philo's thought, the various steps in this upward striving of the soul.

For the man who had neglected his God-given rational heritage, and surrendered himself to the control of his lower nature, the first step was a realization of his position, an awakening to the consciousness that in surrendering to pleasurable cravings he had violated the divinely prescribed order of things for humanity and dethroned the rational element which should be supreme. In this process Philo usually thought of man's own intellect as playing the part of conscience. He spoke of it as the real man, the better self, who in all the critical, moral, and religious issues of life deserved to have the deciding voice.[2] Philo did not, however, view this testing and convicting function of the intellect as a pure exercise of human endeavor, by any means. Recognizing the close kinship of the human and the divine at exactly this point, he considered the human understanding as "intimately related to the divine Logos, an impress or particle or effulgence of the blessed nature,"[3] and frequently in his writings Philo represented the Logos itself as exercising the functions of conscience and arousing man to a realization of his evil ways.[4]

[1] *De Specialibus Legibus* i. 36. Cf. *De Confusione Linguarum* 97.

[2] *Quod Deterius Potiori insidiari soleat* 22 f.; *De Decalogo* 87; *De Fuga* 131.

[3] *De Opificio Mundi* 146.

[4] *Quod Deus sit immutabilis* 134 ff.

Under the promptings of this agency man became conscious of his positive wrongdoings, of his limitations, and above all of his utter humility in relation to the deity. This humble attitude of self-depreciation in the divine presence was, in Philo's opinion, a precondition of progress toward fellowship with God. In a paradoxical statement Philo testified that it was only in this humble frame of mind that he himself even dared approach the divine presence. "When I perceive myself to be but 'dust and ashes' and what is even more despicable, then I have the courage to meet Thee, having become humble, cast down to the ground."[1] The preliminary to the soul's progress toward God was the realization, in the glaring light of conscience, of man's utter inferiority.

The next important step was the active turning away from the life of sensation and passion, desire and pleasure, which had previously ensnared the soul and caused its defection. The human intellect, in order to wing its way upward to the divine, must be freed from all trammels of the body and material entanglements. Not only must the reason be freed from the domination of the senses and restored to its governing position in the human constitution, but it must also learn to distrust itself even and have confidence only in the Uncreated. In words that have a Neo-Pythagorean ring, Philo commented on Genesis 15:5.

The mind that is to be led forth and set at liberty must withdraw from all things, from bodily necessities, from the instruments of the senses, from sophistical reasonings, from plausible arguments, finally from itself. . . . . For it is not possible for one who dwells in the body and among mortal men to have communion with God, but only for him whom God delivers out of his prison.[2]

Later in the same work, Philo addressed an exhortation to his own mind to withdraw from all physical connections.

[1] *Quis Rerum Divinarum Heres* 29.   [2] *Legum Allegoriarum* iii. 41 f.

If you seek God, O my mind, go forth out of yourself, and seek for him. But if you remain in the substance of the body, or in the vain opinions of the mind, you are then without any real wish to search into divine things, even if you do put on the appearance and pretense of seeking them."[1]

Fundamentally, therefore, a profound distrust of sensation and a complete disregard of the body was at the basis of Philo's supreme religious experience, as it was in the case of Hermeticism.

This distrust of the world of sense was but the reverse of a very necessary positive attitude of mind. The turning away from the visible world as unreal must be accompanied simultaneously by a turning toward the invisible as the only reality. At this point Philo's indebtedness to Platonism became particularly evident. These two processes, the turning away from the phenomenal world and the turning toward God, were intimately associated with each other in Philo's thought and writings. He compared the way of sensation to a slippery path on which men stumble and fall, and the way of contemplation and trust in God to a dry high road on which men make progress without hindrance.[2]

In thus disregarding both sensation and reason, man passed beyond the limits of ordinary rational processes. It required a great perseverance of will to follow this Philonian injunction, and Philo himself recognized the difficulties of the situation. He said:

If you choose to make a profounder search and not merely a superficial one, you will clearly discover that it is not easy to put faith in God alone without dragging in something else. . . . . To clear away all earthly influences and to distrust the world of becoming which is of itself wholly unworthy of confidence, and to have faith in God alone, who alone is trustworthy, requires a large and Olympian understanding, one which is no longer enticed by our worldly interests.[3]

[1] *Op. cit.* iii. 47. Cf. *Quod Deterius Potiori insidiari soleat* 158 f.
[2] *De Abrahamo* 263, 268 f.   [3] *Quis Rerum Divinarum Heres* 90 ff.

Philo, like Paul, used the word "faith" to denominate this attitude of trust in God, and if one may judge from the frequency and the emphasis of his references to faith this personal attitude was almost as significant for the Alexandrian Jew as it was for Paul himself. He characterized the attitude as that "of the soul resting and established on the Cause of all things, who is able to do anything, but who wills to do only the best."[1] Philonian faith, then, not only presupposed a complete distrust of self and the world but it issued in a glad confidence centered in the invisible God.[2]

In spite of the handicap with which man started in his physical nature, in spite of a constant tendency to yield to irrational desires and subordinate the reason itself to the dictates of passion, the rational soul of man, according to Philo, was constantly yearning for better things. Man's own intellect, itself an emanation of the divine Logos, was ever busy playing the part of conscience, arousing man to a realization of his weaknesses and inferiority. If, in response to this stimulus, man learned to distrust himself and the world and to throw himself on the invisible God in an abandon of confidence, Philo believed he was in a condition to come in contact with the divine. The question naturally follows, Was there from the side of the immutable God any response to this change of attitude of man's part? Did Philo allow for an approach to man by God to match man's yearning for God?

V

A priori it would seem that any such action from the divine side would be unthinkable to Philo. Considering the fact that the Jewish philosopher conceived of God as pure

[1] *De Abrahamo* 268. For Philo as for Paul the patriarch Abraham was the typical man of faith. Compare *De Virtutibus* 216 with Rom. 4:16 ff. and Gal. 3:7 ff.

[2] *Quis Rerum Divinarum Heres* 9, 26 ff.

being, essentially incomprehensible, devoid of all qualities, except as he was characterized by certain attributes peculiar to himself alone, it would seem improbable that Philo should admit a generally gracious attitude on God's part toward mankind as a whole, or an especially favorable attitude toward those imperfect but yearning souls who were striving for communion with the divine. Yet such was the case.

In general Philo viewed God as the source of all good for humanity. From him, as from an exhaustless fountain, there streamed an overflow of divine mercy that was the cause of everything good in human experience.[1] One of his favorite epithets for God was "He who loves to give,"[2] and he freely expressed the conviction that the only limit to God's graciousness was man's capacity to receive.[3]

Upon those who had abused their God-given endowments but were conscious of their mistake, the deity looked with special favor.[4] In a pertinent passage Philo said that God graciously "makes all things easy" for those who "feel shame and exchange dissoluteness for self-control and loathe the base phantoms which they impressed upon their souls.[5] It was not without the definite assurance of divine help, according to Philo, that the soul started out in quest for the central experience of religion. In a comment on Genesis 46:4 he elaborated God's promise "I will go with you" as follows:

This I do because of my pity for your rational nature, so that by my guidance you may be brought up out of the Hades of passion to the

[1] *De Mutatione Nominum* 58 f.; *De Migratione Abrahami* 30 ff.; *De Cherubim* 13, 27. Cf. *De Plantatione* 89.

[2] For examples see *Legum Allegoriarum* i. 34 and *De Migratione Abrahami* 30.

[3] *De Posteritate Caini* 142, 146; *De Specialibus Legibus* i. 43 ff.; *Quis Rerum Divinarum Heres* 31.

[4] *Legum Allegoriarum* i. 34.   [5] *Praemiis et Poenis* 116.

Olympian abode of virtue, for to all suppliant souls I have made known the way that leads to heaven, preparing for them a thoroughfare that they might not grow weary of the journey.[1]

Like the father in Jesus' parable of the lost son, Philo's God went out to meet the soul that was returning to him,[2] and again like a father he was not satisfied until the soul had been liberated from its bondage to the body and conducted in safety to the freedom of its heavenly mother-city.[3] The God of Philo, beneficent in his attitude toward men in general, was especially helpful to those who turned away the world and earnestly sought fellowship with him.

Notwithstanding Philo's recognition of God's gracious attitude of helpfulness, there yet persisted a distinct emphasis on the transcendence of God. One fundamental assumption that ever remained in the background of his thought and not infrequently came out into the foreground was the conviction that the Uncreated could not come into contact with any created being. In spite of man's aspiration and God's beneficence, there remained a huge gap between the human and the divine according to the Philonian scheme of things. To bridge this chasm the Alexandrian religionist had recourse to the idea of mediation, a conception already familiar to Jews and Egyptians and Gentiles generally, and to philosophers as well as religionists in Philo's day.

To carry on this work of mediation Philo posited three different classes of beings operating between God and man. Chief among them was the Logos, a semi-personification of God's thought or reason. In the theological constructions of Philo, the Logos held quite as important a position as it earlier held in the ethical thinking of the Stoics or the physical speculations of Heraclitus. Next in order

[1] *De Posteritate Caini* 31.

[2] *Legum Allegoriarum* iii. 215. [3] *De Somniis* i. 181.

and subordinate to the Logos were the *powers*, manifestations of the divine energy, who worked what was unseemly for God himself to do in the world. The gnostic affinities of Philo's thought were apparent in this connection. Finally, there were the *angels* who constituted a much more vague category in Philo's thinking than was usual in the case of a Jew. In their mediatorial work Philo assigned these beings an important function altogether helpful to mortals.[1]

He drew a picture of the soul following after God and having as the companions of its journey "those rational powers who are commonly called angels" and the Logos itself.[2] In the progress of the soul toward God, Philo considered the apprehension of the Logos as a preliminary stage to the apprehension of God himself, and he even affirmed, "God can only be grasped by means of the powers which accompany and follow him." In spite of the gap that existed in Philo's thought between the human and the divine, he made ample provision for bridging it by means of mediatorial agencies a part of whose business was to assist the soul in its quest for communion with God.

VI

When, however, it came to this central experience in religion, the mediating agencies were for the most part disregarded by Philo and the human soul was left alone with its God. At this point the one thing that mattered was man's real kinship with the divine by virtue of his intellect. In so far as that rational element came to self-realization, it strove for union with the divine origin of its being; hence there was in the soul itself an inner urge that impelled it Godward.[3] The ultimate goal of the soul's endeavor was

[1] *De Somniis* i. 142. [2] *De Migratione Abrahami* 173 ff.

[3] *De Specialibus Legibus* i. 207; *De Plantatione* 22.

an immediate vision of God himself. This, in Philo's estimation, was the supreme experience of the religious life.
He compared it to the laurel wreath that awaited the victorious athlete. He asked:

> What lovelier or more fitting garland could be woven for the victor-
> ious soul, than the power, with clear vision to gaze on him who is? Truly
> splendid is the prize held out to the wrestling soul—to be equipped with
> eyesight so as to perceive without dimness him who is alone worthy of
> contemplation.[1]

Since God was the ultimate being in all the universe, the
apprehension of him was the very summation of privilege.
He who had caught that vision, Philo said, might well pray
to stay there without change.[2]

Of the supreme importance of that vision for Philo
there can be no doubt. However, when the modern student
attempts to analyze the experience, he finds it very difficult
to get a lucid idea of the thought of the Alexandrian philosopher. Nowhere does Philo himself analyze the experience in any comprehensive way, and his references to it
are so confused and contradictory that it is not easy to
comprehend his ideas on the subject. It is plain, however,
that for Philo the basic conviction growing out of the experience was the realization that God is incomprehensible.
"When the soul that loves God searches into the nature of
the Existent, it enters into an invisible search, from which
the chief benefit which accrues to it is to comprehend that
God is incomprehensible and to see that he is invisible."[3]
The case of Moses was the classical example which Philo
adduced to illustrate this point.[4] In briefest terms, then,
the Philonian vision of God meant a contemplation of the
divine being eventuating in the conviction that he was
incomprehensible.

[1] De Mutatione Nominum 82.   [3] De Posteritate Caini 15.

[2] De Abrahamo 58.   [4] De Mutatione Nominum 7 ff.

With such a negative result, however, Philo himself was ill content, if we may judge from his other references to the subject. In the face of his own theory of the transcendence of God, he persistently asserted, though usually with some reservation, that the direct vision and the immediate apprehension of God were possible for humanity. Some there were who were able to overleap the bounds of the material universe and get a distinct impression of the Uncreated.[1] Philo went farther and in terms of real enthusiasm attempted to describe such an immediate experience of God. In one passage, after prescribing certain preliminary conditions, he showed how the soul might be consecrated as a living sanctuary to God. This was the glorious possibility he pictured: "Then he may appear to you visibly, causing incorporeal rays to shine upon you, granting visions of his nature, undreamed of and ineffable, which are the overflowing sources of all other blessings."[2] The usual comparison that Philo employed in attempting to describe the vision was the simile of light, so familiar in the Hermetic literature. In a more extended description of the experience he said:

A bright, incorporeal ray, purer than ether, suddenly shining upon the soul, revealed the ideal world as under guidance. But the Guide, encompassed by unstained light was hard to behold or divine, for the soul's vision was obscured by the splendor of the rays. . . . . Then the Father and Savior, seeing her genuine longing, pitied her, and imparting power to her sight, did not withhold the vision of himself, in so far as it was possible for a created and mortal nature to contain it.[3]

The concluding qualification in this passage was typical of Philo's thinking. Within the limits of this reservation, he allowed for the immediate contact of the human and the divine and made a real effort to characterize the resultant

[1] *Legum Allegoriarum* iii. 100.

Quaestiones in Exodum ii. 51.   [3] *Praemiis et Poenis* 37 ff. Cf. also 45.

experience. As in this instance the experience was usually described as a process of mental illumination.

Thus far we have considered primarily the intellectual aspects of Philo's vision of God. It had for him, however, a large emotional content as well. The contemplation of the divine being eventuated in an ecstasy which Philo interpreted as a matter of divine possession. He told of rapturous moments in his own experience which especially illustrate this phase of his religious thinking. He wrote on one occasion:

I am not ashamed to recount my own experience. At times, when I proposed to enter upon my wonted task of writing on philosophical doctrines with exact knowledge of the materials which were to be put together, I have had to leave off without any work accomplished. . . . . But at other times when I had come empty, all of a sudden I was filled with thoughts showered down and sown upon me unseen from above, so that by divine possession I fell into a rapture and became ignorant of everything, the place, those present, myself and what was spoken or written. For I received . . . . the most vividly distinct view of the matter before me such as might be received through the eyes from the most luminous presentation.[1]

This famous account from the writer's own personal experience presents an unusual case of mental illumination for a particular task; but the phenomena represented are, in the main, the same as those exhibited in accounts of mystical experiences to which Philo made impersonal reference. Here was the vacant mind, the steady contemplation of a great theme, the sudden flood of ideas, and finally the rapturous sense of possession by divine power. The last factor Philo emphasized in an address to his own soul. He urged:

Go out from yourself filled with a divine frenzy like those possessed in the mystical rites of the Corybantes, and possessed by the deity after the manner of prophetic inspiration. For when the mind is no longer

[1] *De Migratione Abrahami* 34 f.

self-contained but rapt and frenzied with a heavenly passion . . . . this
is your inheritance.[1]

To state the matter very simply and perhaps over simply,
as a consequence of forgetting himself in the thought of
God, Philo experienced an ecstatic sense of divine possession.

One who is familiar with the Philonian vocabulary cannot doubt the importance of this emotional element in his
experience or Philo's own high evaluation of it from a religious point of view. His language is unusually rich in the
vocabulary of ecstasy. Some of his more familiar terms
are *enthousiazein*, "to be divinely inspired," *korubantian*,
"to be frenzied" (like the Corybantes), *bakeuein*, "to be
seized with divine madness," *katechesthai*, "to be possessed
by deity," and the noun forms *ekstasis*, "ecstasy," and
katokōchē, "divine possession," are of frequent occurrence.
In describing mystical experience, particularly in its emotional aspect, Philo used the most glowing terms of enthusiasm. He characterized it as a happy intoxication. To
quote his own paradoxical words, the spirit in a state of
ecstasy "is kindled into a flame of thanksgiving to God and
becomes drunken with that drunkenness which does not
intoxicate."[2] This comparison was a metaphor that Philo
employed more than once. Commenting on the story of
Hannah rebuked for drunkenness during her devotions, he
said, "In the case of the God-possessed not only is the soul
wont to be stirred and driven into frenzy, but to be flushed
and inflamed, since the joy which wells up within and
makes the spirit glow transmits the experience to the outward parts."[3] The quotation suggests what a highly
wrought emotional experience divine possession was for

[1] *Quis Rerum Divinarum Heres* 69 f.

[2] *Legum Allegoriarum* i. 82 ff.   [3] *De Ebrietate* 147.

Philo, and that it was not without its physical accompaniments and manifestations.

It is possible, however, to exaggerate the emotional phase of Philo's mysticism. On the whole the impression one gathers from his writings is that his ecstasy, however deeply felt it may have been, was of a calm and controlled type that was experienced in the solitude of contemplation. Philo's whole emphasis was on the quiescence of the human soul, and his ecstasy was that of one who was being acted upon rather than acting. To state the differentiation in terminology that Deissmann has made classical, Philo, like Paul, was a reacting rather than an acting mystic.[1] Primarily, he viewed the action of God as decisive in the process, and man's experience was but the reaction to this divine activity. The trance of Adam[2] when Jahve removed a rib from his body and made woman therefrom was, to Philo's mind, the prototype of the soul's experience in ecstasy. "The going forth (*ekstasis*) of the spirit," Philo said, "is a deep sleep which falls upon it. It goes forth when it ceases to busy itself with the ideas which impinge upon it, and when it does not exercise activity upon them it slumbers."[3] With special emphasis on the solitary character of the experience, Philo affirmed, "The most secure method of contemplating the Existent is with the soul alone, apart from all utterance."[4] In view of Philo's stress on the passivity of the human spirit in the process, one must conclude that his mysticism was of the quiescent type.

In summary it may be said that Philo's experience of communion with God involved the concentration of all

[1] Deissmann, *Paul. A Study in Social and Religious History* (New York, 1926[2]), pp. 149 ff. See also *The Religion of Jesus and the Faith of Paul* (London, 1923), pp. 195 ff.

[2] Gen. 2:21.   [3] *Legum Allegoriarum* ii. 31.   [4] *De Gigantibus* 52.

man's mental processes on the contemplation of the divine being and the complete loss of self-consciousness in an exultant sense of divine possession.

VII

Did Philo consider this an essentially transforming experience—one that radically changed human nature and made man a new and different creature? There are clear utterances by the Alexandrian Jew on this point which make it evident that he believed the experience was a transforming one as long as it lasted. Philo's theory in this regard was radical. His interpretation of the word "ecstasy" was a very literal one and at the same time quite distinctive. To him it meant that man's rational soul not only left the body but even got outside itself.[1] And when it departed what took its place? Philo was clear on that point also. Nothing less than the divine spirit came in and replaced the human intellect. Commenting on Genesis 15:12, he wrote:

As long as our own reason encompasses us with brightness . . . . filling our whole soul as it were with noon-day light, we remain in ourselves and do not experience possession. But when the light of reason sets . . . . ecstasy and divine possession and frenzy fall upon us. . . . . For the reason within us leaves its abode at the arrival of the divine spirit, but when the spirit departs the reason returns to its place. For it is not fitting that mortal should dwell with immortal.[2]

In this passage Philo cited the case of the prophet as the supreme example of the replacement of human reason by the divine spirit. It was not the prophet, he said, who spoke, but rather the divine spirit who made use of the prophet's tongue and mouth to declare God's will. In view of Philo's sharp differentiation between the human and the divine and his remarkably high estimation of the latter

[1] Note especially *ekstēthi* in *Quis Rerum Divinarum Heres* 69 f.

[2] *Quis Rerum Divinarum Heres* 249. Cf. *De Specialibus Legibus* iv. 49.

in contrast to the former, it is somewhat surprising to find that he does not shrink from pronouncing his prophets divine. The high point of his appreciation of the prophetic type is found in the following statement:

> The prophetic mind, when it has been initiated in divine things and is inspired, resembles unity. . . . . Now he who cleaves to the nature of unity is said to have approached God with the intimacy, as it were, of a kinsman. For, abandoning all mortal types, he is transferred into the divine type so that he becomes akin to God and truly divine."[1]

By virtue of the replacement of the human mind by the divine spirit, Philo believed that a man might be changed from a human into a divine being.

It should be stated immediately, however, that for the generality of men this transformation was not a permanent one, in Philo's estimation, but temporary and intermittent. However much the soul might desire to remain in the ecstatic state of divine possession, most men could not keep so completely concentrated on God and estranged from the world as was necessary in order to retain the divine presence. "He does remain sometimes," Philo said, "but he does not dwell always with most of us."[2] In a passage distinguished for its literary quality as well as for its religious feeling, Philo depicted the human spirit standing as in the holy of holies of the temple, completely enraptured with the sense of the divine presence there in the sanctuary. "But when its divine passion is stilled," Philo continued, "and its ardent yearning slackens, it retraces its course from the realm of the divine and becomes man, lighting upon those human interests which lie in wait for it at the entrance of the sanctuary."[3] Such, Philo believed, was the experience of ordinary men: a temporary impact of the divine spirit which, for the time being, operated to divinize

---

[1] *Quaestiones in Exodum* ii. 29.

[2] *De Gigantibus* 20. Cf. 47, 53.   [3] *De Somniis* ii. 232 ff.

a mere man, but which soon departed, leaving him human as he was before.

Some there were, however, a very few, with whom the divine spirit remained as a permanent possession. These were men of such steadiness of purpose that they could once for all cast aside all interest in created things and mere opinions and reach God with unrestricted and open mind.[1] Moses was the great example of this type of men. He had entered the inmost shrine and there been initiated into the sacred mysteries. And not only had he become an initiate but a hierophant in the mystic cult, a teacher of divine things to those who had been purified. "With such a man," Philo said, "the divine spirit is ever present, showing him the way in every straight path."[2] Philo made many references to men of this type in his writings and characterized them variously. They were the immutable ones who alone had access to the unalterable God.[3] They were the sinless ones who were called divine.[4] These men, he said, were "something new, surpassing description and really divine, existing not by human conception but by inspired frenzy."[5] Much as Philo had to say about them, they were few whom he numbered in this favored class. Only Abraham and Moses and a very few others of the great heroes of his own race were thus classified. But for these exceptions, the permanently spirit-possessed man of Philo, like the wise man of the Stoics, was an ideal figure.

The direct study of Philo's writings, therefore, reveals that while in his thought God and man were so widely separated that mediators were deemed necessary to bring them together, yet as a matter of religious experience Philo did make allowance for the possibility of an immediate

[1] *De Gigantibus* 53.
[2] *Op. cit.* 54.
[3] *Posteritate Caini* 27. Cf. *Somniis* ii. 29.
[4] *De Virtutibus* 177; *De Abrahamo* 47.
[5] *De Fuga* 166 ff.

contact between them. On the one hand he recognized a yearning for God on man's part that expressed itself in a realization of man's utter inferiority, a complete distrust of sensation and disregard of all bodily connections, and a glad trust in God. On the other hand Philo believed that his beneficent God was especially favorable to those who thus sought communion with him. In solitary meditation upon the incomprehensibility of God, Philo experienced a mental illumination that was for him the vision of God. The consequent emotional exaltation he considered to be a case of divine possession. For the time being, at least, the divine spirit replaced the human intellect, and the inspired man became a divine being. The experience, however, was not a permanent one, but intermittent so far as most men were concerned. There were only a very few men, the great Jewish heroes, whom he believed to be permanently in this divine state. For the mass of mankind, however, the transforming experience of mental illumination and divine possession was but a temporary phenomenon. Philo did believe that individual regeneration was possible. Save in exceptional instances he did not believe it permanently possible.

VIII

It remains to inquire concerning the genetic relationships of this peculiarly intellectualized mysticism of Philo. How did it come about that this Alexandrian Jew conceived the possibility of purifying the human soul by various subjective operations and finally having it elevated and transformed to rank as divine? Whence came the influences that convinced Philo of the possibility of such complete possession by the divine spirit as would enable the inspired man to understand the secrets of the divine nature? There are in Philo's own writings references which point the way to a solution of this problem.

The ideal of the spirit-possessed man Philo himself associated with the Stoic theory of the wise man. With obvious reference to thinkers of the Stoic school Philo asked, "Are there not even to the present day some of those persons who have attained to perfection in philosophy, who say that there is actually no such person as a wise man?"[1] But Philo himself would not say this. For him wisdom did exist, and in the prophets and patriarchs of his own race he found the embodiment of this high Stoic ideal. Such men Philo regarded as intermediary between the human and the divine, less than God yet more than man.[2] His conception was strikingly like that expressed in the Stoic *dicta*: "The wise man alone is divine, a prophet; the wise man alone knows God, is a priest, and practices the divine cult."[3]

Granting that Philo's theory of the inspired human intelligence was a Jewish reinterpretation of the Stoic ideal of the wise man, it is important to note the type of Stoicism to which the Alexandrian Jew was indebted. It was not a philosophy pure and simple but a philosophy that had been modified in the direction of religion. Just as Stoic thinkers of the Greek world had made use of allegory to transform myth into philosophy, so in Egypt religionists had made use of allegory to transform Stoicism itself into a semi-religious system. The union in Philo's land and in Philo's era of Egyptian religious theories and Stoic philosophy is exemplified by certain of his contemporaries. There was, foremost of all, Chaeremon the Stoic, Nero's tutor in philosophy and at the same time a priest of an Egyptian sanctuary.[4] Hecateus of Abdera, a Stoic of an

---

[1] *De Mutatione Nominum* 34–37.

[2] *De Virtutibus* 9 f.; *Quis Divinarum Heres* 83 f.

[3] Arnim, *Stoicorum Veterum Fragmenta*, III, 157.

[4] Porphyry *De Abstinentia* iv. 6–8; Eusebius *Praeparatio Evangelica* iii. 4. 1–3.

earlier period, who accompanied Ptolemy Soter on an expedition to Syria, showed his religious propensities by introducing spirit into the constitution of the universe as a fifth element along with the traditional four.[1] Finally, there was Apion, Philo's great opponent and the bitter enemy of the Jews generally. Himself an Alexandrian Stoic he exhibited the application of allegory to the Egyptian God Thoth, "Lord of Divine Words." The admission of Stoic influence upon Philo's thought therefore leads directly to a consideration of the specific religious environment in Egypt which operated to transmute Stoic philosophy into a semi-religious system.

Do the writings of Philo betray a sensitiveness to religious as well as philosophical influences proceeding from his immediate Alexandrian environment? There was one group of religious influences to which Philo's works prove a rather notable indebtedness on his part. These were the stimuli coming from the mystery religions. Scattered all through Philo's productions there are a great number of references which prove beyond peradventure of a doubt Philo's familiarity with this type of religion. Of course he roundly denounced the mystery cults with their secret ceremonies enacted under the cover of night. For him either the teaching or the learning of mystic rites was "no small profanation," and he laid down the absolute rule that none of Moses' disciples might either initiate or be initiated.[2] No loyal Jew could or would assume any other attitude than this one of outspoken denunciation. Philo, with all his mystical yearnings, could adopt the extremist position just because he as a Jew achieved the satisfaction of those desires in his own reworking of his ancestral religion.

Philo found in the scriptures of his race the sacred dis-

[1] Diogenes Laertius i. 10; Diodorus Siculus i. 11. 6.

[2] *De Specialibus Legibus* i. 319.

course that conveyed to him the secret truth which was the essential feature of a mystery. For the interpretation of that sacred lore he made use of the allegorical method, just as allegory was used for explanation in the sacred discourse of the mystery cults. Philo knew, too, of the various functionaries in the mystery ritual and the characters in the mystery drama who assisted the initiates to master the divine wisdom which meant their salvation. But he telescoped these functionaries and summed them all up in a single personage, the guide to the initiate, whom he called hierophant or mystagogue without distinction. In the heroes of his race this Jew found the personalities who served as initiators for himself. Moses was the one to whom he repeatedly referred as the great initiator. God himself had initiated Moses while in the mountain,[1] and thereafter he was "a hierophant of the ritual and a teacher of divine things."[2] Philo acknowledged that he had been originally initiated into the sacred mysteries by Moses. He did not shrink from speaking of himself as a hierophant[3] also, and he urged others to serve in a similar capacity for the uninitiated.[4]

As was the case in the mystery religions, he demanded the fulfilment of certain preliminary conditions before one could attain initiation into his intellectual cult. It is fairly clear that the specific requirements he had in view were of a moral character. In addition to the natural endowment of a good disposition, there must be irreproachable conduct ere one could find the path of life and be initiated into the true mysteries.[5] Philo also followed mystery practice by

---

[1] *Vita Mosis* ii. 71.

[2] *De Gigantibus* 54. Cf. *De Cherubim* 48 f.; *De Somniis* i. 191; *Quod Deus sit immutabilis* 61.

[3] *De Cherubim* 42.

[4] *De Somniis* i. 164.   [5] *Quod Deus sit immutabilis* 61.

laying upon his disciples the charge of secrecy. Those who were adept in the lore of his cult were regarded as an esoteric group, and he addressed them with formulas that were familiar to mystery initiates.[1] From their company all the unworthy were rigidly excluded. He reiterated the command that the initiated must not divulge the secrets of "the veritably sacred mysteries" to any of the uninitiated, lest the ignorant should misrepresent what they did not understand and in so doing expose it to the ridicule of the vulgar.[2] Like the officials of the mystery religions, Philo insisted on secrecy.

For Philo initiation into his intellectualized cult was the entrance into a new world,[3] an invisible country, the intelligible world where "the purified mind could contemplate the pure and untainted nature of those things which are invisible and which are only discernible by the intellect."[4] Hither Abraham went when he "returned to his fathers" and Enoch when "he was not." This was none other than the divine and heavenly region that was the *locus* of immortal life where Abraham and Isaac, having received immortality, had become the equal of the angels.[5] Thus it was possible, through participation in the Philonian cult, to experience a foretaste of the immortal life. The significance of this fact in relation to the mystery religions of Philo's environment is that they too, in their ritual, featured the passage of the soul to another world and in so doing gave a present guaranty of immortality.

Thus the cults of Philo's Egyptian environment exerted a large influence on his figures of speech and his thought-

---

[1] *De Cherubim* 42; *Legum Allegoriarum* iii. 219.

[2] *De Cherubim* 48; *De Sacrificiis Abelis et Caini* 60.

[3] *De Gigantibus* 54, 55.

[4] *De Congressu Eruditionis Gratia* 25.

[5] *De Sacrificiis Abelis et Caini* 5.

forms as well. When we inquire more particularly for the immediate religious influences that stimulated his ecstatic experience of mental regeneration and guided him in his rather elaborate theorizings on the subject, the natural place to look for them is in this same religious environment.

The characteristic contribution of Philo's land to the religious syncretism of the Roman Empire was the cult of Isis. We have seen how this cult gave to the individual religionist the assurance of spiritual rebirth and the guaranty of immortality even while he was alive on earth. By means of certain initiatory rites of great spiritual potency, the neophyte who assumed the rôle of Osiris died to the old life of earth and was revived again to new life, reborn for eternity. These venerable Egyptian rites which from antiquity had been performed in the land of the Nile, for the benefit of the dead and of a privileged few among the living, were in the days of Philo practiced on ordinary folk who sought initiation into the cult.

In the ritual regeneration of this mystery religion, we undoubtedly have an important and immediate source of Philo's theory of mental regeneration. He was acquainted with the potent cult practices of the Isiacists—at least in a general way. He himself was conscious of mystical longings for contact with the unseen, fellowship with the deity, and the transformation of his ephemeral human nature into something more permanent and divine—desires which the Isis cult aimed to satisfy by its elaborate and impressive ritual. As a true Jew, even though a liberal Jew of the Diaspora, Philo could not think of participating in those rites. So he did the next best thing. He rationalized and intellectualized them and found in the experiences of his own mental and emotional life the satisfactions and guaranties that others found in cult practices.

In the rational part of man's nature he isolated a human

element which he believed to be capable of exaltation and transformation and ultimate fellowship with the divine. As conditions preliminary to this process, he demanded a profound distrust of sensation, a great trust in God, and other requirements of similar character. These exercises corresponded to the physical and moral rigors prescribed for Isiac initiation. In the individual's quiet and steady contemplation of the divine perfections, a process which lifted the mind far above earthly considerations and ended in an ecstatic vision of God, he found the regenerative process in the course of which human intelligence was replaced by the divine spirit and man became a divine being. Much more realistically the devotee of Isis, in the rites of his cult, was given a vision of things divine, and, playing the part of a dying and rising god, he believed himself transformed into a divine being. A rite of deification and various other festivities left no doubt in his mind that the regenerative process was complete. For Philo also there were similar assurances. His vision of God eventuated in an emotional exaltation, a sense of being lifted far above earthly things and possessed by divine power. In this state of ecstasy Philo believed himself actually God-possessed, no longer human but divine.

For each important step in the process of Isiac regeneration, Philo had a parallel in his mystical religion. Only he was not at all dependent upon the external stimuli of cult practices. Philonian regeneration was largely self-induced and was normally experienced in solitude. It is altogether probable, therefore, that for his theory of mental regeneration Philo was directly in debt to the Isiac and other mystery religions of his immediate Egyptian environment, and that his own very private cult was a rationalization on the basis of his personal experience of mystery practices with which he was familiar.

The Egyptian origin of the Philonian theory of mental regeneration becomes all the more obvious when the writings of the Jewish thinker are compared with the Hermetic tractates. In both literatures the experience was described as an inward one, involving the phenomena of the mental and emotional life. For the disciple of Hermes, external rites had but slight meaning and for Philo, too, they had scarcely no meaning at all. The items of self-preparation for this experience were practically the same in both cases: man must train himself to consider the world as illusory, to disregard sensation, and to despise his body. In this process of self-discipline the Trismegistic prophet and the Jewish teacher alike stressed the element of human volition. "Have the will, deny the senses, purge yourself!" they commanded. Yet with all this volitional emphasis the transforming experience itself was in the last analysis conceived as a supernaturally conditioned affair. Philo and the Hermeticist as well came to a realization of this regeneration during a period of reverent silence and quiet meditation. They both described the experience in glowing terms of light as a great mental illumination in which they glimpsed a vision of God himself. The immediate result for the Jew as for the Egyptian was an ecstasy which each interpreted as divine possession. In that culminating moment the divine spirit flooded the human soul and temporarily, or permanently, transformed it into divine essence. From start to finish, therefore, Hermetic regeneration and the Philonian vision of God exhibited the most striking parallels.

It is altogether probable that the two were genetically and closely related. Although the Hermetic writings as they stand were later than those of Philo, they preserved antique elements embedded in them which date the beginnings of this religious movement far back in Hellenistic times. Hence, if these two intellectual cults were directly related to each other, Hermetism must be considered the original and Philonism the derived system. Waiving, however, the problem of direct relationship, it is certain that both came from the same Egyptian milieu and were both alike largely influenced by Hellenistic-Egyptian mystery speculation.

Thus the investigation of Philo's mysticism in relation to his immediate Alexandrian environment reveals the fact that in significant ways the thought and the experience of this Jew were influenced by the gentile religions about him. Consciously he remained intensely loyal to the religion of his forefathers. But he was a man of Hellenistic culture and broad sympathies. Hence his writings exhibited a marriage of Hebrew loyalty and Hellenistic spirit. Under the influence of gentile religions he learned to detach the individual man. He came to understand the general longing of Gentiles for personal salvation and the craving of many for mystical experience in particular. The latter desire was his own, also, and in somewhat intensified form. Taught by Egyptian mystery speculation and cult practice, he learned further to interpret his own religious experience in such a way as to allow for a mental regeneration that would bring man into direct contact with God. The Philonian literature, like the Hermetic, shows how strong and extensive was the influence of the mystery religions even among those who were not members of a mystery brotherhood. Of the two the Philonian literature has the greater significance in this particular, because it reveals the influence of gentile mystery practices on the religious thinking of a Jew.

BIBLIOGRAPHY

Bentwich, Norman, *Philo-Judaeus of Alexandria*. Philadelphia, 1910.

Bousset, D. W., *Jüdisch-Christlicher Schulbetrieb in Alexandria und Rom* (Göttingen, 1915), pp. 1–154.

Bréhier, E., *Les Idées philosophiques et religeuses de Philon d'Alexandrie.* Paris, 1908.

Cohn and Wendland, *Philonis Alexandrini Opera quae Supersunt.* Berlin, 1896–1915.

Drummond, James, *Philo Judaeus.* London, 1888.

Kennedy, H. A. A., *Philo's Contribution to Religion.* London, 1919.

Schürer, Emil, *History of the Jewish People in the Time of Jesus Christ* (New York, 1891), Div. II, Vol. III, pp. 321–81.

Stein, Edmund, *Die Allegorische Exegese des Philo aus Alexandreia.* Giessen, 1929.

Treitel, Ludwig, *Gesamte Theologie und Philosophie Philo's von Alexandria.* Berlin, 1925.

Windisch, Hans, *Die Frömmigkeit Philos.* Leipzig, 1909.

Yonge, C. D., *The Works of Philo Judaeus.* London, 1854.

CHAPTER X

THE SOCIAL SIGNIFICANCE OF
MYSTERY INITIATION

ALL religious systems deserve to be evaluated by the pragmatic test of their functional significance for human society. The extent to which they meet the actual needs of individuals and groups in a given period is the measuring rod to be used in estimating their worth. Modern historical study has taught us to view the phenomena of religion in relation to the evolution of the human race and to regard all religious systems, without exception, as socially conditioned products. This applies equally to Christian and to non-Christian systems, and to religions of attainment or religions of redemption like the mysteries. Any given cult that is a going concern develops its peculiar characteristics in response to certain vital demands that are put upon it by society, and these demands, in turn, are but the more or less articulate expression of certain basic social interests that are dominant at that particular period. Hence, in order to understand the needs and desires which found satisfaction in mystery initiations, it is necessary to take a broad view of the general social situation in the Graeco-Roman world and to define, if possible, the outstanding religious interests of Mediterranean peoples in the first century of the Christian era.

I

Graeco-Roman society with all of its complexity was yet a closely knit social fabric unified in large and significant ways. Politically, the Mediterranean world of the

Augustan age was a unit for the first time in history, welded together by three hundred years of military conquests preceding the beginning of our era. To hold this Mediterranean world together in an imperial unity, Rome had thrown over it a great network of military highways reaching to the farthest provinces and centering in Rome itself. Cultural and commercial processes operated even more effectively than military conquests and political organization to unify the peoples of the Mediterranean area. Society under the early Empire continued to be highly Hellenized as it had been during the three centuries previous. Greek continued to be the language of culture and commerce, with Latin as the *lingua Franca* of diplomacy. The sea, cleared of pirates, was a great channel of commerce that led to all the Roman world, and the military highways provided the necessary land routes. Because of the easy means of communication, there was a free mingling of races and classes in the centers of population. In any important Mediterranean city one met Roman officials and native workmen, Phrygian slaves and Greek students, Syrian merchants and Egyptian sailors, all engaged in a common struggle for existence within the bounds of one huge empire.

This free competition on a world scale gave the individual his opportunity. Before the days of Alexander the interests of the individual were quite submerged in comparison with those of the tribe or state. The larger social group was the end-all of existence and personal concerns were properly subordinated thereto. It was a proud thing in one of the city-states of Greece for the citizen to have the opportunity of furnishing a chorus for a civic festival or of fitting out a trireme for the protection of the state. But in the changed conditions of the imperial period all was different. Individual interests came to the fore and those of the state receded to the background. The Roman Empire meant far less to the citizen than the Greek *polis* had meant. It was too large and too far away to be very dependent on his support or to contribute much to his happiness. In the ruthlessness of conquest and the stress of competition, local customs were ignored, traditions were swept aside, and the unsupported individual was thrown back upon his own resources, but with a world of opportunity before him. Happiness and well-being, if won at all, must be won by himself and for himself alone. It was an era of extreme individualism.

In every department of life almost, the changed point of view was felt and recorded. Art featured realistic sculpture and portrait busts. Latin literature became self-conscious and personal, and politics suffered much from individuals who sought to exploit the state for personal gain.

Religion, like the other phases of Graeco-Roman life, felt the effect of these changed social conditions. For the masses of men former religious sanctions and guaranties no longer functioned. In the old, pre-imperial days the individual was well satisfied with the group guaranties that were offered by local and nationalistic religions. To be sure, his relationship to the state deity was only an indirect one —through the group to which he belonged. To be sure, the goods sought were chiefly social benefits which he shared with his fellow citizens. But so long as the gods protected the state and the state protected him he was well content. Successive conquests by foreign powers, however, rudely destroyed this complacency, and the victory of Macedonian and Roman arms wrecked the prestige of merely local and national deities. As racial barriers were broken down and the individual felt himself free to travel and trade in a wide world, he became conscious of needs and desires he had never known before. As a practical matter the time-honored customs of his fathers could not be maintained in foreign lands. New sanctions and assurances of a more personal sort were needed. Thus, in line with the general social movements of the time, there was a distinct breakdown of traditional religion, and national cults, popular in the Hellenic period, fell into abeyance.

But the masses of men did not become irreligious by any means. Instead, they turned to religions of another type and sought satisfactions of a different variety. Their quest was no longer for a god powerful enough to save the state but rather for one who was benevolent enough to save the individual. Oracles were consulted, not so often in the interest of the community but more frequently for the guidance of the individual in his personal affairs. More than ever before the home became a temple and the daily life of the family was filled with the paraphernalia of piety. The shrines of healing gods were overcrowded, and magicians, who were considered the chief mediators of divine power, carried on a thriving business.

In particular, men turned for the satisfaction of personal desires to the mystery group of religions, which were indeed very ancient cults but had hitherto been comparatively insignificant. Most of them came to the Graeco-Roman world from the Orient, with the authority of a venerable past, with an air of deep mystery, and with rites that were most impressive. But the chief reason for their popularity at this time was the satisfactory way in which they ministered to the needs of the individual man. Completely denationalized and liberated from racial prejudices, they welcomed men of all races to their membership. They were genuinely democratic brotherhoods in which rich and poor, slave and master, Greek and barbarian met on a parity. Moreover, they touched the common life of men intimately and in a variety of ways. It is impressive when

one reads the references to these cults in secular literature
to note the complete faith that ordinary folk had in their
mystery gods and how they sought for their divine help
and guidance in matters of health and love and business
and in all the other multifarious concerns of everyday life.

Chief among the personal satisfactions these cults had
to offer was the privilege of a new birth for the individual.
When the neophyte was initiated into the cult he became
a new man—this was the gentile conviction. In earlier centuries, when the emphasis in religion was tribal or national,
this was no special advantage. Then the individual felt
certain of his salvation because of his birth into a particular tribe or race. The Athenian, for example, did not doubt
the peculiar interest of the maiden goddess on the Acropolis both in himself and in his native city. The Jew, even
throughout the prolonged tragedy of his vain struggle for
a national existence, succeeded in maintaining his proud
consciousness of the sufficiency of his racial birth. But the
generality of men in the Roman world had not this confidence either in racial connections or in the potentiality of
human nature itself. For salvation such as the first-century Gentile desired—a salvation that included the immortality of the soul as well as the present welfare of the
body—an essential change of being was felt to be necessary, and this the mystery religions guaranteed by means
of their initiatory rites. Among the basic religious needs
met by mystery initiation, therefore, this should be mentioned as the first. It answered to the current demand for
individualistic as opposed to racial guaranties in religion.

II

It is possible, however, to characterize more closely the
type of individual religious experience which was fostered
by Graeco-Oriental cults of the mystery type. Mystical ex-

perience was a common denominator of them all, and was about as conspicuous in one cult as in another.[1] This fact cannot but impress one as being quite extraordinary because mysticism was essentially alien to the leading peoples of the Roman world. Certainly the Jewish mind was unfriendly to this very subjective type of personal religious experience.[2] With his rigid monotheism, the Jew maintained a clear emphasis on individuality, both human and divine. Furthermore, since he thought of religion in terms of action primarily, his attention was focused on the externality of statutory observance. Latin religion, too, was characteristically as legalistic and objective as was the Jewish, though it was lacking in the minuteness of detailed application. For the typical Roman, religion was a commercial transaction between himself and his gods, and mysticism found little encouragement in such a business arrangement. To the Hellenic mind, also, mysticism had but slight attractiveness because of the balanced appreciation of the Greek for the insignificance and the dignity of man. The thinkers of classical Greece had a full and glad confidence in man's physical fitness to cope with his environment and his mental fitness to explore its mysteries.

[1] The following studies are important for an understanding of mystical phenomena in first-century religious experience: A. W. Benn, *The Greek Philosophers* (1914[2]), pp. 474–522; Edwyn Bevan, *Stoics and Sceptics*, pp. 85–118; Franz Cumont, *Astrology and Religion among the Greeks and Romans*, p. 208; Samuel Dill, *Roman Society from Nero to Marcus Aurelius*, pp. 289–440; W. W. Fowler, *The Religious Experience of the Roman People*, pp. 380–402; O. Gruppe, *Griechische Mythologie*, pp. 1016–41; W. R. Halliday, *The Pagan Background of Early Christianity*, pp. 210–33; E. Lehmann, *Mysticism in Heathendom and Christendom*, pp. 75–97; Gilbert Murray, *Five Stages of Greek Religion*, pp. 153–207; Edward Zeller, *Die Philosophie der Griechen*, Part III, Div. II, pp. 82–217.

[2] For an assembling of the available data concerning mystical tendencies in Judaism, consult the following titles by J. Abelson: *Jewish Mysticism* (London, 1913); *The Immanence of God in Rabbinic Literature* (New York, 1912); art., "Mysticism and Rabbinical Literature," in *Hibbert Journal*, X, 426–43.

This made the short span of man's life a glorious and zestful thing for them. Even so, the destiny of man in Hellenic thought was kept distinct from that of the gods. The reiterated theme of Greek tragedy was this: Would you be happy? Then remember your finiteness and be moderate in your desires and ambitions; else the envy of the gods will bring you disaster because of your presumptuous pride. "Know yourself" was the text of Socrates' teaching, and this was at once a warning to respect one's limitations and a promise that within the limits of human nature itself man could find full scope for the development of his powers. With its reasoned moderation Hellenism had characteristically little use for mysticism.

In spite of all this historical prejudice inherited from the earlier national period, the student finds mystical phenomena everywhere in the Graeco-Roman world. The imperial age was a time when religion was turning inward and becoming more emotional, while philosophy, converted to religion, was following the same trend. There was a cultivated antagonism between spirit and matter and the conscious endeavor to detach one from the other by means of ascetic practices. It was a period of world-weariness and other-worldliness. There was a demand for fresh emotional experience, and the culminating effort was to overleap the bounds of nature and to attain union with the divine in the occult region beyond. These were some of the currents that indicated the general direction of religious thought and feeling when the Christian era began.

They found cult expression supremely in the popular religions of redemption, in the mysteries of Eleusis and Attis and Isis and the rest. Even in the ascetic brotherhoods of Judaism these elements found practical exemplification among the Essenes of Palestine and the Therapeutae of Egypt—so far did the spirit of the times penetrate the inhospitable atmosphere of Judaism itself.[1] More significant still was the philosophical expression of this identical interest. It came to the surface, for example, in the Hermeticism of Egypt and the revived Pythagoreanism of Italy, the latter being characterized by a curious mathematical mysticism accompanied by physical and moral austerities. Ever since the days of Plato the religio-philosophical movement named from Pythagoras had continued a concealed existence in connection with the mysteries of Dionysus and Orpheus. It almost betrayed itself in 181 B.C. by the flagrant forgery of "Numa's Book." But in the next century it appeared frankly in public view at Alexandria and Rome with a new religious literature and a sincere Roman champion in Cicero's friend, the senator Nigidius Figulus. At the time of Christianity's inception it had a more widely known exponent in the far-traveled Apollonius of Tyana.[2] Furthermore, prominent thinkers like Philo the Jew, of Alexandria, and Plutarch the Greek, of Chaeronea, and Seneca the Spaniard, of Rome, all disclosed a high personal evaluation for this kind of religious experience. Each of these writers, in adopting a favorable attitude toward religious mysticism, belied the traditions of his own people, yet earnestly sought to bring his mystical longings into conformity with his own religious and philosophical heritage.

Modern scholars have come to recognize a common element, pronouncedly mystical, running through the writings of these philosophers and have credited this element to a single dominant personality, Posidonius of Apamea, who was born on the Orontes in Syria about 135 B.C.[3] It would

[1] On the Therapeutae consult Philo De Vita Contemplativa.

[2] See especially the discussion of the forerunners of Neo-Platonism in Zeller, Die Philosophie der Griechen, Part III, Div. II, pp. 82–267.

[3] There is no more recent edition of the remains of Posidonius than that by Janus Bake, Posidonii Rhodii reliquiae doctrinae (1810). There is not a better

be impossible to select a single figure who more completely personified the intellectual and religious interests of that age than did Posidonius. He knew the Roman world as few others did for he had traveled even beyond the Pillars of Hercules and his curiosity ranged freely where he had not been in person. He was influential in that world—a teacher of Cicero who sent him an account of his consulship, and of Pompey who twice turned aside from his eastern campaigns to visit his master in Rhodes. In philosophy and religion Posidonius stood for popular eclecticism, mediating between the Orient and the Occident, between astrology and Stoicism. More than any other man of his era he gathered up the masses of popular beliefs and gave them effective literary expression. Child of his age in this as in all else, he felt the contemporary demand for a more inclusive life and sought to assuage it by a siderial mysticism. Hence he is chiefly remembered as the "beholder and expounder of heavens" who found in the enraptured contemplation of the starry skies an assurance of oneness with the divine. Like the astronomer Ptolemy, he could say, "Mortal that I am, I know that I am born for a day, but when I follow the serried multitude of the stars in their circular courses, my feet no longer touch the earth; I ascend to Zeus himself to feast on ambrosia, the food of the Gods."[1] In Posidonius one finds a high peak of mystical enthusiasm; yet he was only one outstanding mystic among many others whom the pagan world knew at the time when the Roman Republic fell to pieces to be reassembled as the Roman Empire.

discussion of his personality and significance than that given by Bevan, *Stoics and Sceptics,* pp. 85–118. For a particular treatment of his astral mysticism consult various references in Cumont, *Astrology and Religion among the Greeks and Romans.* See also Reinhardt, *Poseidonios* (Munich, 1921), and Schubert, *Die Eschatologie des Posidonios* (Leipzig, 1927).

[1] *Anthologia Palatina* ix. 577.

Just why the ever recurrent human quest for larger life should take on a mystical complexion at this time is a difficult matter to determine. There are certain general considerations, however, that have distinct bearing on the case. In the first place, the thought world of the average man had suddenly enlarged to proportions that were frightening. The horizon of a Syrian trader in Nero's time was vastly more inclusive than that of a Macedonian noble who started out with Philip for his conquest of Greece, and this new horizon included a far greater number of facts to be classified and accounted for, and a constantly enlarging group of problems and difficulties to be settled. This expanded thought-world of the middle of the first century was in a very chaotic state. The social structure of an earlier age had been completely wrecked. Greek democracy and Oriental despotism alike had been crushed by imperial power. National and racial distinctions, once considered very important, had been all but forgotten. Whole classes in society had been wiped out. Old things had passed away and what chiefly impressed the ordinary man about the new order of things imposed by Rome was not so much its orderliness as its newness. It is difficult, indeed, to imagine the confusion and perplexity which existed in the popular mind when men found themselves completely torn away from their old moorings, yet unaccustomed to the new social environment. The citizen of the Greek *polis* had lived in a friendly town that was his own; but the Roman citizen found himself bewildered in the crowded streets of a strange city that was everyman's world.

In the second place, the man of the early Empire felt that the ultimate control of his disordered universe was not at all in his own hands, but that it rested with supernatural powers on the outside. Although the people of the Roman

Empire were really well equipped with social agencies new and old for the attainment of their desires, they did not themselves have much confidence in these securities. After all, these were merely human adjustments which governed one's relations with his fellow-men, whereas, according to the first-century point of view, the more important relationships of life were with the controlling powers in the supernatural realm. Whether these powers were friendly or unfriendly or both or either according to circumstances, there was great variety of opinion; but generally speaking there was no doubt of their power. The Epicureans, to be sure, considered this belief in the supernatural to be a blight on the joy of life and harmful to society. But the common man was not at all troubled by skepticism on this point. He was too much concerned with the business of establishing safe relations with the occult powers to debate the problematic social value of supernaturalism. One way he had of accomplishing this was the way of mysticism, whereby he either projected himself emotionally into the supernatural realm and so came into contact with deity, or else by magic and sacrament drew the god down into the human sphere and in this less exalted fashion realized the desired alliance. Not until this *unio mystica* was accomplished did many men feel completely secure in the face of the uncertainties of life.

To such a fearing world as this, which stood in abject awe of supernatural powers, the mystery religions came with the message of salvation through union with the lord of the cult. This was good news, indeed, for such an alliance robbed the unknown spiritual world of its terrors and gave the initiate the assurance of special privilege in relation to the potent beings who controlled the destinies of men. Practically, the lords of the mysteries were the most powerful spiritual beings that gentile religionists of the

Graeco-Roman world were acquainted with. In the background of each of the mysteries hovered the vague form of the supreme power itself: the Anatolian *Magna Mater Deum* or the Ahura Mazda of the Persian system. In the foreground, ready for action, stood the mediator who chiefly made the divine power manifest in life and in nature: the youthful Attis or the invincible Mithra. The mystery gods and goddesses were also potent as netherworld divinities. Persephone reigned as queen of the dead and Osiris presided as judge of the souls of the departed. By means of initiation into their cults, the devotee was enabled to share vividly in the experiences of these divinities and even to attain realistic union with them. Thus, united with the gods themselves, the initiate was in touch with currents of supernatural power which not only operated to transform his very being but also rendered him immune from evil both in this life and in the next. In this way the mystery religions, by means of their initiations, answered to a second great demand of the age—the yearning for the mystical type of religious experience.

III

It should at once be noted that the mysticism of the cults was not of the intellectualized type that one discovers in the writings of Plutarch or Seneca, nor even of the refined, subjective sort, that is evident in the Hermetic writings and in Philo. It was rather of a more realistic, objective, ecstatic, and highly emotional variety. This emotional character of cult mysticism was not fortuitous, by any means, but answered directly to another one of the keenly felt social needs of the age. The first century was a time when the masses of people had a very inordinate appetite for emotional stimulation. This abnormal craving itself can be understood even when its pathological character is recognized. Directly or indirectly it was due, more than to anything else, to the terribly depressing experiences through which society had passed during the wars that filled the years immediately preceding the Christian era.

For four hundred years wars had been unceasing. Greece had no sooner finished her glorious Persian Wars than she started that inglorious internecine strife which ended immediately in the exhaustion of all and the final snuffing out of Greek freedom by Philip at Chaeronea. Alexander's stupendous world conquest had been followed by the petty struggles of the Diadochi and the Epigoni, and thus the eastern world was filled with conflicts which did not cease until Rome's universal conquest. The Romans themselves had gradually extended their rule over Italy by a process of long warfare. They had made the Mediterranean a Roman lake by fighting Carthage to a finish, and finally in their own civil wars they had deluged the whole world with blood. Directly all these military operations had entailed terrible suffering for all classes. Quite apart from the killing or the maiming of combatants there were pitiful consequences for the non-combatants. Breadwinners had been drafted into service. Crops over large areas had been destroyed. Conquered lands had been plunged into debt and bankruptcy, while thousands of men, women, and children, formerly free, had been sold as slaves. The Mediterranean world had known war at its worst, and this long series of conquests, civil wars, proscriptions, and insurrections had produced an untold amount of agony.

The indirect consequences of these military operations were quite as disastrous for the happiness of large numbers of people as were the direct results. One of the most deplorable effects was the practical destruction of the middle classes which had been the backbone of society. This left a bad social cleavage between the wealthy and aristocratic classes on the one hand, and the masses, including the slaves, on the other. Conditions were such that the classes had the opportunity of becoming more wealthy and prosperous, while the proletariat correspondingly became more destitute and wretched. Enormous sums of gold and silver, the accumulated wealth of the east, was disgorged on the Empire. This created a demand for luxuries, raised the standard of living, and multiplied the miseries of the poor. Throughout the period the number of slaves was constantly being augmented. This lowered wages and drove free laborers to the idleness of cities where they were altogether too willing to be enrolled among the state-fed.

With such an unequal distribution of the goods of life, it was inevitable that both extremes in Roman society should feel the need of special emotional uplift and stimulation. The aristocrat felt the need of it because he had pleasures too many, and the poor freeman because he had pleasures too few. In the literature of the time these differing points of view were both fully expressed. On the one hand there was disgust with life, *taedium vitae*, bred of self-indulgence and brought to birth by satiety.[1] It was the weariness that comes when amusements cloy and the means of diversion seem exhausted. "To be ever feeding the thankless nature of the mind . . . . though after all we are never filled with the enjoyments of life . . . . this is to do what is told of the maidens who kept pouring water into a sieve," wrote Lucretius,[2] depicting the mood of too many men whom he knew.

---

[1] Flagrant illustrations of the unbridled self-indulgence of the new-rich may be found in the familiar account of Trimalchio's dinner given in the *Satyricon* of Petronius, who had the opportunity of knowing this side of life if anyone did. The selfish hedonism of this class in society is perfectly summarized in a six-word Timgad inscription, each word of six letters: *Venari, Lavari, Ludere, Ridere, Occest (hoc est) Vivere.*

[2] Lucretius *De rerum natura* iii. 1003 ff.

On the other hand there was genuine sensitiveness to suffering in this age born of a sympathetic understanding of its pain and an earnest attempt to provide alleviation. The demand for solace in time of calamity was so great that the office of consoler became almost a profession and the closing days of the Republic saw the development of a curious literary type, known as consolation literature. Crantor, who originated this literature, wrote a book for a bereaved parent which Cicero pronounced "a golden book, to be learned by heart," and the latter on the death of his daughter formulated a *consolatio* for himself. Plutarch wrote such a consolation to his wife, while Seneca, the prince of consolers, went far toward making the art a science by the psychological study of individual cases. Formulas of sympathy were developed for calamities of all sorts: for ill health, old age, financial disaster, confiscation of property, exile, and most of all for death itself. It was a period when all classes were sensitive to emotional needs, but chiefly the inarticulate masses who were most miserable and knew not how to express their misery.

Here was religion's opportunity. Some cults strove to meet it while others did not. Generally speaking the officials of state religion remained unresponsive, and the marble gods of Greece and Rome had no word for men in agony. Judaism, which had itself gone through a prolonged martyrdom, should have learned from suffering to minister to personal need, but it had not. Its hope was still a national one, not personal.

But the religions of redemption that came from the east furnished exactly the emotional satisfaction that the age demanded. Hence they were popular. They told men of savior-gods that were very human, who had come to earth and toiled and suffered with men, experiencing to an intensified degree the sufferings to which flesh is heir. These savior-gods had known the agony of parting from loved ones, of persecution, of mutilation, of death itself. In this hard way they had won salvation for their devotees and now they stood ready to help all men who had need. The rites of these mystery religions were impressively arranged to represent the sufferings and triumphs of the savior-gods. Thus it was possible for the initiate to feel as his god had felt, and sometimes more realistically, to repeat the archetypal experiences of his lord. His initiation was a time of great uplift that elevated him above commonplace worries and gave him an exalted sense of security. In after days the memory of that great event remained with him to buoy him up amid the hardships of his daily lot, or in such special crises as might come to him. The third great contemporary need which mystery initiation supplied was that of emotional stimulation through the mystical experience of contact with a sympathetic savior.

IV

The majority of gentile religionists, however, were not satisfied with a merely emotional assurance that the desired mystical union had taken place. Something more tangible and objective was required to supplement the evidence furnished by subjective experience. This was in accord with the vivid realism of contemporary thought concerning divine beings and spiritual processes. Greeks and Romans both conceived of their gods very concretely and humanly. They gave them admirable plastic representation and sought to secure their favor by rites that were correspondingly realistic. At the beginning of the imperial period when the uncertainties of life made men feel more dependent than ever on supernatural assistance, the operations whereby they strove to assure themselves of the desired aid became, if anything, more realistic than ever.

Records of the Augustan revival in religion illustrate

this tendency in a hundred different ways.[1] We read of statues whose lips, hands, and feet were worn smooth by the persistent and devout osculations of worshipers. To the naïve thought of uneducated people these statues were identified with the divine beings they represented and were treated accordingly. High and low alike shared in the realistic point of view. The Emperor Galba kept a necklace of pearls and precious stones to adorn his favorite goddess Fortuna on his Tusculan estate. When he suddenly decided to give it to Venus instead, Fortuna appeared to him in a dream and threatened to withdraw her favors. In genuine fright Galba rushed off to Tusculum to make amends to Fortuna.[2] Seneca, on a chance visit to the capital, was aroused to indignation when he saw the statues of the Roman trinity attended as if they were living persons and found women there awaiting the pleasure of Jupiter because they believed themselves loved by him. Philosophers generally had as little patience with these practices as Seneca had; but occasionally there was a Maximus of Tyre who would speak a tolerant word for these ingenuous expressions of religious devotion.[3]

In such an age and amid people who thought in these vivid terms, the rites of religion, in order to be satisfying, had to partake of the same pictorial quality. They had to give actual and dramatic representation of the processes they were intended to typify and induce. This was what the ceremonies of the mystery cults did, and this was another reason for the great attractive power of the cults. Most of their rites had come down in traditional forms from an immemorial antiquity. Originally performed

---

[1] The realistic phases of the Augustan revival are well represented in the general bibliography cited on page 11.

[2] Suetonius *Galba* 18.

[3] Maximus Tyrus *Dissertationes* viii.

among primitive people in order to assure the revival of vegetable life in springtime, they were enacted in these later imperial days for the higher purpose of assuring the rebirth of the human spirit. Yet, among the masses at least, the efficacy of these ceremonials was as little questioned as it had been in their original setting.

The baptismal rite, in particular, whether by water or blood, was regarded as marking the crucial moment in a genuinely regenerative process. Once reborn the initiates were treated as such; their birthday was celebrated and they were nourished in a manner appropriate for infants. Childish rites they seem, yet to the uneducated and simple-minded of the first century A.D. they were fraught with spiritual significance. The semblance of mystic marriage and the partaking of consecrated foods were other realistic sacraments in which the neophyte found assurance that he was really and vitally united with his lord and endowed with the divine spirit. What gives the modern student pause when he is inclined to smile at the naïvete of these practices is the sincere conviction of pagan initiates that their spiritual transformation was not only represented but was also really accomplished by these dramatic ceremonies. By means of initiatory rites of great impressiveness the mystery cults were enabled to satisfy another conspicuous demand of the age, the desire for realistic guaranties in religion.

V

The personal transformation which was the initial feature of cult mysticism had its ethical as well as its religious aspect, and this responded to a demand of the age for a blend of ethics and religion. It is somewhat difficult to define the ethical interests of gentile religionists in the first century, for the early imperial period was a time of great moral disorder and confusion, paralleling the stress and strain in other areas of life. This moral anarchy is comprehensible, for it grew out of the same social conditions that determined religious developments in this period. In the *polis* of Hellenic days, political, moral, and religious duties were all integrated, and the citizen found sufficient guidance for the performance of his obligations in community institutions, ancestral customs, and state laws. These had divine sanction for him and no other authority was needed. With the wrecking of that corporate life, however, morals were divorced from politics and the individual was left to himself without external authority to guide his conduct. The continuous social upheavals of Hellenistic and republican times, the free mingling of populations in commerce and conquest, and the enormous increase of slavery furthered the process of cutting thousands of human beings loose from moral restraints. No wonder men were groping after new norms for the conduct of life at this time!

It is ordinarily assumed that society in the middle of the first century was conspicuously lacking in ethical interests and had sunk to the lowest point of moral degradation. This impression is gained chiefly from two sources, from Jewish and Christian writers on the one hand and from Roman satirists on the other.[1] Obviously, however, the former were prejudiced witnesses from the start, and the latter confined themselves to a one-sided view of only one class in Roman society. When the student turns aside from such biased and limited views to consider the general trend in society as a whole, he discovers that it was not only a period of moral anarchy but of ethical awakening

---

[1] Paul's fulmination in Romans 1:18 ff. is one of the most familiar of the Christian sources. For pagan views giving a similar impression from different points of view, consult the comedies of Plautus and Terence, the satires of Juvenal and Martial, and the biographies of Suetonius.

as well. Interest was alive on moral questions. It had shifted from politics to ethics. Philosophy had come down out of its theoretical basket amid the clouds of speculation and was walking on solid earth once more. It was under-taking to do for men what religion too frequently did not do—to give guidance in problems of conduct. There were moralists in plenty who were castigating vice and holding up models of virtue for imitation.

Almost every characteristic vice in Roman society was being met with the most vigorous protests and sometimes by active measures for amelioration. Slavery was a curse to that society, cultivating a cruel spirit of indifference to human suffering. But brutal masters were in a minority, and slaves had the right to acquire property and purchase their freedom. Legal enactment assured them of protec-tion against cruelty, and an increasingly humane public opinion prevented grosser abuses. It is true that Roman amusements were debasing. The theater was obscene and the amphitheater with its gladiatorial combats was beast-ly; but Cicero testifies that many regarded the amphi-theater as cruel and inhuman;[1] while Plutarch, Seneca, and even Petronius joined in a chorus of personal condemnation of gladiatorial combats. It is true that marriage at this time was carelessly contracted and easily annulled; but inscriptions and literature both prove that marriages of love were at least as common as marriages of convenience —consider Pliny's graceful love letters to his Calpurnia and the *Laudatio Turiae*, which tells of forty-one years of happy married life. Moreover, there was an impressive and unanimous demand on the part of all moralists and philos-ophers that equal virtue should be required of men as of women. It is true that there was much infanticide in Ro-man society. Children were exposed and abortion was free-

[1] Cicero *Tusculan Disputations* ii. 17. 41.

ly practiced. But Paulus, the jurist, branded these practices as assassination and "against the voice of nature and the voice of conscience." Moreover, one of the primary concerns of moralists was for the exemplary training of children. It is only too true, also, that the Romans knew of nameless sins. Yet the philosophers did not hesitate to denounce the epicenes who practiced them, and Dio Chrysostom was only the first to attack prostitution as a legalized vice.[1] A balanced view of the whole social situation therefore shows high ideals and exceptional interest in moral problems.

There was at this time a particular demand for greater concreteness in ethical teaching. Abstract instruction was not popular, but the formulation of definite precepts was desired instead; hence the teachers of the time studied the writings of philosophers and moralists to find texts and maxims to use with their pupils. To some, ideals seemed more useful than particular precepts. So careful catalogues were made of virtues and vices, and the former were summarized in certain cardinal qualities especially to be desired. These ideals, however, proved generally too elusive, and there was a call for living examples which could be referred to as demonstrations of the practicability of ideals. This became the great teaching point of the age—the citation of examples. Each system had its own particular hero, Orpheus or Pythagoras; but Socrates, most of all, came to be regarded as a personification of the ideal for humanity. Seneca urged his friend Lucilius to keep before his mind constantly the picture of some upright man and to live always as if in his presence. The practical Roman regarded this as an excellent method in education and he had his sons taught by appeal to the examples of the past. Biographies were written with this didactic purpose in view.

[1] Dio Chrysostom *Oratio* vii. 133.

Notably was this the case with Varro and Plutarch in composing their parallel lives of Greeks and Romans.[1] The first century A.D. was an age of hero worship when concrete, living examples were called for.

Stoicism, the leading philosophy of the Empire, was in a strategic position to meet the general ethical demands of the time.[2] It had its first development in Greece just after the old landmarks of Hellenic morality had collapsed; for it was in 320 B.C. that Zeno, of Citium, arrived in Athens where he was to end his days lecturing in the Stoa Poicilē. As a thoroughly Hellenized system, it appeared in Rome where it was disseminated by Panaetius through the Scipionic circle. Its Semitic earnestness accorded well with the stern severity of the old Roman character. Seneca, the Spanish prime minister, and Epictetus, the Phrygian slave, are outstanding figures showing the hold that Stoicism had on all classes in Roman society at this time. With such a cosmopolitan background, Stoicism was well furnished to supply the Roman world with new ethical norms consonant with the spirit and needs of the age.

It essayed to do so on the purely naturalistic basis furnished by human nature itself. According to Stoic teaching the chief end of existence was virtuous living, further defined as living in accordance with the dictates of reason. This brought all rational beings under a single ethical standard, at once individualistic and universal in scope. It made all men the sharers in a common world citizenship. Thus the good of every creature became the individual's good, and their hurt became his own. The call for explicit precepts of a moral character was met by Stoic

---

[1] Plutarch *Timoleon*, Introduction.

[2] For original Stoic literature read especially: Epictetus *Discourses* and *Manual;* Marcus Aurelius *Meditations;* Seneca *Moral Epistles;* Von Arnim, *Stoicorum Veterum Fragmenta.*

manuals that are still highly valued. Its ideal of virtue was analyzed into component elements, wisdom, justice, courage, and temperance, and these in turn were extensively subdivided. There was no lack of ideals in Stoicism. It had its ideal wise man, who acted without desire and made no mistakes; but Epictetus and his contemporaries were constantly referring rather to the example of Socrates—so concrete were they in their teaching.

The Stoics, more than others, were outspoken in their denunciation of social evils. Their antidote for slavery was deliverance by right thinking and complete indifference to outward circumstances. The virtuous man only is free and the only slave is he who is in bondage to bad habits, so the Stoic taught. It was the Stoic Seneca who said plainly, in reference to a double standard of morality, "You know it is injustice to demand fidelity from your wife while you seduce another man's wife," and other Stoic utterances as pointed might be quoted in regard to gladiatorial combats, prostitution, *paiderastia*, and the other vices of Nero's time. The Stoic teachers, who served as moral directors for the rich and missionaries to the masses, knew better than any others of their day what the moral weaknesses of their fellow-men were.

For him who had the will to endure its rigors, the ideal of Stoicism was satisfying. But that ideal was strenuous, almost impossible, and inhumanly high. The true Stoic must always follow the pure light of reason and be guided by duty, not desire. Passions must be exterminated and emotions crushed as perturbing influences which would hinder achievement. To attain the ideal, man must depend on himself alone, for the Stoic knew of no power external to himself that could help him. In the struggle for wellbeing, he had to act as his own savior. The ethic of Stoicism was completely rational and naturalistic. It lacked the authority of revelation and had no other sanction than that furnished by human nature and experience. In its very strength was the fatal weakness of Stoicism; it did not deal in supernaturalism, and that was the only coinage that had general acceptance in the first-century world.

Conditions of life were such at that time that most men did not have confidence in their own unaided ability to achieve character. They had "lost nerve," to paraphrase Gilbert Murray's expression, and they looked away to the supernatural realm for the powers that controlled personal conduct as well as the more ultimate destinies of mankind. What the men of the first century wanted was not so much ideals, but the power to realize those ideals; not a code of morals, but supernatural sanctions for morality. In the last analysis, it was the divine will, and not human welfare, that was the generally accepted criterion whereby the validity of any ethical system was tested. Accordingly, the religion which could furnish supernatural guaranties along with its ethical ideals had a preferred claim to first-century loyalty.

The stern morality of Judaism, like that of the Stoa, was not unattractive to many Gentiles; but the element that fascinated them was not the inherent excellence of Jewish rules for living but the fact that they had venerable sanctions bearing the impress of divine authority. The Law of the Jews was quoted as the *ipse dixit* of Yahweh himself and the scriptures were referred to as authentic documents proving the genuineness of the representation. Such confirmation was impressive to men who were seeking for divine authority to make moral conduct obligatory. The religion of the Egyptian Hermes, also, was one that offered supernatural guaranties for its ethical ideals. In the process of Hermetic rebirth, the powers of God drove out the hordes of vices and left the regenerate individual divinely empowered for right living.[1] That was Mithraism's point of strength also and accounted not a little for the vogue it continued to enjoy for some time after the beginning of the Christian era. The "commandments" of Mithraism were believed to be divinely accredited; for had not the deity himself revealed them to the ancient Magi? One of the chief reasons why the high Mithraic ideals of purity, truth, and righteousness had real attraction was because Mithra himself was the unconquerable champion of these ideals and the ready helper of men who were willing to join with him in the eternal fight of right against wrong, good against evil. Mithraism was the outstanding example of a mystery religion which gave supernatural sanctions to the demands of plain morality.

The mysticism of the mysteries came in effectively at just this point to give both realistic content and divine authorization to the ethic of the brotherhood. The ideals of the group found personification and embodiment in the divine lord or lady who was the object of cult worship. Osiris was the model righteous man who functioned in divinized state as the judge of the departed. Hence the Isiac initiate, reborn as a new Osiris, was supposed himself to exhibit the Osirian type of righteousness. So, too, in the other mystery systems, the initiate realistically united with his lord and, actually transformed by virtue of that union, had his ideal incorporated within himself as a part of his very being. Thus, in the end, mystical experience became the theoretic basis and practical incitement to good conduct. In this close articulation of mysticism and morality the cults made an important and distinctive contribution to the ethical life of the age.

It has been a general habit among Christian writers in both ancient and modern times to depreciate the ethical

[1] *Corpus Hermeticum* xiii. 8. ff.

significance of the mystery religions and to emphasize instead the ceremonialism and theurgy which characterized their cult practices. This habit developed first of all from the apologetic tendency to exalt Christianity by damning its rivals as much as possible. A fairer view of the case reveals the fact that in the first century the well-developed mystery religions like nascent Christianity were vividly responsive to the awakened conscience of the period and were reinterpreting their rites accordingly. Moral as well as spiritual cleansing was attributed to ablutions and lustrations, and ethical as well as essential regeneration was sought in the bath of the *taurobolium*. According to Celsus —and Origen has no word to say in contradiction—the Eleusinian herald demanded of candidates for initiation not only clean hands and intelligible speech but also purity of conscience and a good life.[1] This is an eloquent contemporary tribute to the moral influence of the mysteries. Yet it is only one instance out of many that might be cited.[2]

When the mystery religions are viewed in their contemporary relationships, it is possible to distinguish in each instance the peculiar contribution of each to the moral development of the Mediterranean peoples. Orphism, true to its initial character as a reform movement, moralized the process of metempsychosis and placed exaggerated emphasis on the idea of retribution in the future. Mithraism, with its ideal of aggressive, militant virtue, had great appeal for practical-minded people in the Roman world. Isiac brotherhoods, with their restrained asceticism, registered characteristic protest against the immoral practices of the peri-

[1] Origen *Contra Celsum* iii. 59.

[2] Consider particularly Andocides *De Mysteriis* 125; Aristophanes *Ranae* 455 ff., 1032; Cicero *De Legibus* ii. 14; Epictetus *Discourses* iii. 21; Horace *Ars Poetica* 391; Pindar *Olympian Odes* ii; Plutarch *De Iside et Osiride*.

od. Each cult in its own way lent the sanctions of an ancient religious system to the demands of contemporary morality and in so doing made adjustment to the ethical requirements of the age.

VI

The ultimate pledge that the mystery religions made to gentile religionists pertained not to the present but to the future. It was the assurance of a happy immortality. That was a matter about which there was very general and very genuine interest in the first-century world.[1] Whatever attitude a man might adopt on the question of continued existence after death, he could not well avoid the issue. The inevitable fact of death, together with the palpable injustices of first-century life, forced it upon his attention. As a symptom of the widespread interest in this problem the great variety of opinion which existed in educated circles may be cited. Some there were who succeeded in maintaining an absolute and consistent negative on the question. Others were just as positive in affirming immortality. Still others wavered between the two opinions.

There were philosophic sects which definitely and finally rejected all future hope. The Peripatetics, true to the scientific spirit of their founder, refused to speculate about the existence of a soul that their reason could not conceive or define. The Skeptics, true to their name, and the Academics, now turned skeptical, either doubted the possibility of a future life altogether or else suspended judgment on the problem. But these schools were not of great impor-

[1] The following works contain important discussions of the first-century belief in immortality: Franz Cumont, *The After Life in Roman Paganism*, 224 pp.; Samuel Dill, *Roman Society from Nero to Marcus Aurelius*, pp. 484–528; L. R. Farnell, *Greek Hero Cults and Ideas of Immortality*, pp. 383–402; W. Warde Fowler, *The Religious Experience of the Roman People*, pp. 380–402; L. Friedländer, *Roman Life and Manners under the Early Empire*, III, 282–313; C. H. Moore, *Pagan Ideas of Immortality during the Early Roman Empire*, 64 pp.

tance in the early Empire. The Epicurean philosophy, however, was still influential, and its advocates were sincere and thoroughgoing opponents of any belief in immortality.[1] Holding consistently to the atomistic materialism of Democritus and Epicurus, they maintained that the soul came into existence at conception, that it grew with the body, and at the body's death it passed into nothingness once more, dissipated like the other bodily elements. This annihilation the Epicureans did not dread because death destroyed all sensibility. On the contrary, they warmly praised their master for liberating men from the terror of future punishment and teaching them that death was not a frightful thing but a blessing. Lucretius, in pure Epicurean vein, exulted in the opportunity of driving from men's hearts "that dread of Acheron which troubles human life to its inmost depths, and overspreads everything with the blackness of death, and permits no pleasure to be pure and unalloyed."[2]

There were not a few both among the high and the lowly who were attracted by this article of Epicurean faith and made it their own. According to Sallust, no less exalted a personage than Julius Caesar, the pontiff of Roman religion, opposed the death penalty for the Catilinarian conspirators because, he said, "Death puts a period to all human ills and beyond the grave there is no opportunity for either anxiety or joy."[3] The elder Pliny, a most useful and industrious citizen whose lot was a very favorable one, was vehement in his rejection of the idea of a future life. To him it was an invention of human vanity that robbed

---

[1] For ancient expositions of Epicureanism read *Diogenes Laertius*, Book X, and Lucretius *De rerum natura*. Usener, *Epicurea*, is a convenient collection of source materials.

[2] Lucretius *De rerum natura* iii. 38 ff.; vi. 764 ff.

[3] Sallust *Catalina* 51 ff.

death of its virtue and doubled the pain of dying.[1] Latin
poets gave graceful and memorable expression to similar
views. *Carpe diem* was the motto that Horace recommended. Catullus, at his brother's grave, took an everlasting
farewell of him, and he anticipated that sometime night
would close on his love for Lesbia also: "Suns can set and
rise again, but we, when our brief light is extinguished,
must sleep for an eternal night."[2]

That Epicurean ideas were disseminated among the
lower strata of society is shown by rude and simple grave
inscriptions, many of which express unbelief in any future
existence. "We are mortal; we are not immortal," was the
terse confessional of one.[3] This idea was reiterated in more
extended form, emphasizing the thought that man returns
to the same sort of non-existence from which he came:
"Once I had no existence; now I have none. I am not aware
of it, I care not." "We are and we were nothing. See,
reader, how swiftly we mortals go back from nothingness
to nothingness."[4] In some instances the state of non-existence was contrasted with the conditions of earthly life to
the disadvantage of the latter. The following is a jocose
example: "What remains of man, my bones, rests sweetly
here. I no longer have fear of sudden starvation; I am
exempt from attacks of gout; my body is no longer pledged
for rent; and I enjoy perpetual and free hospitality."[5] In
some cases, however, the contrast was in favor of this life;
for the advice, "Eat, drink, be merry, come!" was many
times repeated among grave inscriptions.[6] Such epigraphs
testify to a vulgar and sensuous deterioration of original

[1] Pliny *Historia Naturalis* vii. 55. [2] Catullus v. 4 ff.

[3] *Corpus Inscriptionum Latinarum* Vol. XI, No. 856.

[4] *Op. cit.* Vol. V, Nos. 19–39; Vol. VI, No. 26003.

[5] *Op cit.* Vol. VI, No. 7193.

[6] *Op. cit.* Vol. II, Nos. 1434, 1877, 2262.

Epicureanism during this period. But the really pathetic maxim among them all was one that was so often repeated it was sometimes represented by initial letters only: "I was not; I was; I am not; I do not care."[1] This was an epigraphic formula frequently used for slaves and gladiators to whom death must have come as a blessed release. Inscriptions of this general character indicate the acceptance of the Epicurean solution by quite a number among the lower classes. Yet, even so, the proportion of such inscriptions was not large in comparison with those which expressed hope regarding the future.

There were many among the cultivated classes and more among the masses to whom the negative answer of Epicureanism was less than satisfying. Those who were philosophically inclined turned backward for the confirmation of their faith to the classical arguments of "divine Plato" who had made the first great attempt at a rationalization of the belief in immortality. Cato of Utica, who by his death became an ideal figure for later Stoicism, spent the night before his suicide in reading the *Phaedo* of Plato. This same book was the last consolation of many another man who was the victim of proscription or of imperial tyranny. Cicero testified to the lasting influence of Plato in his day.[2] There were many others also who like Cicero preferred to be wrong with the Greek idealist on the question of immortality rather than right with those who criticized him.

One sect in particular, the Neo-Pythagoreans, held Plato in special reverence and granted him a place next in honor to the founder of their order. These strange sectaries substantiated the belief in immortality by the authority of

---

[1] *Non fui, fui, non sum, non curo* (Dessau, *Inscriptiones Latinae selectae*, Nos. 8162 ff.)

[2] Cicero *Tusculan Disputations* i.

a revelation in definite scriptural form, bearing the names of Pythagoras and Plato. In detail their beliefs and practices were like those of their predecessors, the Pythagoreans of south Italy and the Orphics of Greece. They believed the soul to be divine and therefore immortal. By generation the soul was imprisoned in the body, and so long as it remained there it was in danger of corruption and of successive sojourns in this evil world. The whole aim of their practice was to secure the soul's liberation from the body and from the cycle of physical rebirths. By ritual purifications, moral discipline, and the practice of piety they believed this could be accomplished; so that, when the soul was freed at death it would ascend through the heavenly spheres to dwell with the blessed gods. To the Neo-Pythagoreans, death itself was a spiritual rebirth to immortality. In one of the most familiar documents of the Augustan religious revival, the sixth book of the *Aeneid*, the court poet of the Roman Empire gave lasting literary expression to the revived Pythagorean hope. This pagan apocalypse is a curious medley of Orphic-Pythagorean beliefs with an admixture of Platonic and Stoic ideas and various other elements more primitive; but it does give a vivid and picturesque impression of hopes and convictions that were cherished more or less extensively by Vergil's contemporaries.

A large body of first-century thinkers, however, were not satisfied with either the fantastic beliefs of the Neo-Pythagorean sect or the nihilism of Epicurus. Many of the most earnest souls of the time wavered in doubt, inclined toward belief, and found in the varying and ill-defined positions of Stoicism a harbor of refuge. At one point the Stoics agreed with the Epicureans. They had no fear of Hell. "There is no prison house, no lake of fire or river of forgetfulness, no judgment seat, no renewal of the rule of tyrants."[1] On one other point they were generally agreed among themselves, that the ultimate destiny of the soul after death was reabsorption into the primal divine substance whence it had originally come. In Epictetus' memorable phrase, the soul was "a fragment of God." It was "fiery spirit" (*pneuma purōses*),[2] and by virtue of its very origin and constitution it could have no other end than to return to its divine source. To quote a Stoic grave inscription: "The holy spirit which you bore has escaped from your body. The body remains here and is like the earth. The spirit is naught else but God."[3] Most Stoics were of the opinion that one day the universe would be reduced by general conflagration to its primal fiery state and a new cycle of existence would then begin.[4] The question was, What would be the fate and condition of souls in the interim? Here most of the leaders disagreed. The older Stoics had little to say on the subject. Under the influence of Pythagoreanism and astral mysticism, however, the later Stoics became more definite. Posidonius, for example, was sure they would pass through a period of purification, and rising to heaven's height, would delight themselves by watching the stars go around. In general, then, the Stoics allowed for only a limited future existence before the soul merged once more into God.

Among the educated classes of the first century, therefore, one finds all shades of belief and unbelief, but almost universal interest in the question of the future. There were many who like Cicero, or Seneca, included within their own experience a changing series of beliefs. In the days of their

---

[1] Seneca *Dialogorum Libri* vi. 19. 4; Epictetus ii. 6. 18; iii. 13. 15; Cicero *Tusculan Disputations* i. 16; *De Deorum Natura* ii. 2.

[2] Epictetus i. 14. 6; ii. 8. 11.

[3] *Corpus Inscriptionum Latinarum* Vol. XIII, No. 8371. Cf. Vol. III, No. 6384.

[4] Cicero *De Deorum Natura* ii. 46.

happiness neither of these philosophers had much concern with the subject. But as years brought wider contacts and misfortunes of one sort or another, they both developed a more positive attitude. In 45 B.C. when Cicero was having his troubles in public affairs, he suffered a cruel blow in the loss of his only daughter Tullia. The bitterness of this personal experience persuaded him that his daughter still lived among the gods, and he resolved to erect in her memory not a tomb but a shrine. Writing to his friend Atticus from gloomy Astura on the shore of the Pomptine marshes, he confessed this determination, half apologetically:

> I wish to have a shrine built, and that wish cannot be rooted out of my heart. I am anxious to avoid any likeness to a tomb . . . . in order to attain as nearly as possible to a deification. This I could do if I built it at the villa itself, but I dread changes of owners. Wherever I construct it on the land I think I could secure that posterity should respect its sanctity.[1]

In the *Consolatio* addressed to himself at about the same time, he dwelt upon the divine and eternal nature of the soul in words suggesting Pythagorean inclinations. Cicero, then, was a type of the educated man who was not ashamed to stand in the crowd of those who "were stretching out their hands in longing toward the farther shore."

If there were doubts among the educated on the question of the future life, the masses generally were not perturbed by them. So far as we can gather, they had much more faith in immortality than their leaders were inclined to have. Plutarch maintained in so many words that the Epicurean negation of the future hope was repugnant to the majority. In contrast with the skeptical and material-

---

[1] Cicero *Ad Atticum* xii. 36; cf. *Ad Familiares* iv. 5; vi. 4. See also the imaginative exposition of astral immortality in the *Somnium Scipionis* at the end of Cicero's *De Republica*. The first of his *Tusculan Disputations* reviews the Platonic arguments for immortality.

istic epitaphs already cited, there are many touching inscriptions expressing confidence in immortality and reunion. One found on the grave of a married couple represents the wife as saying: "I am waiting for my husband." Generally speaking, the more traditional Greek and Roman ideas regarding the future seem to have persisted among the common people. Take, for illustration, a simple item of popular belief, the myth of Charon, that "grim ferryman of the muddy pool" to whom every dead man must pay an obol for passage money. Lucian said of this belief: "The mass is so preoccupied with the idea that, when a man dies, his relatives hasten to put an obol in his mouth to pay the ferryman for his passage across the Styx, without first finding out what money is current in the underworld." Further arrangement was made for the future happiness of the dead by supplying them with the things they had needed or enjoyed most in this life. Hence, the belongings of the deceased were frequently cremated or buried with them, and sometimes definite provision was made for this in first-century wills. With an acceptance of the idea that the soul continued to exist after the death of the body, men longed for the assurance that this future existence was a happy, and not a miserable, one.

What religions were there in the first-century world to give men assurances in regard to the future of the individual? Not the new emperor worship, surely; that was concerned with a present salvation within the empire. Not Judaism, either, for Jews were still tenacious of their racial consciousness, and their future hope was predominantly national and Messianic.[1]

The one group of first-century religions which did specialize in future guaranties were the mystery cults from Greece and the Orient. Originally intended to assure the

[1] See R. H. Charles, *Hebrew, Jewish and Christian Eschatology.*

miracle of reviving vegetation in the springtime, they were perfectly adapted to guarantee the miracle of the spirit's immortality after physical death. These were the cults which in the form of Dionysiac and Orphic brotherhoods had first brought the promise of a happy future life to Greece in the religious revival of the sixth century B.C.[1] But Greeks at that time were too well satisfied with a life of present salvation to be much concerned with the future. The Orphic teachings regarding immortality, however, were taken up by the Pythagoreans and moralized by Pindar and rationalized by Plato. In Hellenistic times the Greek cults merged with similar religions from the east which offered equivalent guaranties, and in this syncretized form they came into their own. In the early imperial period they were more popular than ever, for they gave positive and definite answer to the questioning of the common man about the future. Their answer had the authority of revelation and it included the guaranty of divine aid in the realization of that blessed after-life which they vividly depicted to their devotees. Altogether the mysteries were unusually well equipped to meet the contemporary demand for assurances regarding the future.

When consideration is given to the fundamental character of the interests represented by the mystery religions, one can well understand their popularity in the Graeco-Roman world. In an era of individualism, when men were no longer looking to religion for guaranties of a racial or national order, the mystery cults offered the boon of personal transformation through participating in rites of initiation. At a time when men were seeking a larger life

[1] On the relation of the Dionysus-Orphic cults to the belief in immortality, see particularly: L. R. Farnell, *Greek Hero Cults and Ideas of Immortality*, pp. 373–402; E. Rohde, *Psyche, Seelencult und Unsterblichkeitsglaube der Griechen*, Vol. II; B. I. Wheeler, *Dionysus and Immortality*.

through contact with supernatural powers, the mysteries guaranteed absolute union with the divine beings who controlled the universe. In an age when men were craving emotional uplift, mystery initiation gave them such encouragement as they could scarcely find elsewhere. At a period when realism characterized thought in all departments of life, the religions of redemption offered men realistic rites to guarantee the actuality of spiritual processes. When supernatural sanctions were sought to validate ethical ideals, the mystery cults provided a unique combination of mysticism and morality that was practically effective. When, as never before, people were questioning about the future fate of the individual soul, the mysteries, through initiation, gave guaranty of a happy immortality. At every one of these points the gentile religions of redemption were effectively meeting the needs of large numbers of people in Graeco-Roman society.

BIBLIOGRAPHY

ANGUS, S., *The Environment of Early Christianity* (New York, 1921), pp. 1–139.

BAUER, A., *Vom Griechentum zum Christentum*. Leipzig, 1917.

BAUMGARTEN, POLAND, AND WAGNER, *Die Hellenistisch-römische Kultur*. Leipzig, 1913.

BENN, A. W., *The Greek Philosophers* (London, 1914[2]), pp. 474–522.

BEVAN, EDWYN, *Later Greek Religion*. New York, 1927.

CASE, S. J., *The Evolution of Early Christianity* (Chicago, 1914), pp. 48–77, 331–69. *The Social Origins of Christianity* (Chicago, 1923), pp. 79–160.

DEISSMANN, A., *Licht vom Osten*. Tübingen, 1923[4]. English translation, *Light from the Ancient East*. New York, 1927[4].

DILL, SAMUEL, *Roman Society from Nero to Marcus Aurelius*(London, 1920[2]), pp. 289–528.

FIEBIG, PAUL, *Die Umwelt des Neuen Testaments*. Göttingen, 1926.

FRIEDLÄNDER, L., *Darstellungen aus der Sittengeschichte Roms in der Zeit von August bis zum ausgang der Antonine*. English translation,

Roman Life and Manners under the Early Empire. New York, 1908–13.

FOWLER, W. W., *Social Life at Rome in the Age of Cicero.* New York, 1909.

GEFFCKEN, J., *Aus der Werdezeit des Christentums.* Leipzig, 1909.

HALLIDAY, W. R., *The Pagan Background of Early Christianity.* London, 1925.

HATCH, EDWIN, *The Influence of Greek Ideas and Usages on the Christian Church.* London, 1897.

MURRAY, GILBERT, *Five Stages of Greek Religion* (New York, 1925²), pp. 153–207.

STAERK, W., *Neutestamentliche Zeitgeschichte* (Leipzig, 1912), 1–177.

WENDLAND, PAUL, *Die Hellenistisch-Römische Kultur.* Tübingen, 1912.

INDEX

Abraham, 252, 257

Academics, the, 289

Achaemenides, the, 147-48

Acts, 14

Adonis, 137-39, 171, 178

Adonis, festival of, 138, 185

Adonis and Aphrodite, cult of, 30, 87, 137

Aelian, 78

Aeschines, 102

Aeschylus, 13, 46, 92, 105

Agnosticism, 4

Ahriman, 146

Ahura Mazda, 9, 143-46, 157, 274

Aidoneus, 111

Alcibiades, 24, 47, 77

Alcmene, 19

Alexander, 13, 68, 87, 119, 178, 275

Allegory, 229, 254-56

Ammon, 212

Ammonius Saccas, 196

Amon, 179

Anactoron. See Demeter, chapel of

Andanian mysteries, 29, 39

Andocides, 24, 64

Angels, 244

Antiochus, 202

Antonines, the, 1, 2, 147

Anubis, 170, 174, 175

Aphrodite, 137-38, 178. *See also* Adonis and Aphrodite, cult of

Apion, 255

Apocalypse, the, 14

Apologists, Christian, 1, 162; mystery, 26

Apollo, 21, 23, 28, 41, 86

Apollodorus, 48

Apollonius, 39, 270

Apotheosis, 16, 20-22, 110, 117, 127, 136, 165, 192, 258, 295

Apulian vase paintings, 94

Apuleius, Lucius, 7, 25, 31-32, 124, 140, 186, 187, 189-90, 192-94

Archigallus, 120, 130

Aristides, 26, 193

Aristobulus, 229

Aristophanes, 45, 64, 86, 92, 119

Aristotle, 21, 60, 93, 212

Arnobius, 77, 117, 128

Artemis, 14

Asceticism, 104, 108, 166, 188, 196, 213, 222, 269, 288

Asclepeia, 23

Asclepius, 197, 206-7, 212; cult of, 22-23, 28

Ashtart, 30, 137

Ashtoreth, 137

Astarte, 137

Asterius, Bishop, 53

Astrology, 147, 149, 203, 223, 271

Atargatis, 139

Atheism, 1, 8

Athena, 56, 70, 86, 95, 267

Attalus, 120

Attis, 32, 87, 116-20, 122-29, 131-37, 171-78, 269, 274; cult: *see* Cybele-Attis cult; confessional, 133; festival, 116, 121-22, 128-29, 131; rites: *see* Great Mother, rites of

Augustine, 26, 132

Augustus, 6, 11, 16, 18, 40, 222

Avesta, 143-44, 146, 157

Baals, Syrian, 9

Bacchae or Bacchi, 73-74, 76-77, 80-81, 83

Bacchanals, 72, 74-75, 79-80, 82, 84, 88

Bacchic communion, 75; experience: *see* Dionysian experience; feasts, 76; literature, 74; revel, 77, 79-80, 82, 86, 87